The Strategic Heart

The Strategic Heart

Using the New Science to Lead Growing Organizations

Michael H. Shenkman

QUORUM BOOKS
Westport, Connecticut • London

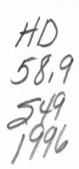

Library of Congress Cataloging-in-Publication Data

Shenkman, Michael H.
    The strategic heart : using the new science to lead growing
organizations / Michael H. Shenkman.
       p. cm.
    Includes bibliographical references and index.
    ISBN 1-56720-078-8 (alk. paper)
    1. Organizational effectiveness. 2. Corporate culture.
    3. Leadership. I. Title.
    HD58.9.S49   1996
    658.4'012—dc20   96–587

British Library Cataloguing in Publication Data is available.

Library of Congress Catalog Card Number: 96–587
ISBN: 1-56720-078-8

First published in 1996

Quorum Books, 88 Post Road West, Westport, CT 06881
An imprint of Greenwood Publishing Group, Inc.

Printed in the United States of America

The paper used in this book complies with the
Permanent Paper Standard issued by the National
Information Standards Organization (Z39.48–1984).

10 9 8 7 6 5 4 3 2 1

A paperback edition of *The Strategic Heart* is available from
Praeger Publishers, an imprint of Greenwood Publishing Group,
Inc. (ISBN 0–275–95620–2).

Contents

Figures   vii

Introduction   ix

I. Unleashing the Power of Your Organization   1

1. Complexity: A New Model of Organization   3

2. Values   19

3. Mission (I): Purpose and Commitment   33

4. Mission (II): Action and the Arrow of Value   49

5. Choice   65

II. Unleashing the Power of High Performance   79

6. Flow: From Work to Peak Performance   81

7. Engage   93

8. Responsibility (Not Jobs)   109

9. Envision   123

10. Aspire   139

11. Conclusion   157

Appendix: Conifer Group, Sample Organizational Documents   171

Bibliography   175

Index   177

Figures

4.1 Conifer Group's Core Actions   51

4.2 Conifer Group Arrow of Value   53

4.3 Detail Arrow of Value   54

7.1 Results-Producing Coach   101

10.1 Producing Roles   147

10.2 Organizational Roles   148

10.3 Strategic Roles   151

11.1 Driving Toward the Center of Influence   159

A.1 Conifer Group Complete Arrow of Value Chart: Detail of
"Integrate and Assemble Systems"   173

A.2 Scheduler's Critical Success Factors   174

Introduction

Perhaps it is time the "work ethic" was redefined and its idea reclaimed from the banal men who invoke it. It is time for our species, it would seem to go on to other matters. Human matters.

—Studs Terkel, *Working*[1]

THREE FALLACIES

What do business decision makers say they need most from employees and managers today? "We need people to work smart, to prioritize, to do the important things first." And, "We need people to be flexible and ready for change." People on the line, in turn, demand decent pay and sensible benefits, yes. However, more often than not we hear them talk about another level of concern: "We want our opinions to matter." And then, "We want to have a sense of where we're going as a company. We want to contribute and be recognized for that contribution."

These longings are really quite in sync. Everyone concerned wants to be a part of a business that really accomplishes something, that is challenging and productive. Shareholders and owners want the business to be profitable, to maintain leadership in its field and to protect margins sufficiently to sustain innovation. The company's managers and employees want their products and services to be well-received, and they want good decisions about future investments to be made by management.

And yet, in the consulting work I have done over the past fifteen years, owners, managers and their line workers frequently act at cross purposes. Owners seem to make investment and strategic decisions that make no sense to line employees, and managers make the work more difficult by changing priorities, changing the rules or not communicating; managers seem detached and listless to the owners who are crying for drive, energy and a sense of urgency. Line workers act like clock punchers—in at nine, out at five.

This alienation is too bad, and it is not necessary. The disconnect grows out of narrow mind-sets into which we have been straitjacketed for too long: (1) businesses are rational places, and running them is a matter of tracking the numbers and using logic alone; (2) managing businesses is a process of coordinating its different parts so that they run together like a machine; and (3) businesses are constantly under pressure to be ruthless and opportunistic with regard to competitors and, if necessary, to employees.

While these tenets were once operating truisms of business thinking, they have outlived their usefulness. Just as the truism that the world was flat became a fallacy by dint of the exploits of Magellan and Columbus, so too have these truisms become fallacies of business practice. Computer networks, and educated work force and new ideas about our world in general and management in particular have made it both possible and necessary to move beyond them.

FALLACY NUMBER ONE: BUSINESSES ARE PRIMARILY RATIONAL ENTERPRISES

Managers are schooled to use their "Strategic Minds": They learn how to crunch numbers and how to calculate risks and opportunity costs; they learn to gather and sift through information to keep abreast of competitors; they learn the language and nuances of high finance deal-making. Along with these lessons go fancy-sounding terms and acronyms: EVA (Economic Value Added), subordinated debentures, TQM (Total Quality Management) and many more. The premise of all of these efforts is that business is a head game, a rational process that becomes irrational only when things go wrong. That idea is misleading at best and, at times, dangerously wrong.

This attraction to cold, dispassionate rationality has a long and venerable tradition in our culture. Ever since Galileo, Descartes and Kepler showed that we could understand the motions of the stars by means of experimentation and mathematical formulae, we have tried to export that conception of science into everything we do. Since World War II, with the growth of academic business education, we have become enamored with "Scientific Management," which promises that everything of importance that happens in a business shows up on the balance sheet. From there it logically follows that if you put strict controls on every aspect of operations, a business will reap its maximum profits.

To the contrary. Ask any real-life manager and you'll hear that things happen too fast for most things to be known by any one person, and especially by a senior manager far from the firing line. No matter how much the most knowledgeable person can anticipate, there will always be the ragged edges of unpredictability. Regardless of on what level you approach it, life in a business is a volatile, heartfelt affair.

In fact, I would venture to say, no level or aspect of business life can be considered a predominantly rational enterprise. Take partnerships, for instance. As in any living process, partnership agreements become outmoded as partners age and new blood comes into the business with motivations, values and priorities in life that are quite different from those of the founders. Yet, successful partnerships survive the transitions to a new generation of leadership when there is a genuine, emotional bond between people that enables them to transcend the limitations of the "rational" framework. And, correlatively, partnerships do break up when emotional issues pile up, are swept under the rug and remain unaddressed, eventually becoming irreconcilable.

Or, consider life on the "firing line" level of the business. In all honesty, for how long can people work like machines, each doing the same task over and over? If the work progresses smoothly from one task to another, you can be sure people will soon get bored; if the work is choppy, fragmented and interrupted constantly, people get stressed and burned out. How rationally do people behave when new innovations are introduced? The answer,—"Not very."

On the sales level, despite the neat microeconomic models taught in universities, what is a rational decision for a customer? Is it to buy the cheapest products, or those of the highest quality? What product does make the most sense for them in terms of how "useful" or "helpful" it is? If people made buying decisions rationally, would there be a cigarette industry, for example? Despite these obvious facts, many decision makers try to treat their businesses as rational endeavors, manageable exclusively by the numbers, improvable by mechanistic tools. Rarely are managers judged or promoted on the basis of their "people skills," so they drive toward what they are evaluated on—that is, the bottom line.

Successful businesses, we consistently observe, are anything but "rational places." They exude emotion; people trust one another and look to one another as resources that can be counted on. People hug, they cry, they talk about their feelings about work. People up and down the organization make decisions and respect others' decisions based on emotional concerns. They are also fun places: Not the "theme park," sidetracked-from-life fun, but fun in the sense of being places where there is an opportunity to experience and share with others elevated and uplifting energy and action.

FALLACY NUMBER TWO: A BUSINESS CAN RUN LIKE A MILITARY UNIT OR CAN OPERATE LIKE A MACHINE

If the decision maker's organizational model is that of a machine, the company will be driven by efficiencies. Things will be expected to be done in the fastest, most economical way. Overlap or redundancy will be a cardinal sin. Management may be relatively flat, but the people at the top still think of themselves as the machine's designer, architect and/or software all rolled into one; the people below do the work. When these models are in play, I find decision makers are quite amenable to faddish ideas; they try little tweaks to the system that, they expect, will get the machine running faster, more efficiently. When a crisis hits or a decision has to be made, it will be demanded that people work more efficiently; a new program is announced and fancy signs touting slogans like "Can Do" appear.

The mechanistic model fits well with the presumption that businesses are rational places. If businesses are rational, they can be controlled, manipulated, tweaked. Strategies can be centrally developed and managed with hierarchical authority. But since businesses are most definitely not rational places, the model ends up being forcibly superimposed on the organization. Not only are workers' and managers' lives emptied of their internal drive and passion, their contributions are demeaned by being pigeonholed into narrow, mechanically repetitive jobs.

These presumptions are strangling businesses. Warren Bennis observes,

Life on this turbulent, complex planet is no longer linear and sequential, one thing logically leading to another. It is spontaneous, contrary, unexpected, and ambiguous. Things do not happen according to plan, and they are not reducible to tidy models. We persist in grasping at neat, simple answers, when we should be questioning everything.[2]

As we will see, there are new ways to envision how a business operates and organizes people to accomplish goals. These new ideas unleash the potential of what organizations can make happen in their markets and energize the people who do the work. These ideas appeal not just to the mind, but to the heart, the "Strategic Heart," as well.

FALLACY NUMBER THREE: BUSINESSES MUST BE RUTHLESS AND OPPORTUNISTIC

While they are portraying themselves as doing their best for "their people," many managers, just beneath the surface, really believe that they are not responsible for decisions that may hurt people. The ethical universe of managers such as these is ruled by an iron logic of competition: "All is fair." Deals are cutthroat; you can get fired; people are out for their own advancement and enrichment and will stab you in the back to get what they want; businesses are places of politics, not ethics.

Of the three fallacies about business, this one is the most damaging. Not only is it wrong, but this preconception undermines the very enterprise it purports to protect. This misconception undermines any possibility of constructive organizational transformation and especially of attaining the goal of this book—to have people perform beyond expectations, with energy, insight and enthusiasm. It kills the commitments between managers and employees and other stakeholders that can lead to innovation, value and profits.

The workplace can be a positive, constructive, meaningful part of life. In fact, given the decline of many of our socializing institutions such as family, church and local government, the workplace may be the best place, and may be the only place, to realize goals interdependently, working side by side with people of different backgrounds, education levels, races, countries of origin and organizational responsibilities. On the one hand, I can definitely cite examples where misplaced loyalty on the part of a business owner or manager has led to a decline in a business's performance. On the other hand, in the pages that follow, I will cite many more numerous situations wherein a company that is known for being run on an equitable, moral and highly humane ground does so without any diminution in managerial prerogatives in terms of hiring, firing or moving people into different positions.

These businesses not only survive, they thrive on change and challenge. People are not threatened by these changes; rather, the business provides a structure from which to undertake them. Businesses that succeed are what the management scholar Robert Burgleman calls "opportunity structures."[3] They are platforms from which people can accomplish something they feel is worthwhile and life-enhancing. To do this, they are willing to invest exceptional emotional energy and committed attention as well as extraordinary time.

What employees and managers ask from a company is that they get a chance to contribute something, that their efforts amount to something and be recognized. When this is provided to them, their loyalty is cemented and their performance remains solid. It is quite natural that over time a company may move away from needing a particular skill set, or it changes priorities in a way that changes its employment needs. Employees and managers affected by the change can be given a choice: if they can change and adapt, they make the cut; if they can't, they move on. A company's tradition of fair, equitable and moral treatment of its personnel, accompanied by good documentation of fairness in a particular case, gives decision makers room to make tough decisions because people know they were taken into consideration and that the choices are difficult for everyone. After tough choices are made, a fair and morally sound business can mourn openly for a time and then move on to new challenges.

Businesses must adapt and respond to difficult and sometimes painful challenges. Employees know this. Losing a job is painful, but most employees don't look to businesses to guarantee their livelihood forever. Workers are really asking for a different quality of commitment from employers that includes:

- Genuine recognition and appreciation of their current contributions and their potential to contribute in the future.

- An effective and reliable process that incorporates their ideas into the practices of the business that really matter.

- A genuine attempt to foster adaptation, over a reasonable amount of time, to anticipated changes.

- Frank and truthful evaluations of current performance.

- Truthful accounts of how the business is developing and what changes are likely to happen.
- If termination is envisioned, then a provision for a reasonable transition.
- Constancy in hard times—as soon as trouble hits, the company does not immediately pull the plug on them.

The challenge is to be fair, moral and reasonable, not saintly or perfect.

COMPLEXITY, FLOW AND THE GROWING BUSINESS ORGANIZATION

It is time to move beyond such a static, narrow and ultimately destructive worldview and take advantage of the wider possibilities opened up by the new modes of thinking now coursing through the networks of the scientific world. This book presents those ideas in the belief that they provide new answers to the questions and problems that all of us face in our work lives. It proposes a new outlook on the purpose of a business's organization. It will show how an organization is not a down-side consequence of responding to growing markets and rising customer excitement. An organization is a means to liberate human potential in collaborative actions that drive toward achieving large-scale goals. Far from creating the ennui and boredom we have succumbed to in the bureaucracies of the past, growing business organizations unleash the power of the human spirit in each of us and can thereby benefit us all.

This is a bold assertion. Yet, all around us are examples of organizations that respond in miraculous ways to their environmental challenges. They adapt, learn and grow. They develop incredible skills and command respect, even awe, in what they are able to do. These are very complex systems, bursting with energy that borders on the chaotic. They are also highly organized, self-determining and self-perpetuating entities that are very successful at adapting to changing circumstances. The systems that effectively adapt and thrive in a changing, competitive environment are living systems—like ourselves and our fellow creatures—and complex social systems like societies, nations and business organizations.

Recently, scientists have made these living, changing, developing systems the object of critical study. It is this work that we believe opens up new avenues of thought about what a business organization makes possible in the lives of those it touches.

Complexity: A New Way of Thinking

A group of scientists from a wide range of disciplines—chemistry, physics, biology, cybernetics, the social sciences, economics—has been developing an understanding of evolving, environmentally adaptive systems that use available resources in order to grow into new, more complex forms. Their work has also resulted in a whole new style of scientific thinking. We are used to the traditional brand of science that reduces the variety of life, materials and forces we enjoy around us down to the most basic particles and fragments. However, when the explorers of complexity look at the world, they move in the opposite direction. They see how apparently simple, "nonconscious," subatomic particles of matter, when energized into a near-chaos state of activity, can actually organize themselves (around various kinds of attractors) to form grand and complex systems—galaxies, living organisms, human beings, institutions and whole societies.

That outlook is called "Complexity." Rest assured that the name does not allude to complicated formulae, undecipherable prose or a maze of cross- and inter-connected patterns. The name "complexity" is actually shorthand for a style of thinking that has as its premise that matter, even at its most primary and irreducible level (is that quarks?), is predisposed, under certain circumstances, to combine with other particles and organize into entities that have greater complexity.

The evolution of complex systems points to a factor for which traditional, mechanist and reductionist ways of thinking were unable to account: Evolution creates entities that are more capable, adaptable and creative than anticipated by any of the original components that constituted the system. Organized systems, such as galaxies or human beings, are entities in which the whole is, in fact, truly greater than the sum of its parts. Scientists conjecture that is characteristic of complex systems stems from that fact that it is not a system's total size or mass that makes it capable of organizing into self-sustaining and growing entities but rather the highly energized state of its comprising elements.

The picture scientists create can be summarized this way: Highly energized material gathers around some stable and attractive agent. As long as the energy can be sustained and a suitable attractor for that energy is available, the universe evolves to form "emergent" entities of greater complexity. That is, emerging from the gases and dust of the "Big Bang" come stars, galaxies and solar systems. And, from these more complex materials, develop life, intelligence and, eventually, intelligent, human social systems that have taken charge of their own evolution. Each new, "emergent" system evinces capabilities that can hardly be imagined as emanating from those constituent parts (Who could imagine that consciousness would emerge from the firing of billions of neurons in the brain?). In the new science, the whole is significantly, qualitatively greater than the sum of the parts. And, according to this model, there is no end in sight to the potential of this evolution.

Businesses most certainly qualify as complex, emergent social systems that evolve and adapt to their environments (i.e., markets). Businesses are self-organizing, complex entities that capitalize on the energized performance of their constituents (owners, managers, vendors) in order to be more effective in their markets, take on new challenges and command greater impact in the lives of their customers and other stakeholders. The more that business decision makers take into account the kinds of thinking that describe how systems become more complex—meaning more capable of adapting to and generating change in their environments—the better they will be able to guide their organizations toward success and profitability. Complexity, as a discipline of observations and knowledge and as a style of thinking, offers decision makers an opportunity to look at their organizations in a positive light.

But in most businesses today, the organization is regarded as an afterthought. The company is growing and adding people and processes, so the thinking goes that it must divide its organization into more parts, break down into more manageable components. The process becomes one of adding a new box under the president, naming a new vice president to go into the box and then adding more boxes under that one. In more radical designs, decision makers may go so far as to "spin off" an entirely new company, creating a more "entrepreneurial" business unit instead of adding to the existing one. This only creates more bureaucracy. Another option always under consideration is "downsizing." This may seem like an odd response to growth, but nevertheless the thinking goes that investment in automation and hyperspeed communications will permit growth with fewer people and lowered payroll.

All of these options have their place in the arsenal of organizational development approaches. But most often we see these models applied inappropriately. These approaches to adjusting an organization to new competitive realities reflect precisely the kind of thinking that neglects the power of organizations to be constructive factors in the process of making businesses successful. Companies that build mechanistically or downsize precipitously often reach the condition called "corporate anorexia": they have depleted their store of knowledge, experience, talent and enthusiasm to the point that growing again costs far more than the investment in incremental change would have cost. Reaching this state of affairs, however, is a symptom of a larger problem that I would call "organizational aphasia," the inability to see a business's organization as a source of creativity and strength.

These decision makers have forgotten that organizations amplify individuals' talents by organizing their energies into larger entities with greater capability, flexibility and adaptability. These ideas key off the ideal of the "entrepreneur in the garage" who, with no bureaucracy, no hierarchy—just complete freedom—arrives at the invention of the century. The Steve Jobs and Steve Wasniaks of the world creating a personal computer, are, in fact, rarities. More likely, inventions and innovations spring from the trials and errors of interconnected collaborators. Up to a point, the more connections and the more fruitful the experimentation, the more likely the efforts will bear fruit in the form of a commercially successful product. The job of the decision maker is discerning what level of organization, size, energy level and resources are most fitting to meet a certain challenge.

I see the discipline of complexity as offering decision makers the best antidote that has ever been available to this organizational "aphasia." Instead of reductively analyzing organizations down to their most uncreative and limited component, the complexity model provides decision makers with a metaphor and way of thinking about people and organizations that is expansive, creative, egalitarian and open-ended. This idea holds tremendous power for unlocking a business's energies, internally and externally—freeing the talents and capabilities of everyone in the organization in completely new ways.

Complexity is the subject of Part I of this volume. We will first discuss the major tenets of complexity and then see how top decision makers can put certain practices into place that envision the organization as an evolving, complex system, increasing in capability and adaptability and not as a machine. We will see how the organization's values, mission, core actions and ability to engender choice make room for the kind of change and challenge that generate lasting success and profitability.

Flow: The Lure of Challenge, the Joy of Growth

Working in a mechanistic way saps our energy. When put in situations that demand this kind of behavior, people have no choice but to disconnect from their inner lives. They crank the stuff out or oversee the processes by means of which others crank the stuff out. Today, businesses are demanding more attention, more dedication, more commitment from their people. Trying to run "lean and mean," managers are pressing their people to work longer hours and work "smarter"—do more tasks more efficiently.

There is little choice: We do need dedicated attention and high performance from people. However, there is a great deal of choice as to how we achieve these goals. For employees to be energized, focusing and stretching beyond their comfort zones, managers need to treat them as the experiencing human beings they are and not means to generating a certain level of output. You can force people to stretch themselves for only so long. People are really effective, and sustain that level of performance for long periods of time, when they are challenged and engaged in something that has meaning and accomplishes something worthwhile.

This is my argument with the "reengineering" and "process" brand of consultants that have made headlines of late. They feast on the three fallacies we began with. They see people as being cogs in the great machine, as performers of steps in the great process of production. You improve performance, they say, by cutting fat, giving the survivors bigger jobs, automating and rationalizing. "Not so," I would argue. You get greater performance from people by immersing them in the vital, value-creating relationships in which the business has to succeed each and every day. It is these relationships that present real challenge and offer the opportunity for creativity and validation of one's value.

"Enrich relationships" (rather than pare-down processes) is the mandate of the line manager in today's businesses. Time and time again, I find that as people are promoted into line manager positions, they seem to lose their way. When they were line workers, they were determined to become managers and have authority and not just be accountable to someone else's standards. When they are promoted, however, these new managers are often perplexed and at a loss as to how they add value to the company. It becomes harder for them to understand just what it is they are supposed to do each day. Now that someone else is "doing the work," what do they do? Do they make sure things are done right? Do they count and measure what others do? Do they think of new ways to reorganize their groups? How do they get people to work better, faster, smarter?

In Chapter 7, I show how line managers add value by helping people fully engage in their work—experiencing it in a way that adds to their sense of excitement and expands their vision about themselves as productive people who contribute to the well-being and success of a larger entity, the business. Line managers assure that people have proper resources: They negotiate with other managers to pave the way for new ideas; they put people together into effective groupings so that there are few distractions and they can maintain a clear picture of what needs to be done.

There is nothing "soft" about this approach. It is just that the emphasis is not on outputs and numbers and "efficiency" in the narrow, cost-saving sense, but rather on the idea that achieving peak performance on the job requires conditions in which people can achieve a quality of experience, which precludes that they feel bored, stressed, put upon and burned out.

There are, for instance, signposts and indications—some quantitative, but mostly qualitative—that an effective manager can notice and act on in order to help people achieve to standards of high performance. We call them "Critical Success Factors (CSFs)," and they will be the focus of our attention in Chapter 8. CSFs are indicators for evaluating an action that is embedded in the moment-by-moment results of each person's work. The workers themselves are the best monitors of whether or not these indicators are showing up in the plus column. The manager's job becomes one of noticing them with the worker, reinforcing their importance and thinking, with the worker, of actions that have a better chance to achieve desired results.

Managers aren't soft-pedaling their concerns or downplaying the crucial roles of monitoring and upholding standards for outstanding performance. They work frankly and directly with the worker about achieving the kinds of responses and results the action is supposed to evoke. And even more, these indicators, qualitative though they may be, have the advantage of appearing long before any significant quantitative measurement can be made. Managers are engaged in the work, aware of what the work is really producing each and every day and able to provide relevant, collaborative feedback to the workers at all times. So the manager acts proactively—a nearly universal hallmark of managerial success.

The idea of CSFs, and many of the other concepts we present here, are based on a model of experience called "Flow." Its premise is that the most valuable work that people do for a business also produces the kinds of experiences that result in peak performance and transform work into enjoyment and enjoyment into achievement. The term "flow" was coined by Mihaly Csikszentmihalyi, a University of Chicago researcher, teacher and department chairman. In his two books, *Flow*[4] and *The Evolving Self*,[5] he describes how people in flow experience a sense of timeless engagement. They forget the narrow egotistical parts of themselves that crave control and power and become focused on the energy, drive and moment-by-moment progress that their actions are producing. Their minds and bodies are in sync, "psychically organized" as Csikszentmihalyi describes it. Their performance is unassailably outstanding and productive. This is the quality of experience we seek to harness in the context of the growing business organization that is adding complexity and capability.

As Csikszentmihalyi makes clear, the phenomena of flow and complexity are linked:

> Enjoyment alone will not lead evolution in a desirable direction unless one finds flow in activities that stretch the self. Therefore *seeking out complexity* [his italics] is also necessary. Continuing curiosity and interest, and the desire to find ever new challenges, coupled with the commitment to develop appropriate skills, lead to lifelong learning. When this attitude is present, a ninety-year-old is fresh and exciting; when it is lacking, a healthy youth appears listless and boring.[6]

Flow and complexity go together because businesses cannot evolve in a desirable direction just because people are enjoying themselves. Creating warm and happy environments, all the rage these days, is neither necessary nor sufficient in order to achieve the business's goal of creating more value for customers and sustained profitability for the company. What is effective is creating situations and environments in which people can frequently achieve flow. In Part II, we document concrete steps that elevate others to achieve peak performance and productivity. We will offer managers descriptions of the qualities of experience to which they need to pay attention if they are to take the lid off and do the work at peak levels of performance. We will show how different kinds of organizational practices lend themselves to creating the environments in which peak performance has the best chance of materializing.

CREATING THE STRATEGIC ORGANIZATION

My experiences as a consultant with Mage Centers for Management Development drive the pages that follow. Mage works with managers of companies in transition: from small to becoming large; from one generation in a family to the next, or one generation of partners to a new generation; from private to public. Our method is to coach managers toward personal growth while helping them to implement the strategic organizational changes that have to be made. During the course of this work, I have encountered managers who genuinely understand how to create organizations that compete successfully and enrich the lives of the people in them at the same time. They understand that a healthy and growing organization not only amplifies each person's ability to perform tasks but also makes it possible for the business as a whole to operate over a wider field of endeavor, to reach and affect more people in different ways, to create value in more individualistic and more comprehensive ways.

These organizations are primed for change. Not only do the individuals in the organization know that they may do things differently tomorrow than they do them today, they have had a major role in determining what they will be doing differently. Change is not a threat to their job, it is their responsibility. Managers look to their people to do more than crank stuff out and solve the problems put before them. They want these people to think of what needs to be produced in the future and to demand that measures be adopted so that problems don't recur. The organization is a platform for change, providing both the resources that amplify the talents of individuals and groups and the continuity to make the changes stick.

It isn't surprising that most managers, at all levels, have only the most perfunctory understanding about what organizations make possible. Up until now there has been very little general understanding about how complex systems work. All kinds of organizations, from the inorganic celestial systems, to the simplest organisms to the most advanced social systems, were thought to constitute merely a more complicated confluence of mechanical, one-dimensional, linear forces. The results of that kind of thinking for businesses has been the mechanistic, static views on organizations we have outlined. Managers have not been given reason to consider their organizations as worthy of attention. Their focus is on getting the organization out of the way so that profits can be made. Minimizing organization, as well as the thought given to it, has been the rule of thumb.

Complexity and flow open up our ability to become literate and experimental in designing and leading organizations. They provide decision makers with signposts and working principles that highlight the right kinds of actions to take to foster vital, dynamic and creative responses to challenges in the marketplace. They provide us with guidelines by which we can identify and build on an organization's "emergent" properties which, in turn, can be used to break through the barriers of any one person's limited imagination.

To that end, *The Strategic Heart* sketches out a way for decision makers to encourage and develop those qualities of human experience that lead both to a strong performance ethic in individuals and to the ability of the organization to assume risk and create change. On one level, the idea of *The Strategic Heart* is that a business's growth and development is a matter of pulling together many different people's talents and perspectives into a vital, thriving organization. People don't pull together on the basis of rationality. They rally around a compelling emotion. Growth—for individuals as well as for organizations—is emotional and heartfelt from start to finish. Rationality is usually a means to divide, reduce, replace. These are negative and degrading actions, not the actions that create new ideas around which people rally. Those that try to work by strictly rational principles create degrading emotions: frustration, discouragement, isolation, detachment.

In our complex, pluralistic, diverse society, one person's good rational reason is easily outargued, outbid or discredited by another's experience. People come together in today's world because there is an emotionally compelling reason to do so. They believe in a mission; they trust and esteem its leaders, rallying around them because these people point the way to accomplishing something great. And, along the way, they see opportunities for their own personal growth and enrichment. *The Strategic Heart* draws decision makers' attention to the kinds of energies that excite and inspire people, moving them and their colleagues to create organizations that can move toward new horizons of accomplishment.

On another level, *The Strategic Heart* points to the qualities of leadership that create organizations that can continually act strategically in their markets. Acting strategically means creating change. Leading strategic organizations means guiding a company's managers and employees through sustained, continual change so successfully that they make it possible for customers to try new products, attempt new actions, do things in new ways. *The Strategic Heart* points beyond the so-called "learning organization," that is, an organization that is able to adapt to change, to the *"strategic organization"* that amplifies and sustains the energies, openness and aspirations of its people so that they can collaborate in creating new opportunities. These organizations have the courage and the ability to aspire to the same level of greatness we admire in our most esteemed heroes, institutions and epoch-making ideas.

Senior Managers

The new disciplines of complexity and flow not only make it possible for decision makers and their employees to work more successfully, they change the work that needs to be done. The disciplines we cite here do not support laissez-faire management styles or completely flat, egalitarian organization. However, the kinds of qualities that constitute managerial attention and hierarchy do change. Senior managers, who are the primary focus of Part I, do not simply monitor results at a higher level and a more abstract and pre-digested (quantified) form. They are not simply designers of new "org. charts" who approve purchase orders over a certain dollar amount. Senior managers are living "attractors," focusing the near chaos action, energy and enthusiasm generated in the strategic organization. They keep the people of the organization within the intentional (mission- and values-based) boundaries and also provide the structure that captures the ideas, initiatives and innovations that drive strategic change. When they are successful, senior managers lead by evoking the "strategic values" that propel an organization into new areas of endeavor and challenge. As we will see in Chapter 10, they demonstrate and embody the constancy and concentration that keeps people moving together with determination as the changes unfold around them.

Skillful senior managers elevate the performance of everyone around them by giving people a sense of confidence and comfort even as they are moving into new, risky and challenging situations. To do this, senior managers have to get beyond the confines of their "Strategic Minds." Analyzing markets and competitors, crunching the numbers on the spread sheet, monitoring and measuring quantifiable outputs from working units provide information that is often inaccurate and is always too late to be useful in the competitive struggles of the international marketplace. Successful senior managers (some of whom are profiled in this book) consistently reach out with their own passion and embrace the requirements and potentials of the "Strategic Heart," including the values that unify people (Chapter 2), the mission that spells out how the business intends to affect people's lives (Chapter 3) and the concerted focus on the actions that will accomplish that mission (Chapter 4).

The "Strategic Mind," mired as it is in the lingering shadows of events that have long since passed, often fails to look up to see what is emerging over the dawning horizon. A strategy, after all, only exists to assure that the right things get done in order to create change. Any strategy worthy of the name attempts to mobilize people's talents and energies to accomplish things that have never been done before, at least by those now executing the strategy. Strategies consciously marshal resources to change situations, circumstances, behaviors and events. The "Strategic Mind," in my experience, never gets to the point of realizing the fullness of opportunity—it is only capable of assessing the static terrain and the already digested experiences of the past.

The Strategic Heart is, above all, an attitude of the thriving organization that incessantly pushes forward. The experiences it draws on for its insights are living and vital—culled from the interactions that happen every day on the business's firing line (Chapter 5). The plans don't make something happen. Energy, will, heart, risk-taking and action make things happen. Its plans are sometimes sketchy and incomplete, and instead it relies on the innovating and spontaneously adjusting talents of working people to make things work. Its limitations are determined only by the company's ability to invest and leverage its organized resources.

Line Managers

Line managers have to pay attention to how the specific "subsystems" of the organization perform. As we will detail in Part II, they concentrate on maintaining the focus and concentration it takes to keep employees working at an effective level of performance day after day. They do this by fulfilling "organizational values" that leverage the resources that are already in place in order to create new connections with customers and other stakeholders that challenge and ultimately expand workers' capabilities (Chapter 7). Their actions assure that choice, readiness and innovation are values acted upon and esteemed by everyone in the organization (Chapter 10). In terms of the complexity model, line managers are the keepers of that near-chaos condition that keeps a person's spirit alive and thriving against the tides of inertia or overwhelming competition. Line managers assure that the high energy output and risk-taking that people on the line have to sustain are worthwhile for everyone involved. By their constant and knowledgeable attention to each person's daily exertion, by their overt, consistent and demanding support of innovation and by their ability to modulate and channel workers' energies into real possibilities for success, they protect the business's vitality over the long term (Chapter 9).

The New Managerial Work

Each type of manager has a role in keeping a business thriving and successful. As we will discuss in Chapter 10, the hierarchy that is envisioned in the disciplines of Complexity and Flow are ones that elevate a different kind of leader than was valued in the traditional mechanistic models. It is not that the monitors and directors—the authoritarian skills of managing a machine—are not employed. At some point in any manager's day, these skills are called for. But they are not valued as qualities worthy of promotion for their own sake.

The "production skills" that had once been the province of the clock-watching monitors of the assembly line are hopefully internalized by each worker in a self-monitoring style of work. One only begins to travel the road of management by demonstrating the ability to work for others and truly affect their working lives, as learning and growing individuals. Then, one begins the journey as a facilitator and broker. In this role, a young aspirant searches out and devises ways to help others find the resources and arrange the situations that can produce growth for them and excellence in service to the values and mission of the company. At the top of the hierarchy are the exemplars, mentors and masters who seem to embody the will of the whole organization as they move people into realms and challenges that they have never faced before. In short, to move up the hierarchy of a strategic organization—a business that is modeled using the disciplines of complexity and flow—a manager has to demonstrate the ability to marshal and multiply the human spirit of challenge and growth.

Armchair quarterbacks don't make it in business. You either act and it works, or you're out of business. Managers have to respond to the fact that these actions require a heartfelt exertion of risk-taking adventure; that is, a "Strategic Heart." This means that managers are willing to challenge everyone around them and that they themselves are willing to be challenged. They require of others a willingness to venture, to be at risk, to experience change; and they are willing to forgo their own comfort and control when others step up to accomplish something great. These managers, at all levels of the organization, are able to build the kinds of structures and practices that balance the safety of the rational plan with the passion it takes to challenge the unknown. How to strike that balance and maintain it over the long haul is the subject of the chapters that follow.

NOTES

1. Studs Terkel, *Working* (New York: Avon Books, 1972), p. xxvii.

2. Warren Bennis, *On Becoming a Leader* (Reading, MA: Addison-Wesley, 1994), p. 24.

3. Robert A. Burgleman, "Corporate Entrepreneurship and Strategic Management: Insights from a Process Study," *Management Science* 29, no. 12 (December 1983): 1353.

4. Mihaly Csikszentmihalyi, *Flow* (New York: HarperCollins, 1990).

5. Mihaly Csikszentmihalyi, *The Evolving Self* (New York: HarperCollins, 1993).

6. Ibid., p. 248.

Part I

Unleashing the Power of Your Organization

Chapter 1

Complexity: A New Model of Organization

It is quite remarkable that we are at a moment both of profound change
in the scientific concept of nature and of the structure of human society
as a result of the demographic explosion. As a result, there is a need for
new relations between man and nature and between man and man.
—Ilya Prigogine, *Order Out of Chaos*[1]

THE MEANING OF ORGANIZATION

The new science of "complexity" promises nothing less than a new, revo-
lutionary way to understanding the world around us. Scientific descriptions provide explanations for how things work in a rigorous, testable way. Up until now,
that has meant reducing things to their most basic, and ultimately meaningless,
units. Complexity obeys the scientific tenets of rigor and testability, while it
also tells us how dynamic and changing systems create, evolve and grow.

Complexity is actually shorthand for a variety of descriptions of the ways
complex systems develop. Complex systems include many of the structures we
see around us, from crystals or hurricanes to organisms and societies. Since
many people from different scientific fields observe one or another aspect of a
phenomenon, they each name what they see differently. Ilya Prigogine, a Nobel
Laureate chemist, calls the complex systems he observes "dissipative structures," because they consume and then dissipate energy in order to perpetuate
themselves. Murray Gell-Mann, the Nobel Laureate physicist (who named physics' most basic particles "quarks") calls the phenomenon "algorithmic information complexity," because these systems reduce the information gathered into
simplified formulas (such as scientific equations), which can be used for gathering, sorting and using information for survival. Another name that mostly

biologists and sociologists apply, and that comes closer to what we have in mind, is "complex adaptive systems," pointing to these systems' abilities to respond to environmental conditions.

In all cases, however, these pioneers cite certain elements that are consistent in the complex systems they are describing. We will describe them below and show how businesses organize people, machines and ideas into complex systems. From these descriptions, we can get a taste for how well this model of complexity provides a new way to understand events in the life of doing business.

We no longer need to see the business's organization as a cost-creating inconvenience; we no longer need to see the people in the organization as adjuncts to machines that crank stuff out. These narrow and stifling concepts of business organization can be cleared away so businesses can meet the technical and social challenges that loom in the next century. To do this, decision makers need to appreciate the kinds and qualities of energies that are needed to accomplish large-scale goals. So, before we can hope to provide a new vision of how to unleash the power of human insights and energies, we need to reorient ourselves to the context in which this vision can be realized. That is the purpose and intent of Part I.

Using the insights of complexity, we will see how a growing organization is a business's most productive asset. We can appreciate the dynamics of growth and see how adding complexity actually increases the ability of everyone involved—managers, employees, customers and other stakeholders—to act together in a collaborative effort that benefits all.

EDGE OF CHAOS

In his seminal book, *Order Out of Chaos*,[2] Ilya Prigogine describes how order and organization arise out of energized, chaotic situations. When matter is cool, at a low level of energy, it is in a state of "equilibrium." Equilibrium is the state in which we find the static, gross bodies we experience as the physical things around us. These bodies don't interact with the environment. They don't change of their own volition over time. If you took a piece of granite from a New Hampshire quarry and dropped it in a Brazilian rain forest, nothing would happen to it. Eons later, it would still be that piece of granite. These materials, as we know, change only by decay, submitting to the inexorable laws of entropy and eventually wearing away or dissolving into the environment around them.

We also know that when matter is overenergized, when it is heated to extremes or when it is subjected to an extreme impact, it burns up or explodes. Excitation takes matter "off the chart"; it goes "nonlinear," obliterating any hope of maintaining internal cohesion or historical continuity with its former state.

When matter is energized to just the right level, however, it behaves in a completely different way. When atoms and their constituent parts are excited by light or heat, for instance, but not so excited that they fly apart, they can some-how "sense" what other materials are in the vicinity, but beyond the boundaries of their own atomic unit, and can respond to them. Furthermore, these excited and energized particles are able to combine with the atomic particles of these more distant materials to form new structures. In this "far from equilibrium" (but nonexplosive) state, matter tends to become sensitized to its environment, and it also combines with other materials in that environment into more complex structures.

Order only arises out of highly energized situations. Not all chaotic situations give rise to organization (an "attractor" is necessary, as we will see momen-tarily), but a complex system has to be a high energy place. The material or system persists in a condition that is active and highly sensitized to what is around it, but not so chaotic as to drive it to fall apart or to explode. Michael Waldrop, a writer and reporter on the emerging science of complexity, says these systems are in "a certain kind of balance between the forces of order and the forces of disorder. . . . These systems are both stable enough to store infor-mation, and yet evanescent enough to transmit it."[3]

With this observation about the nature of living systems, complexity offers a key insight of startling freshness about business organizations. Living, thriving, strategically capable organizations have a touch of wildness about them. There is no "business as usual" at these places. In every corner of the business, in every department and functional unit, plans are underway to change the way things are done. Every day, there are e-mail messages posted about new ways that the company is solving problems and forming terms to make internal changes or plot new responses to the market. Organizational charts are useless and replaced with "maps" that lay out who is involved in working on this or that situation for now. Lines of communication are alive, humming and buzzing, because there is so much to learn each and every day.

Business organizations can be characterized along a continuum in the same way we plotted matter in different states of energy. At one end is the low energy bureaucratic organization; in the middle is the high energy, strategic organiza-tion; and at the far end is the entrepreneurial organization that approaches non-linear explosion. When a business is settled in its low energy ways, habituated and bureaucratized, it labors with a heavy, leaden quality. It moves slowly, accomplishing little, and it senses little of what is happening around it—how customers are responding to its actions or how effectively employees and man-agers are performing. Leadership is constant and rigid. If such a business isn't blind to what is happening around it, it still doesn't have the heart to redeploy its resources and rethink how it does things. In the 1980s, we saw what happened to tired and flaccid businesses when international competition hit home with a vengeance. They disappeared.

In the other direction, when a business is out of control—for instance, its sales far outstrip the ability of its organization to absorb them—it flies apart. People aren't in touch with what is happening, they perform erratically and without consistency. Quality and customer focus get lost. The business collapses in on itself.

When the business strikes just the right balance between growth and its capacity to absorb the changes that come with that growth, it has achieved the status of being a strategic organization. It is an exciting, high energy place, bursting with activity while also maintaining itself at some level of equilibrium. Every action does not lead to a predefined result; there is not one-to-one correspondence between a process and an outcome, but the people are alive, in touch with their surroundings and customers and eager to find innovative solutions to problems that are more demanding.

These people are acting with what we call their "Strategic Hearts." They are alive with ideas and pushing hard, using the organization's resources and leverage in the marketplace to make something worthwhile happen. They are acting to be effective now and, at the same time, moving themselves and those around (and above) them toward new challenges. This attitude of the soul is the absolute basic and primary condition for the emergence of the growing, driving organizations we are describing.

ACTIVELY CONSUMING RESOURCES

To remain in this "far from equilibrium" state, all complex systems consume resources. There is no free lunch, especially in the world of complex systems. By consuming resources, burning up energy in a controlled, modulated manner, complex systems confound the "entropy" described by the second law of thermodynamics. This law states that as heat and energy dissipate, all things run down over time, order dissolving into chaos or into a uniform, formless soup. By absorbing sunlight or eating other organisms, plants and animals hold back the forces of entropy for a time. An animal's prey supplies food that is converted into slowly released fuel that sustains the predator's life, allowing it to move, respond, learn, reproduce and perpetuate its species.

Businesses consume many kinds of energy. They consume physical resources, fossil fuels and the like to power machines and appliances used to perform their activities as well as the energies of human labor. Businesses also consume a higher level of energy. They consume a general social resource we call "wealth." Wealth is partly measured by the government's Gross Domestic Product. It is the amount of accumulated resources that are available today as a result of the whole society's efforts. But wealth is an even more encompassing term, since it includes a society's human resources in the form of trained, educated and able people who can apply their talents and energies in an informed, organized and modulated way to the benefit of others. When that overall social wealth exceeds the resources that had existed yesterday, the society's economy is growing. Wealth represents the bounty of our social economy, a pool of energy that is readily available and adaptable for human and business consumption—and businesses do consume it.

Organized systems also store up some of what they have consumed, transforming it into energy at a later time. This ability to store material and consume it at a later time allows us to get through times of famine. It also allows organisms such as humans to use some of their time for purposes other than searching for food. For a business, stored energy comes in the form of *profit*.

Profit represents a kind of contractual relationship between a business and its customers. People allow business to charge a bit more for an item than it costs to make because they accept this as the way the business preserves, and hopefully improves, itself. Businesses depend on people being willing to pay profit-sustaining prices, and people depend on businesses to reinvest those profits in better products and services. By drawing on these stores of energy, businesses create new products and services and a more diversified array of human activities. Some of these activities are completely new, others are familiar activities made easier, more pleasurable or at least less onerous.

Of course we have painted a rather benign picture of businesses and their consumption of resources. In the process of evolution, organisms tend to *over-consume* resources and so put their environments in jeopardy. Gypsy moths, for instance, eat themselves into periodic near extinction by stripping trees bare of the leaves they depend on for sustenance. Businesses also abuse their environments. The ecological movement is our social response to the need to moderate these demands on resources so we won't overconsume ourselves out of existence. New environmental businesses are also arising to take up the job of incorporating environmental protection into the commercial, profit-making sphere.

The idea here is that profit-making businesses can always find ways to translate their consumption activities into profit-making opportunities that exploit the environment. Restraint, in this scenario, is only a way station on the path to new enterprises. While in the short run, we as a society have done a great deal to reclaim our waters and land, we'll have to see how well this idea pans out in the long run. Business will always consume resources, however, and society will have to learn how to balance its competing needs, one of which is profit-making institutions.

MULTIPLICITY, ATTRACTORS AND EMERGENCE

Attractors

Because their energies coalesce around an ''attractor,'' complex systems do not merely fly apart, dispersing into oblivion. An attractor can be anything from a stable molecule in a chemical reaction to a robust and compelling idea in a society. In the latter case, people's individual actions and energies are elevated, excited, even aggressive, but they keep the larger social entity intact because they intend to support the guiding idea. An attractor adds an element of ''intentionality" to the near-chaotic swirl of activity. It integrates that activity into a form that is capable of using energy to sustain itself and adapt (and adapt to) the environment around it.

Higher complex systems, and especially very complex systems such as organisms and societies, are characterized by the fact that they *unify a multiplicity* of different kinds of systems, each of which specializes in performing one or another function. This combination does not merely function together the way a car's engine and transmission combine to move the vehicle. To create complexity, the combination of the constituents' actions *emerge* into a capability that can only be described as being qualitatively beyond what any sum of similar or different parts could accomplish.

Emergence

For instance, consciousness is an *emergent* property of the combination of billions of neurons firing in the brain. There is no way the electrochemical reactions of the neurons themselves or in combination foretell the emergence of consciousness. The latter "emerges" out of the firing of these units, however, because they have been ordered, sequenced and organized. As Mitchell Waldrop muses, "Somehow, by constantly seeking mutual accommodation and self-consistency, groups of agents manage to transcend themselves and become something more."[4]

Complex, emergent systems "transcend themselves" by organizing around a "hierarchy" of attractors. Simpler actions—atomic or molecular—are guided by simple and basic materials that act as attractors; the combined actions of more integrated systems are guided by attractors of a higher order. The simpler actions are not overwhelmed or eliminated by the higher ones, but are unified and coordinated in an intentional act by the attractors that are effective at higher levels. This manner of organization, called "emergence," provides for the complete open-endedness of complex systems' evolution. There is no limit to the number of attractors that can be incorporated into a system, and there is no limit to the continuum of moving from point attractors to the more complex and abstract attractors. "There is no fixed limit of complexity, either in biological or in socio-cultural evolution," says author Klaus Mainzer.[5]

In the movement toward more complexity, both aspects—the multiplicity of individual subsystems and their unification into a new emergent entity—are important. First, there are a multiplicity of different kinds of systems interacting in specialized ways with different aspects of the organism's life. Integrating these functions into a single, simplified, flowing life form is just as crucial since that allows the organism to act quickly, decisively and appropriately to changes and dangers in the environment. A hitter's split-nanosecond decision to swing at an incoming fastball (or slider) comes to mind. The end results of these coordinated, integrated and locally guided responses are the flight of the eagle, the attack of the panther or Ted Williams's swing of the bat—all graceful, seemingly effortless actions that are incredibly complex and demanding and far beyond what any component of that system can do on its own.

Values and Mission

A business is a complex system that also has different disciplines that it uses to sustain itself: for example, sales, finance, facilities and management. A great deal of managerial energy is spent keeping these functions running smoothly. The mental picture conjured up here is a manager acting like the instructional code for a computer or the designer of a machine. The managerial mandate in this model is to monitor, control, coordinate, communicate, measure.

From the standpoint of complexity, however, that old "scientific management" has had its day—and good riddance, I might add. With the kind of competition businesses are facing each and every day, those managerial functions have to become "autonomic"—built reflexively into the tissue and bone of the business. In terms of complexity, these conceptual and intentional "attractors" of action have to be built into the moment-by-moment practices, into the habits and expectations of each worker. This is the idea of self-management we all have heard so much about and that we support wholeheartedly. The people doing the work that fulfills the purpose of the company have to be ready to immediately respond in a fluid, spontaneous, novel and integrated way to the changes that are happening all around them—on their own.

To create a strategic organization, people have to coalesce their individual actions around "attractors" that coordinate the business's actions on a higher, more subliminal plane. For a business, that transindividual level of attractor, which guides the intentions and creates meaning from the assemblage of discrete, individual actions, is described by its *values* and *mission*. The senior managers in an organization embody the values and mission and act as symbols of their daily importance.

Values constitute the business's highest, most compelling and most durable attractor. They demarcate the range of accepted and permitted actions that the company will support and condone in any situation. Each action that a person has to take during the workday cannot be prescribed in advance. The company's values act as an attractor by pulling actions in a certain direction and deflecting them from other directions. They create a field of approved intentions, of supported expectations that if kept in mind point to a way to resolve issues. Even mistakes within those values are permitted. After all, even the best hitters strike out, but they know their job is to swing at the ball. Thus, when people identify with deeply rooted company values, they feel free to decide and act "instinctively."

The mission of a company has a two-sided "attractive" quality. For one, it is the "attractor" that a company sets out to create in its markets. By virtue of doing certain things, as specified in the mission, people will be attracted to what the business has to offer. Internally, the mission forms the attractor for unifying the multiplicity of actions the company needs to take to meet the demands of customers and markets. In this role, the mission defines what everyone in the company intends to make happen in its markets and for its customers each and every day. The business may not accomplish all of this on any particular day, but each and every action performed by each and every person in the company each and every day has no other intention but to accomplish that action eventually for the benefit of customers (and ultimately other stakeholders in the company).

How a business disseminates and activates its values is the subject of Chapter 2; how it creates a compelling, unifying and action-creating mission is the subject of Chapters 3 and 4. In these chapters, we will see how the values and mission of a business's life unify the company's individual, corporate actions with the expectations and norms of the society and markets in which it operates. Just as an organism's species gives it a place and a role in an environment, the business's values and mission give it its role in a market.

Senior managers succeed when they are able to embody the company's values and mission. Often characterized as marking the difference between "leaders" and "managers," this ability to embody what is as yet only envisioned is not a matter of charisma or power, but of daily focus and attention. Senior managers who act as attractors for strategic organizations concentrate on the issues, relationships, and resource decisions that push everyone toward challenges that are real, compelling and have the chance of success. How senior managers act as exemplars, mentors and masters of strategic change is our focus in Chapter 10.

The complexity model opens up a new way to view the role of managers in regard to their people and to the kind of organization they are creating. Instead of enforcing the rules, in a strategic organization, managers elicit the aspiration of individual employees by reaching into their hearts and encouraging them to step up and swing, take that chance and make something happen. Instead of acting like enforcers, they embody the role of "attractors" that coalesce a complex system. The manager isn't just keeping score or time. The manager helps workers achieve individual success by acting as an attractor that integrates the resources of the organization for the benefit of all. In the second part of this volume, we will see how the iron-fisted taskmaster that used to pass as a manager fades away. Instead, a different skill emerges as the distinguishing mark of the successful manager—that of putting the right people together in the first place, so that they are working together each step of the way. The taskmaster who thrived by taking the business's organizational machinery is supplanted by the "results producing coach," who simultaneously works to increase the complexity, capability and prowess of the whole business organization and everyone in it. The new world of business has truly spawned a new managerial regime.

ADAPTIVE/LEARNING

The edge of chaos, as we have said, is a high energy state in which matter seems to become "aware" of its wider surroundings and is able to combine with other molecules and atoms to form more complex structures. When already complex organizations are in a far from equilibrium state, this ability to be aware becomes an ability to *learn.*

John Holland, one of the early members of the Santa Fe Institute—a complexity think tank—sees in this capability of complex systems a natural drive, a propensity to create "perpetual novelty." In fact, he notes, if a system ever winds down to equilibrium, it isn't just stable, it's dead. I am reminded of the old Bob Dylan line, "He who isn't busy being born is busy dying." That is an exact description of complex adaptive systems, or growing organizations. They are "constantly revising and rearranging their building blocks as they gain experience."[6] Some patterns catch on and are perpetuated in the system, others aren't successful or reinforced and die off.

Strategic Organizations

All of these revisions mean change. Sometimes the revisions and reshuffling of the building blocks result in gradual changes. But over time, the changes accumulate and a whole new system or subsystem emerges. A "quantum leap" occurs and whole new capabilities and new sets of market possibilities emerge. It is this ability that gives rise to the name "complex adaptive systems." Organizations can change instantaneously to avoid dangers or life/integrity-threatening events; and, over time, they can change even more drastically, changing their genetic material and so evolving new capabilities, new body forms and, eventually, whole new branches of species.

In this discussion, businesses that are capable of creating change within themselves and in their markets are "strategic organizations." By designating that kind and quality of organization, I want to highlight the fact that if businesses aren't changing, they are dying. It's that simple. If a business's customers aren't demanding changes and improvements in its products, services and business practices, some managers might think they finally have it right. They can relax because things are stable, going smoothly. Nothing could be farther from the truth. Equilibrium and stability aren't necessarily positive vital signs for a business. What is really happening is that customers of that capability have moved on to competitive products or have left that particular capability behind for another way of doing things.

Markets as Complex Systems

The complexity model lets us look at how businesses perform in their markets in a new light, with profound consequences for business strategy. We are all familiar with the traditional model of business cycles that looks at an "industry" and sees it going from a period of flowering, growth and a profusion of suppliers to a condition of dwindling down. Businesses disappear as the industry settles into static, marginally growing niches. The steel, auto and textile industries are typically used .as examples of this. This model presumes that businesses are machines that crank out products and markets are the collection of those machines competing for buyers to sop up their limited output.

The most efficient machines survive and the market settles into the patterns that accommodate the way people buy its products. The profits are derived from gains in internal productivity and efficiency and by holding up prices through control of market share. There is no need for strategy or strategic behavior that envisions and embraces change. Managers simply have to find ways to eliminate costs or devise competitive tactics that nibble at margins of market share.

If, instead, we look at these companies as complex systems that are, in turn, parts of even larger complex system (i.e., markets), all of which are dedicated to providing certain kinds of value to customers, our perspective can change. A steel manufacturer is producing a substance called steel in one shape or another (beams, sheets, ingots), but the *value* being created is that a type of material that can be used for many different items is available to other manufacturers. The steel industry has declined as other kinds of materials have been produced that have additional benefits to manufacturers—more pliability, lightness and plasticity, for instance.

As building materials proliferate beyond steel, the market does not shrink and dwindle. These new innovations add variety to the range of quality, cost and suitability of materials that people can use in different endeavors. Plastic, aluminum, ceramics and silicon compounds all enter the fray. The market becomes capable of producing "increasing returns," as W. Brian Arthur, an economist who is using the complexity model, calls this phenomenon. A market is able to offer a wider array of choices to people, at better prices and quality, thus increasing the market's complexity and enhancing the value offered therein to customers. If a steel company declines, it is not because the market "matures," but because its decision makers faced these changes with an utter lack of imagination and used mechanistic models to plot and execute strategy.

There are rows and rows of books and articles helping managers notice patterns in the marketplace that can be exploited to gain market share. "Competitive Strategies" that find ways to leverage costs and pit one vendor against another to get that lowest price are a dime a dozen—and help that much. Then there are the books that espouse organizing humanistically rewarding achievement or allowing for upward criticism of managers. The intended result is more "productivity" and "high performance" in doing the same things over and over again. It's just that people feel better now and then while doing them. None of these antidotes for bureaucratic organization lead to strategic behavior from employees or add to an organization's capability.

This book provides tools that can be used to manage in a new way. If we are successful here, today's managers will realize they can let go of their preset limitations about their work, get beyond today's issues and plan, strategize and grasp and then articulate the meaning of the events that are shaping tomorrow. The strategic organization does not merely adapt to what has happened to it, it goes out to shape what will happen to others (competitors and customers). Managers must be the energizers that keep the business's senses alive, tingling and crackling with new information and visions that drive to the heart of what its stakeholders (customers, employees, owners, the community and others) demand. Nothing less.

THE VISION

The complex systems model applies to any business that intends to grow, add value to its offerings and bring something of significance into the lives of its customers. It more aptly describes business life than does the rationalistic, narrow, hierarchical and authoritarian mechanistic model into which we have squeezed businesses for all these years. Instead of seeing businesses as cold, impersonal grinders that spit out materials and burn people up, they are seen as gathering places for diverse human energies and talents. Instead of seeing markets as dwindling and shrinking, they can appear as fields of opportunity. Instead of seeing customer demands as trials and threats, they are openings into a process that engenders responsiveness and change in an organization. Instead of seeing people as "variable costs," they can be viewed as the primary resources that enable change, growth and responsiveness.

Here are some of the important ramifications of the model we will follow and develop further in the chapters that follow:

1. A growing business organization is always on the edge. Complex systems only develop and grow when they are in that special state called *beyond equilibrium.* Things are crazy; people are driving against deadlines and pressing customer demands. Employees are challenged, fired up and maybe even a little anxious or irritable. Businesses that are growing and succeeding are highly *emotional* places. If all the t's are crossed and i's dotted; and if everything is known and set, the organization will be like a rock, or at best a crystal—fixed in time, at the mercy of the living, moving, predatory forces around it. Bureaucratized, settled and complacent businesses are ripe for takeover and loss.

The lesson here is that managers can neither organize the turmoil out of a business nor manage it into perfection. Successful, strategic organizations make mistakes. But when a business's basic intentions are clear cut, it can encounter many different circumstances, make mistakes and wrong turns and still keep on the track. Mistakes are an occasion for learning—an encoding of new messages. Businesses cannot proceed by being right all the time; they have to proceed by knowing what is important and valued and using this as a standpoint to learn about the world being encountered.

To be sure, certain emotions are destructive to the productive efforts on which a business counts. Jealousy, egoism, holding grudges and the like are not emotions that energize organizations. We'll spend the second half of this book discussing the kinds of emotional energies that do contribute to creating "Strategic Heart" and dynamic organizations (responsibility, engagement, envisioning and aspiration). The organization builder's job is to find ways to encourage and support these positive emotions, usually by exemplifying them, and help people who feel them find the resources and allies that will lead to success.

2. *Successful businesses evolve toward greater complexity.* This doesn't mean the organization gets more complicated or difficult to manage; it means that decision makers create emergent, *strategic* organizations that grow in their ability to accomplish more difficult tasks and thus are more able to have greater and greater impact on the lives of their customers and markets with each passing day. They release what Murray Gell-Mann calls "potential complexity."[7]

These organizations unleash the possibilities that can emerge when people's strategic hearts are tapped. This happens when individuals' energies are organized and combined with technology into a unified, adaptive system that responds creatively to situations and problems. A business has to be able to take full advantage of its nonphysical assets: the intelligence, adaptability and ingenuity of its people. People are the assets that should command a manager's attention. Machines can never do more than they were designed and built for. People, however, eagerly seek out situations in which they can stretch and grow.

For employees to take risks in a business situation—where their livelihoods (and egos) are on the line—requires a new way for managers to work with them. Managers have to forego the propensity toward authority and top-down monitoring of preset goals and open up to the idea of acting as "complex attractors" that embody the business's values and personify its drive to succeed in its mission. The challenge to managers is to foster learning and development throughout the organization in a way that flows powerfully toward accomplishing the business's explicit purpose and intention.

The complexity model redirects our attention, therefore, from the mechanical processes that build things more cheaply to the need to increase the business's capability, flexibility, depth and reach. Machines cannot increase their own capability and adaptability. Only a living, complex organization—a highly energized system organized around high-level, complex attractors (values and mission that are embodied in managers and leading employees)—can make the changes that accomplish something we are proud of.

3. *The Complexity model implies "cooperation" every bit as strongly as it acknowledges the power of competition.* Not only is there competition among companies that make similar things and so compete for customers and resources, but a business is embedded within another complex system called the market. The market is an evolving entity as well. So the competition is not only between business that already exist; it also goes on between the companies that already exist and the new ones that come along and change those markets, create new ones and wipe out others.

The good news is that rarely does a new development just come out of no-where. New products and markets evolve out of the ones that already exist. Businesses do have an opportunity to see these developments and assess what the opportunities are for their response. The challenge is that the right technical solution is not always the customers' first choice. Instead of the naive and limited idea of competition being a matter of the "survival of the fittest" and all the amoral behavior that implies, the complexity model tells us that competition is a matter of the "survival of the most fitting"—the company with the way of behaving, producing and understanding what the public requires is the one that will win.

Cooperating with others is every bit as critical a component for success as is effective competing. A business has to work closely with others and honor their needs and understandings of those needs in order to succeed. This spells the death knell for the idea of the amoral business. A business must come forward not only with products and services worth buying, but it must also present itself as a welcome member of its community. It must serve that community and its sense of possibility and aspiration. Each slap of callous behavior takes a bit of adaptability and veracity away from the business. People will migrate to those companies who stand for something of value. For what other kind of company can lay claim to *producing* value?

4. The complexity model thus tells us that everyone in a business must learn new things, formulate new understandings of the situation and their role in it and then act on these new images. Ultimately, the most severe competitor a business faces is not another business or an unknown business but its own organization, with its habits, comfortable channels of authority and control.

The demand posed by the complexity model is not merely to reorganize or "reengineer" toward new and more efficient processes. Complexity challenges decision makers to envision greatness for their businesses, to invest in a new future—one that has never been known before. The challenge is to conduct business with heart, with a "Strategic Heart" that really connects with its world, its possibilities and dreams and then goes out and makes them happen. Where once organization was synonymous with control, stasis, predictability and bore-dom, complexity points the way to create organizations that are:

Open: Decision makers that build strategic organizations are able to listen, capture, take in and implement new ideas and experiment. They accept failures but garner from these experiences valuable lessons that ultimately lead to success. They are guided not by the things that the company makes but by what the company enables its customers to do. They are always seeking to find ways to help them do those things better.

Dynamic: Decision makers that build strategic organizations look at their businesses for the long term and attack opportunities for creating something new and worthwhile. They see their businesses as "opportunity structures"[8] that create a platform for excitement and aspiration. They listen to customers and employees or anyone else that can point to new ways to view and understand their role in their markets and communities.

Innovative: Everyone in the organization is able to find new ways to do things and has the support and managerial coordination to make these changes effective, while preserving the core intentions of the company's values and mission. The workday is no walk in the park: there is a lot to do, and sometimes it is hard to figure out how to do the work, no less complete it. Still, there's no clock watching, and the day speeds by. One leaves work tired but feeling it was worth it and it is leading somewhere.

Ethical: Not only are these organizations ethical in the narrow sense of doing no wrong, they go out of their way to demonstrate flexibility and appreciation of the customer's situation. That doesn't mean giving away the store. It might mean spending time with an angry customer or even creating some internal discomfort to make a customer's or employee's rightful grievance heard. The strategic organization builder is always looking for ways to forge new and more robust connections with the people that the company will be counting on in the future.

Possible or Pangloss? For some, this may seem to be a one-sided, rosy view of business: business without its warts, without its abuses. I plead, "Guilty." As a consultant who deals daily with business problems, I, too, have occasionally been angered and outraged at greed-driven, irresponsible business behavior that stunts individual and organizational growth. But more often than not, I have been truly moved and inspired by the positive contributions that progressive, humanistic managers have made possible for everyone associated with their businesses—customers, owners, employees and their communities. I am using the complexity model to point out the kinds of ideas that will lead more business decision makers to create positive, constructive working environments for people.

I have yet to see a business that doesn't benefit from these ideas and, in applying them, become more productive and profitable, as well as a better place to work. This new model, based on liberating people's talents and energies, their vision and aspirations, frees managers to work in new ways. Businesses need not be dreary places where an individual's dreams have to end as the price to pay for an honest day's wage. Businesses are creative enterprises of a high evolutionary order, and as such have unlimited horizons of mission and opportunity before them. Businesses as organizations do not always rise to the full potential of their vision; but those decision makers who fail to aspire to that vision usually bring their businesses down with them.

The vision proposed in *The Strategic Heart* is that of business organizations that create value on an individual, corporate and social scale. For all their warts and shortcomings, I have walked in the halls of businesses that do this every day, and I have thrilled to the vibrations of the energy these organizations unleash. This book shares that excitement with you.

NOTES

1. Ilya Prigogine, *Order Out of Chaos: Man's New Dialogue with Nature* (New York: Bantam Books, 1984), p. 312.

2. Ibid.

3. M. Mitchell Waldrop, *Complexity: The Emerging Science at the Edge of Order and Chaos* (New York: Simon and Schuster, 1992), p. 293.

4. Ibid, p. 289.

5. Klaus Mainzer, *Thinking in Complexity: The Complex Dynamics of Matter, Mind and Mankind* (New York: Springer-Verlag, 1994), p. 269.

6. Waldrop, *Complexity,* p. 146.

7. Murray Gell-Mann, *The Quark and the Jaguar: Adventures in the Simple and the Complex* (New York: W. H. Freeman and Company, 1994).

8. Robert A. Burgelman, ''Corporate Entrepreneurship and Strategic Management: Insights from a Process Study,'' *Management Science* 29, no. 12 (December 1983): 1353.

Chapter 2

Values

If you over-esteem great men,
people become powerless.
If you overvalue possessions,
people begin to steal.
The Master leads by emptying people's minds,
and filling their cores,
by weakening their ambition
and toughening their resolve.

—Lao-tzu, *Tao te Ching* (3)[1]

THE SUCCESS OF THE MOST FITTING

Complex systems do not erupt spontaneously, out of nowhere. They emerge out of the conditions, materials and opportunities offered by their immediate environment. Over successive generations, complex systems evolve so they are able to fully exploit what the environment offers for sustenance, shelter and support. Each species hones its skills and develops sensory organs and bodily forms in order to be even more successful in its environment niche.

No system encompasses everything or takes advantage of each and every aspect of an environment. One being may fly and eat insects, while another slithers along the ground and gobbles up small mammals whole. The one that flies cannot slither, the one that slithers cannot fly; they grow in specialized ways that reinforce their respective choices for survival. In this way, each individual organism has its own unique shape and behavior.

Since Charles Darwin published his *On the Origin of Species by Means of Natural Selection* we have accepted the idea that living systems have evolved from simple forms to beings of greater complexity and adaptability to their environments. As organisms become more complex, they also gain flexibility in their ability to adapt and survive. Whatever limitations the human species exhibits in other ways, it excels in survival because of its supreme ability to use technology to adapt to just about any terrestrial habitat, and now to extraterrestrial habitats as well. When humans make choices, exhibiting preferences for some aspects of their behaviors, habitat and food resources over others, we say that they are demonstrating or acting on their "values."

Values and "Attractors"

In our everyday conversations, the idea of "values" often seems to be a fuzzy one. When seen from the perspective of organized systems, including living organisms, the idea does become clearer. As we said in the last chapter, complex systems coalesce their exuberant, near-chaos energies around "attractors." Attractors can be either point particles that give rise to molecules or complex, nonphysical entities such as goals, desires or ideas. Whatever form they take, an attractor is something around which beyond-equilibrium energies cluster themselves.

An already complex organization, such as a human being, is likely to have many points around which it clusters its energies. Food gathering (self-sustenance) coalesces a great deal of our energies, since no human being could survive as a self-organized system if it did not give this attractor its full and due attention. But it hardly constitutes the sole attractor of human energies. Physical entities such as money or property command high attention for some, while spiritual pursuits and humanistic service do so for others. For humans, these "values" constitute a kind of attractor, a high-level, abstract attractor that determines and selects behaviors and choices, while not excluding or depreciating the more immediate food and shelter levels of values.

Thus, people and organizations usually operate under the sway of several attractors. Many religious people also like to eat well; many money-seeking people also like abstract challenges like games and puzzles. Business decision makers are clearly focused by the need to create profits, and most of them also esteem "humanistic" treatment and regard for employees. Complexity not only allows for multiple attractors, evolution toward increasing complexity demands it.

A Business's Values

When we work with clients on a business's values, we make it clear that the values we are trying to articulate are not ideals. A business's values summarize what decision makers want their people to actually do, each and every day, in pursuit of the organization's most essential goals, needs and dreams. The stated values express concerns and identify the necessities of the people's organized life that spur them into action or enable them to choose one course of action over another. They define the boundaries of commitments the business makes to a wider world. At the same time, they define the strands of connections that the company makes to that world.

These issues are often raised by consultants and/or academics under the rubric of a business's "culture." A culture supposedly summarizes an organization's "way of doing things," meaning the patterns and assumptions that underlie actions and decisions. And since the key judgment for decision makers in a growing company is "what do I change and what do I preserve," as we move forward, this offers them a useful tool for analysis. The idea of a business's culture opens up conversations about the feelings, attitudes and traditions that either contribute or impede an organization's effectiveness. Clearly, the form of organization changes as a company grows. In many of the circumstances we see, as a company grows, adding positions, processes and equipment, people find they have more and more to do in their daily jobs, and yet they are less and less involved with the "big decisions" that are made. "This company used to be a family, but now it's getting big, like a bureaucracy," we often hear. No culture can remain the same under these stresses. So the old culture is out the window. Now what?

This highlights the limitation of the idea of "culture" as a useful concept for guiding organizational growth. When people talk about their "culture" they overemphasize the habits and structures that comprise the status quo as opposed to focusing on the latitude that values permit as changes become necessary. When companies grow, they may also have to change the values under which the company had succeeded. When a company expands its markets, it deals with a wider spectrum of customers, for instance. It may have to adjust the values that it projects in order to accommodate a wider spectrum of beliefs, customs and lifestyles.

A growing business succeeds because its choices and actions (i.e., its values) have been fitting and appropriate. The company's decision makers have to understand who their products and services are really connected to and how those customer define service, reliability, integrity and courtesy. In a process of change, the company remains connected to the old customers while encompassing the new ones by making choices that resonate with what most people that are involved with the company are viscerally attracted to. The business acts in ways that brings forward new forms and new processes that connect it to things that are clear and important for their customers' well-being. As far as the customer is concerned, the company's values have remained intact even as it has changed and grown.

Values at Work

Values are the most basic and essential attractor for any organization, precisely because they define for people how they can act in a way that is meaningful and appropriate for those who have a stake in the company. Values express that special way each and every person in a company can decide and act as individuals, and by doing so strengthen their connection to things that are larger and more meaningful: the company, then the customers and other stakeholders, and finally the wider community in which they live and raise their families. The power of values thus cuts two ways in terms of offering decision makers discretion in guiding organizational change.

On the one hand, values can act as limiting factors on the actions decision makers can take. Conflicting values from two different companies often undermine the success of mergers and acquisitions, for example. In addition to the insecurities around whether or not they'll have a job in the future, employees also don't know how to interact with their old customers now that a new boss is calling the shots. For instance, a customer service rep might wonder: "Do I toe the line or give the customer a break? What are the guiding values here? Do we put the customer first or the company's bottom line?" Employees don't know whether or not a decision is right or wrong, so they sit on their hands and wait to be told what to do. In the meantime, opportunities slip by, customers are alienated, profits slip and the merger implodes.

Customers of merged or acquired companies say, "It's not the same company anymore," because of unexpected disappointments or affronts that the new "parent" company foists on them with more bureaucratic policies and procedures (or automated voice messaging services). The merger may have succeeded in providing capital gains for the seller, but it failed to fulfill expectations of customers and employees and the new owner as well, because the values have changed and people don't know how or on what basis to make necessary decisions. The connections that define the company's essential relationships break down and anticipated profits dwindle.

On the other hand, an organization that operates on the basis of its values, rather than on the basis of what products or services it sells, creates for itself the widest possible range for its decisions and actions. By redefining in widening terms the nature of the company's highest values, decision makers expand their options. They use values as a framework in which to undertake change and manage the business's growth, by showing the continuity of its actions and choices even as its products, services or the organization itself are revised. When they do this successfully, new capabilities can be added because people don't fear they will be replaced; new positions, equipment and procedures can be integrated into the company without resistance, because people can see how they strengthen their respective abilities to act on those values.

The role of middle managers, as we will see shortly, is to emphasize "interactive" or "organizational" values that stress the necessity of people working together to accomplish something great and worthwhile. They want people to make decisions about their work and generate new options and ideas for innovation; and they want their people to be primed for change and challenge, not perfunctorily checking off tasks. Senior managers personify different, but complimentary values. They demonstrate "strategic" values in all their actions, personifying the conviction that the future is bright if acted upon with a sense of shared commitment, openness and aspiration. This hierarchy of values creates a dynamic atmosphere in which learning, growth and competitive fitness thrive. A management group that projects and faithfully acts on these values creates the strategic organization that succeeds; the management group that fails to grasp this essential aspect of their work struggles and sometimes fails.

The story we tell next is about a poorly functioning department in a growing furniture retailing company that we were asked to help. Several reorganizations—new managers with all the usual "reengineering" measures—had been tried to no lasting or meaningful effect. We saw a group of people that, in the course of their company's astronomical growth, were on the verge of losing touch with the company's values. It is not that these people were acting destructively or dishonestly. They had lost sight of the connection between what they did in their daily tasks and what the business organization as a whole was trying to accomplish. They just didn't see, or didn't think about, how their actions were a part of the company's value structure. Treating organizations at the core of their values is often the first step that needs to be taken to assure continued success. Often, when these issues have been well addressed, everything else falls into place.

LEADING BY VALUES

Terry was shocked by the astronomical growth of Barry's Sales. The company had started as a local family enterprise that was well known in its base city for good prices and excellent service and had now grown to become the region's largest family-owned retail company. In the last two years, it experienced 30 to 40 percent growth per year.

Terry is a successful, self-taught professional who, over the span of a fifteen-year career at Barry's, rose through the ranks to become chief buyer. His operation, called the Purchasing and Receiving Department (PRD), started with just himself. At the time of this story, the department had swelled to twelve people (now, two years later, it has sixteen). He, like other lifelong employees, had the value of "the customer is always right" bred into his bones. The lore of the company included many heroic tales of offering same-day delivery to a newlywed's apartment, making repairs to many-year-old merchandise without questions being asked and providing merchandise that could only be purchased from a competitor.

The company had three locations in the region—a fourth and fifth were on the way—and the parking lots were always jammed with people waiting for spots to park. "I don't understand why they wait in line to park," Terry said. "We never have sales, our prices are always the same. Except for our closeouts, we'll always get them what they want. But the customers line up as though this is their last chance. Well, it's great for us."

The PRD was at the core of the company's operations, managing the inventory at all the stores. It ordered the merchandise (for both stock and custom items), scheduled deliveries and made sure that received merchandise was up to spec and that it was all priced, tagged and tracked properly. It also handled relationships with vendors including returns and order changes. The work the people in the PRD performed was hard and extremely demanding. It required an unusual combination of talents. On the one hand, these people needed an intuitive awareness of the big picture—what the stores company-wide were doing in a line of merchandise. On the other hand, they needed to pay attention to the smallest details of each and every order—and there could be hundreds of these to process each and every day.

At Wit's End

Terry coped with his elevation to management in the same way many promising, recently promoted managers do: he multiplied, divided and delegated tasks in a rational, machine-like manner. First, he multiplied his tasks by the demands of the business's growth and filled in the slots. Then he divided the tasks into jobs, according to the number of people that were available. Finally, he "delegated" those tasks to the few people he knew and trusted.

Terry had his people working like bureaucrats. They cranked out paperwork and enforced the rules: quality assurance, delivery times, proper colors, checking shipments against packing slips and those against invoices. He hired conservatively, based strictly on technical "competence," so any new person could jump right in and get started with a minimum of training. To deal with the department's growth, and so he could pay attention to more global purchasing issues, he hired Ron, a systems analyst, as a manager to oversee the day-to-day operations of the department. A good-hearted guy, knowledgeable in furniture, Ron was expected to keep things running like a clock.

It didn't work out that way. Terry made several attempts at integrating the new manager into the group, but the group resisted. He tried several different organizational schemes, including having longer tenured members of the group take on supervisory roles, but the results always seemed to be the same: internal backbiting, hostile cliques, a growing reputation for being a surly and uncooperative group. They kept score as to whether one person was working longer or harder than another, who was getting undeserved credit or who was being overlooked. They scrutinized suggested changes in their jobs down to the last detail to determine what effect it might have on personal status or one's place in the pecking order. Cynicism was setting in fast.

From their perspective, the company was growing all around them, but they were going nowhere; they worked hard to get things done, but no one appreciated them. "This manager comes in," one member of the group said, "and tries to enforce the rules, but he doesn't know the business as well as we do."

People were preoccupied with their piece of the action, they protected their turf and their jobs. The department was stuck and discouraged. Terry was at a loss and a bit defensive about his seeming inability to set things right.

The situation was all the more painful because his group performed a service of tremendous and pivotal value to the company. If this group fell behind, the company lost customers, financial control and control of where its merchandise was. The people in the department were very good at their jobs and deeply experienced. They put in an intense eight hours. They usually left at five, but during the Christmas season, they accepted the occasional necessary Saturday work. The work had value; the people were good at it—but no one related to their work as though it had value, and no one related to the people in the department as though they created value for the company.

In the meantime, Terry never lost his human touch. He listened to their stress-driven complaints; he intervened to resolve the interpersonal conflicts that came up—and they came up often. In Terry's mind, and in the minds of his people, emotions were one side of life and work was another. They were separate and distinct, like the banks of a river. They resided side by side, and they never touched. But at this point, Terry had hit a wall. His quick mind and easy manner, his humane instincts and intense dedication to the company and the people in the department—strengths that got him this far—seemed to be working against him. To deal with the personal conflicts and internecine warfare, Terry relied on his sensitivity, his ability to act as a confidant. But this wasn't working either. People came into his office all the time, complaining about this or that, telling tales of how others weren't doing their jobs. It was time-consuming, and ultimately degrading for everyone involved. Terry and his more senior managers came to the conclusion that something else had to be done.

PUTTING THE VALUES INTO THE WORK

Mage was called in to see if we could help this new manager succeed in these trying circumstances. In our observation, the problems went much deeper than the manager's alienation. As we put it to Terry, he and his people had lost touch with what it was that made their jobs matter to themselves and to the customers—internal and external—that they served.

Typically, a mechanistic approach to Terry's problem would be to "reengineer" the department: do another reorganization, put a new manager in place and hope for the best. As we saw it, this company had all the elements of being a dynamic, fun, energizing place to work. It was growing; the owners were new at running such a large company, but they cared about customers and cared about their employees—providing generous benefits and profit sharing; there were new opportunities for advancement everyday; and the business was clearly on the upswing for the foreseeable future.

When seeking to build "complexity" and add capability into a company's life, we start with helping people find a way to put their heart back into their work. We wanted the people in the PRD to see that their work is connected to values—to something that they cared about personally—and that their company makes them personally proud to be doing their work. We wanted to bring these connections to the fore and let them take precedence even over what specific tasks they performed in the course of their jobs. Then, when the people were fully reinvested, we would see what kinds of reorganization would be necessary.

We met with the group weekly for two-hour sessions. In each meeting, concepts were introduced and an assignment was made to be worked on during the week (although some were to be done individually, eventually, most of the assignments were to be done in working groups) and then reviewed. We started our process by asking the group to answer three questions: What values that the company espouses do you esteem most? What are some of the things that get in the way of living up to those values? And finally, what can you do to help the company live up to those values?

We went around the table, listening to each person's list of values and the stories they told to illustrate their convictions. Since values are not ideals that people articulate and then live up to, but instead are real attractors that affect behavior in everyday life, they can only be discovered in stories that people tell about how and why they make the decisions they do. In these stories, people tell others, and hear for themselves, how they discovered what the real operating and effective values are in their lives. It is a very powerful process.

All of the people in the group said that they esteemed the value of customer service the most. Some told stories of how proud they were to work at Barry's when their friends told them about their experiences in the store. They were all proud to tell their friends and family to shop at Barry's, knowing that the news about their experiences would always be good. ''Barry's creates a fun experience. When people come here we don't treat them like all we want is for them to buy our stuff,'' one PRD member said. (Indeed, while customers are waiting at the loading dock to pick up merchandise, their cars are washed!) ''When I get bad service somewhere else, it bothers me more than it does my friends. I know how it's supposed to be done,'' said another. Also mentioned was how the company (and especially Terry) cared for the employees and how often genuine attempts were made (not always successful) to get everyone in the company to work as a team.

Growth was taking its toll. The pressures of time were getting in the way of fulfilling those values. With the organization growing bigger, things took longer to get done, the red tape was more entangling and ever more segregated departments lost touch with each other. When we asked if they felt they personally contributed to the problem, each person fully acknowledged complicity and responsibility. We discussed their reputation of not being receptive to suggestions from others or how they can appear to be negative and even hostile at times. They also noted how their internal bickering was detracting from their work.

This was no intellectual exercise. These were hard sessions. Many operational issues got caught up in a web of frustrations. Because one was angry at another, communications were truncated or nonexistent. Finger-pointing had become routine; they looked over each other's shoulders to see who was working or doing personal business. There was a great deal of pent-up anger, and it was vented in these meetings, sometimes with bare knuckles. There were tears from those who had been hurt and from those who realized how hurtful they had been.

The next sessions were devoted to making individual commitments to do one thing that could change things for the better and would contribute to fulfilling the mission. They saw how acting these ways really detracted from what they themselves cared most about. Several people vowed to have a positive attitude and to "leave my problems at home." Another said, "I'm going to mind my own business, stay away from gossip and negativity." Another vowed to make sure to acknowledge what the department does well and show appreciation.

Our aim was to help the people in the group see how each person's actions, day in and day out, helped the company fulfill the values they themselves held in esteem: to achieve an unsurpassed reputation for outstanding customer service. We wanted them to focus on these value-fulfilling actions, not the discrete tasks they performed in order to complete those actions. We asked them to think beyond the tasks they did—the forms they completed, the orders they filled or verified—to see how their work made it possible for Barry's Sales to offer outstanding customer service.

That was not hard to do. Not only did they do things that made this reputation come alive—like special ordering products and negotiating aggressive deliveries from vendors to meet exceptional customer needs—they realized their work enabled others to make those promises of exceptional service because they were the ones that delivered on them. Fulfilling the values of the company started with them. They just had forgotten or hadn't thought about the fact that this reputation can only be earned if they work to fulfill those values.

They began to see that their work did not just add up to the sum of the functions they performed. In fact, those functions would certainly change or even disappear or at least be replaced with growth, new technologies, new ideas, successive reorganizations. Their work, no matter what combination of tasks it included, was to help the vendors, suppliers, delivery people, accounting and sales people on the floor get what they needed on time, at the best price. From their work emerged the core—the heart—of Barry's success, nothing less. They were the ones who made it possible for everyone in the company to fulfill the values that Barry's projected into the community and on which its success arose.

WHAT VALUES DO FOR A COMPANY

It is really worth it to spend time working to enumerate these "soft" things and create value statements? In making that decision, it will be worthwhile to consider these facts about what values mean to a business.

1. Values are not ideals. They are realized and recognized in the stories that describe the incidents that have made our actions and efforts worthwhile.

When we think of values as attractors, as factors in our lives that coalesce many diverse people or desires into a unified focus, we can see the difference between values and ideals. Ideals are statements about actions, results or outcomes that you keep aiming at but may never attain. Values, however, are achieved and proven in actions each and every day. Values constitute the necessary actions that help everyone hang together, to take the risks and the hits that come with accomplishing the worthwhile intentions of the company.

Value statements summarize those actions everyone knows to be necessary and those actions that they depend upon each other to perform every day. There are always stories about how values were revealed or proven. A customer was surprised and grateful, a short-term sacrifice was made, but months later that customer returned because the gesture was remembered and appreciated. By telling and retelling the stories, our true values are revealed and proven. In these stories, we find out what really spurs our actions and feeds our spirits. No matter what a manager may write down as a company's values, what the company is really willing to do, learn and sacrifice for defines its true values.

2. *Values are about achieving a balance between competing claims or choices. They spell out all the factors, competing and contradictory though they may be, that we deem worthy of our attention and energy.*

We value those people and things that we hold in esteem and deem worthy of respect. In a business context, if profit is not held as a value by decision makers, the business will soon fade away. However, if profit is the only thing an owner esteems, employees, customers, vendors and the community are not particularly highly valued. The business will most likely also fade away under these circumstances.

As we said, a complex system can have many different attractors, all of which are necessary at different levels. Sometimes the needs and claims of these attractors conflict. Sometimes our basic need to survive conflicts with more spiritual values we may hold about life. In the movie "Survival," victims of a plane crash high in the frozen Andes were able to survive only by eating the flesh of comrades who had died. This practice was utterly repugnant to the civilized values of each of them; still more basic values—that of having food to eat—had to take precedence in this emergency.

Values frequently conflict in business. How do you reconcile humanistic values with regard to employees with the need to press them for performance or to possibly lay them off during a recession? These are hard to reconcile. It is folly for decision makers to declare values that don't take these kinds of conflicts into account. It is simply realistic to acknowledge and declare that since a company has to live with sometimes contradictory values, its efforts will be directed at trying to strike a balance among them.

Again, the difference between values and instincts is precisely that values don't have to be "hard wired" so to speak, guaranteeing a specific, single outcome. If we think of the psychologist Abraham Maslow's hierarchy of needs as a hierarchy of values, we can see that lower-level values, such as shelter, food and security, are satisfied concretely and naturally (if one thinks of the commercialized products that satisfy these needs as being "natural"). Higher needs, however, such as love and self-actualization are more abstract. Each individual will have to name and define the qualities that satisfy those needs and fulfill those values for them.

Likewise, a business has a hierarchy of values, some of which can be stated simply, like the need to maintain profitability, while others, such as those mentioned above, need more explanation and qualification. Because these "higher" values are more abstract and conceptual, however, they can be formulated in ways that express the striving for balance and still be compelling.

One of the best statements of this came from a values writing process we led with a large insurance company. Management wanted to make a strong statement about the fact that their employees were valued and respected, but the need to perpetuate the business and meet the demands of their competitive environment also had to be taken into account. Their statement on this subject became:

The loyalty of our employees, reflected by the longevity of their service and in the excellence of their performance, is a great source of pride. This achievement reflects a mutual awareness that each working day we always have to do whatever is necessary to meet the sometimes stressful demands required by our commitment to outstanding service and need for long term profitability.

At the same time, we must always hold our behavior to each other up to the highest standards of mutual respect, fairness, and appreciation of each individual's uniqueness. While we always expect the best from each other, we allow for mistakes and human frailties.

We believe that our employees take full responsibility for the quality of their work, and count on their willingness and generosity in their offering to do whatever is needed to provide quality service to our clients and companies.

Looking at a business's values in a wider social context, there are conflicts that are perennially vexing. Of the many reasons why the recent "downsizing" of companies has caused such disruption in our society, none is more significant than the shocking revelation of the true values of many of our largest and most esteemed corporations. The rationalistic, mechanistic drive to become "lean and mean" has undermined the connection between people's working lives and their place of work. Putting out time, effort, energy and sacrificing so that customers have something worthwhile, they find, has no redeeming value in the eyes of corporate decision making.

However, as a consultant who works with senior managers every day on these kinds of decisions, I appreciate the decision maker's side of the story. A business must uphold its mandate to be profitable and competitive; otherwise it creates neither products, value nor jobs. When productivity gains are both possible and necessary, and there are too many people, what are decision makers to do?

The answer lies in appreciating the hierarchy of values a business organization must maintain. At the middle level, where productivity gains are salient, the values of maximizing the use of organizational resources may call for changes in staff structure. If only the values of productivity or efficiency are salient in a company's decision making, layoffs will follow. In our model, however, there is another level of "strategic values" that can mitigate that outcome.

The values we urge for senior managers entail keeping the company investing and moving into new areas that promise growth, not reduction; creating jobs, not eliminating them. When changes need to be made, there are opportunities for people to take or decline, as they choose. As one executive said recently, "You can't downsize your way to greatness." The only viable answer to downsizing is fully embracing the responsibility entailed by the values of strategic growth and change. Sometimes achieving a balance means creating the weight— the innovation that creates jobs—that keeps the scales even. The idea is not to preserve jobs, but to create value, wealth and profits.

3. Values express what we choose to do as freely deciding, independent, thoughtful and mature people.

Decision makers too often look at a person's resume for schooling and experience and choose whether or not to hire based on that information. They are looking to find the right kinds of skills to fit into a slot in a mechanical process. We find that hiring people on the basis of a more intuitive understanding of their values is often more productive. When it is said people don't change, I think it means a person's values don't change. If a person shares a company's values, deficiencies in education, training or experience can often be made up. But when a person's values are different than the company's values, changes are hard or impossible to make.

Let's say two companies—a sales and distribution company and a personal services company—are interviewing two of the same people for customer service positions. Sam loves to help people, but he's never been too good with numbers. He may not be a good fit in a sales and distribution company, for instance. When a conflict needs to be resolved, he might tend to feel badly for the customer and give away the store. When Sam's decisions are constantly second-guessed, a bad situation develops in which everyone gets hurt. Based on his values, Sam would probably do well in a personal service business where it is often necessary to bend and negotiate for the client. On the other side of the coin, Lonnie loves to help people, too, but sees negotiations as a game where a point or two here or there decides who has won. Lonnie's values may be a better fit in the sales and distribution company and would probably not be a very good fit in the professional services firm.

It is people's values that will determine how they will act, decide and thus represent the company. Those moment-by-moment decisions can't be supervised. People's values have to be trusted. This same formula cuts the other way. How can a manager be sure the decisions being made are in line with the business's choices and priorities? Things happen too fast for decisions to be reviewed and assessed individually through a long, ever more restricted chain of command.

Decisions that are made on a strictly economic or situational basis will reflect the inconsistencies and random nature of the way the world works. This is the mistake many turnaround specialists make as they strip companies down to the bare bones in the name of "saving" it. They put the company in the position of being able to generate sales but not to build and sustain relationships with customers. They forget that people can get goods and services anywhere. What makes for a successful company is one that strikes a chord with people, sparks their imagination or elevates itself into some kind of special position with its customers. Companies that can just make and sell things don't survive; the ones that build and sustain relationships do.

There is only one source of answers that can be relied upon to work in a way that provides the consistency and power needed to have the decisions be made and to have them stick: make the business's real, operant and heartfelt values perfectly clear. If a person knows what the company's values are, that customer service rep or that division manager knows that the decision fits and builds on what the company ultimately wants to happen.

A final note on this point. A growing business needs people who represent a spectrum of values. There are many different kinds of things that need to be done in a business. For these things to be done well, people have to put a high value on them. For example, I appreciate the importance of financial discipline. Still, on those close calls, I would lean toward giving in to marketing or client service at the expense of some financial discipline. To enforce that discipline, a company would need someone who puts the financial order of the business above short-term good feelings. On the other hand, this person has to appreciate other values as well, appreciating that the long-term viability of a client relationship or, sometimes, the long-term viability of the firm may require an occasional fall from iron financial discipline. A strong organization blends talents and values to the greatest extent possible. A successful growing company finds ways to blend personal values into meaningful and compelling organizational values.

4. Values show how an organization goes about creating itself.

Values are never about idleness. Living things, have to affect their environments (either changing them or preserving them against encroaching changes), they have to act. I am defined to others by virtue of the actions I feel compelled to make. Value statements, then, declare what I am paying attention to in the course of my actions, and so define who I am, what I think is "good" and, therefore, how I come to be known in the world.

Decision makers sometimes have to incur short-term losses. They have to placate a client, apologize for a mistake or correct a defect. These actions all diminish the bottom line. Still, if they acted otherwise, they would set precedents with employees and customers that could cause far more harm down the road. Reputations could be tarnished, trusts broken. The business being created day by day with such actions becomes like Marley's chain in Charles Dickens's "A Christmas Carol," dragging that business into oblivion.

But another strength of focusing on enduring, human values is that when they are well understood and proven day in and day out, people will allow for mistakes and will offer their forgiveness and forbearance. Because people know that the company's soul is intact, they forgive the small stuff. They allow for difficult times, times for adjustment and working out of issues. They allow for learning. That is exactly the way the people in the PRD reacted to Terry. He was respected and deeply trusted. They forgave his management gaffes because they "knew where his heart was." When he elevated his values into his management decisions, people responded with celebration. Everyone gained in the process.

Where those values are not present or where they are suddenly betrayed, all latitude for forgiveness is lost. Many high-tech companies once promised lifetime employment, but when they suddenly had to retrench and lay people off, they disappointed everyone. Many of these companies disappeared, not so much because their sales dipped, but because the wellsprings of their values dried up. No one believed that there was anything the company would return to after hard times—just money in, money out, employees hired, employees let go. These people discovered the hard way that a money machine is not a business.

In the face of rapid and dramatic change, values also act as a company's compass, as a stabilizing force. Values are the most durable guides for sorting out events and instantaneously assessing situations. People always know where they stand when they operate from a set of values that are truly followed. If there are differences of opinion, that's not only fine, that's good. Values allow for a lot of room for disagreeing, amplifying the possibilities in a situation and working together to find meaningful solutions that propel the organization forward.

NOTE

1. Lao-tzu, *Tao te Ching* (3), trans. Stephen Mitchell (New York: HarperPerennial, 1988).

Chapter 3

Mission (I): Purpose and Commitment

The journey of a thousand miles begins
from beneath your feet.
Rushing into action you fail.
Trying to grasp things, you lose them.
Forcing a project to completion,
You ruin what was almost ripe . . .
The Master simply reminds people
of who they have always been.

—Lao-tzu, *Tao te Ching* (64)[1]

"WE'LL DO IT OR DIE TRYING"

Every living being contends with changes in its environment. Some changes are slow and gradual, allowing organisms a chance to adapt over many generations of evolution. Other changes—such as those wrought by human intervention or natural catastrophe—are instantaneous and global. Wholehearted effort is required in nature just to cope with these changes, no less succeed or achieve dominance for a while.

Still, those complex entities called businesses try to go nature one step better: *Businesses actively undertake projects and actions that intentionally change their world.* No other creature or group of creatures I know of actively sets out to create disturbing and destabilizing changes in its environment as its way of life. Where once an economy or culture could expect major changes to take place one or two times in a generation, businesses now generate continual change, rolling from one industry to another, changing one way of doing things, then another. Although we've become more or less accustomed to these business-wrought changes, the process is actually quite new, getting up to a full head of steam only after World War II, and becoming institutionalized in the 1960s.

Business-Driven Evolution

The business prescription for instigating massive social evolution goes something like this: Alexander Graham Bell creates a device that allows people to talk instantaneously wherever they are, for example. The telephone is developed and perfected over time, its capability and applicability to many aspects of our lives deepens and spreads. This single invention eventually becomes the vast telecommunications industry we know today. As it works its magic, the industry combines with other businesses and institutions—governmental, educational, even religious organizations—to assure that the environmental changes it has wrought will be permanent, that it will never fall back to conditions that are inhospitable to its way of acting and/or producing. For instance, it is impossible for us to envision a world that does not have commercial telecommunications available. Thus, starting from this single invention, a whole system of capabilities emerged, creating irreversible massive changes in the lives of everyone throughout the world.

What a monumental undertaking. Still, we can safely predict that the increasing pace of technical change and the organizational development required to keep up with it—no less to exploit it for the increases in productivity that it augers—is not going to diminish. From the business's standpoint, the accelerating pace of change is not a clear and simple blessing—it cuts two ways. In one direction, the business decides on the changes it is going to precipitate in people's lives. A software company changes the way a process is done, the way a product works or the way people can use basic services like banking, grocery shopping or receiving medical care. But then it cuts the other way. The same business has to contend with changes coming from the other direction, from the changes being forced on it by other businesses that are also creating change. In terms of the complexity model, this impetus to change supplies exactly the kind of energy that keeps organizations at the edge of chaos: energized, sensitized and primed for growth, making organizational readiness for change a requirement and not a nice to have option.

Certainly, we pay a social and individual price for this incessant churning of (under the banner of enhancing) our lives. Anxieties about the lack of job security and the obsoleting of our employable skills, not to mention the financial pressures entailed by the need to upgrade and update our own ''home economies,'' are an unwelcome adjunct to this process. Can we see a positive side to this churning, in addition to the possibilities offered for increasing individual and social net product? From an organizational perspective, an energizing spark to revitalize the way we work can be a positive force that refreshes the way we do our daily work and leisure activities, despite the short-term upset it causes. Incessant change can be a good thing, that is, if there is a guiding thread of increasing benefit to it all.

In that light, our question has to be, "What keeps a growing business organization on a positive, constructive track as it goes about generating change for others and contending with changes others have forced on it?" The company doesn't have instinct to guide it, nor genetic inheritance. In most cases, even marketing studies aren't reliable. The successful businesses that we have seen are guided by selecting from among its decision makers' diverse and knowledgeable visions about how the talents and energies of its people can improve upon the way its customers do things at home and at work. Individually, these "visions" may be right or wrong, but collectively, they supply a reservoir of ideas and initiatives that are vital and alive. Their envisioned changes may or may not end up being an improvement in some people's eyes—markets and history make those judgments on a case-by-case basis. But the businesses' visionaries—at all levels and in all positions in an organization—push ahead. They act as though they were on a mission; and, in fact, they are.

What a Mission Is—and Is Not

The mission summarizes what every member of a business organization strives to make happen in people's lives—events and experiences that would not happen without the business's actions. The business's mission states what the business will either accomplish or die trying to accomplish. Nothing less. If the mission isn't worth getting up in the morning to do, the organization will be overwhelmed, either by the indifference paid to it in the marketplace or by a competitor that is focused and concentrated on making something special happen in people's lives. The mission states the company's unassailable *intentions*. It makes clear what everyone in the company is committed to make happen, to change by virtue of their collective actions. Part of those actions are bringing individual visions together and melding them into a plan of action.

A mission is not an "ideal," however. Ideals are often thought of as being dreams, utopias that are worthwhile and inspiring thoughts for all of humanity and the world, but in all likelihood will never be accomplished. If we tried to attain all of our ideals we'd burn out, become cynical, or both. For all that, however, ideals are just as easily disregarded, since they are only goals that are strived for. For that reason, they are rarely guides to the real actions that we actually undertake each and every day. A mission statement, in contrast, has to be completely real, compellingly attainable and thus be able to convey what everyone realizes must, in reality, be done. It forcefully articulates what the organization is *actually accomplishing* in its markets—each and every day, with each and every action it performs—to affect, improve and change people's lives.

Creating Value

That purpose and those actions may, and indeed hopefully will, intend noble and worthy outcomes for customers, employees, shareholders and others. The mission gets whatever altruism it contains from the fact that its actions are bringing about something that attracts others and offers them something that elevates their lives, adds a dimension of fulfillment, or a dream of fulfillment, they did not have available before. Businesses create something positive, not because they make a good product, but because they appeal to an aspect of human life that transcends mere physical need.

We humans spend a great deal of time satisfying basic, life-sustaining activities, but we do not limit ourselves to merely doing these things. Not only do we think about how we do these things, judge them and evaluate our actions, we seek out ways and means to make changes to our behaviors and habits. When we perform these reflective, evaluative, higher level, learning and growing functions, we are acting to sustain and enhance an abstract and nonphysical identity known as the "self." This "self" is not a material thing, like our physical body. Instead, it is the prime example of an "emergent" entity, an abstract and transcendant phenomenon that becomes real as a result of the interactions between our complex biological and social systems.

At this stage of our evolution, our biological needs do not preoccupy us. Instead, we spend our time and energy acting on the demands made by this "self." We go to schools to enrich our "self's" compass of understanding and choice; we buy clothing and cosmetic products that bring out qualities about ourselves that we like; we buy tools, houses, cars and other things and go to masseuses, tennis lessons or other service providers that not only meet the basic physical needs of survival but also enhance our image and give us some pleasurable moments.

Many other creatures exhibit a sense of self to the extent that they will fight for their own physical survival and for the survival of their young or their group. But, we humans take it one step further; that is, no other creature on earth has evolved a system of trade, commerce and manufacturing that changes or modifies both the environment and its own behavior in order to meet the requirements of its *nonphysical* needs. Businesses provide materials and services that help people survive on a physical level, of course. However, only a small percentage of our businesses produce basic, unbranded products such as foodstuffs, commodities or raw industrial materials. Businesses in our culture arise and grow at the pace and with the impact they do because they are able to respond to the peculiar, higher level, more abstract needs of a *person's emergent and freely determined sense of "self."* They create things and services, that is true. But it is not the things themselves that spur success—no matter how attractively designed and packaged they are. People select products and services in order to maintain and/or enhance their sense of a being that does particular things in certain ways, with certain likes, dislikes and styles. Responding to these higher level requirements, businesses create *"value."*[2]

Businesses create value when they offer successful new products and services that enable people to enhance their sense of self and the feeling of that self's well-being over and above what they were able to experience before. For instance, as I am writing in my New England home in the depths of winter, the way I have to shovel snow comes to mind. Shoveling day after day by hand, I expend calories galore (that's good), but I also incur backaches and often get in very grumpy moods that are quite harmful to my familial relationships. Then along comes the "snow blower." I expend much less personal pain and energy clearing snow, and I have much more time to do other valuable things, like writing this book. By making this time available to me, back pain-free time, businesses have created "value" for me. In the meantime, because I buy a snow blower at a premium price, I create profits for the businesses involved with this product. The more activities businesses transform actions that are central to my sense of living well into entities or services I can buy, the more they are able to create value and hence, profits.

Creating Value Is the Mission

We have spent all of this time developing the idea of value to get to the point of why businesses need missions. Frankly, when businesses only created life-sustaining commodities, they didn't need mission statements or a sense of mission. They just needed capital, machinery, laborers and a place to put them all together. What was possible was never an issue; necessity kept the goods moving out the door. This all changed, however, when businesses moved beyond producing subsistence goods into the realm of the creating value by envisioning and creating new ways for people to live and interact. Many businesses make lots of things very cheaply and efficiently that end up on scrap heaps, the business's owners in bankruptcy court; and ideas are a dime a dozen. Who cares if a business has decided to make or provide one thing or another? A business only exists because people have incorporated its products and services into their ways of life and these customers want more. Decision makers now have to make a clear and compelling case for their vision of how things could be done, improved, enhanced and enriched. They have to define their mission.

A mission has an intrinsic sense of elevation and inspiration because it appeals to this higher level of human identity and self, offering a way to improve the lives that people envision for themselves. The mission identifies to everyone how the business goes about creating value. It does not consist of a shopping list of products and services or a to-do list of tasks. It can't be boiled down to the day's agenda, but neither can it be blown up to meaningless hyperbole. The mission describes the actions, in the here and now, the business's people *intend* to accomplish by virtue of their concentration, commitment and consistency each and every time they turn on the computer at their desks.

The mission appeals to a business's stakeholders—its customers, managers, employees, shareholders and others—because it makes clear that actions being envisioned and undertaken will have an effect on their sense of self, their self-esteem, their enjoyment and their engagement in life. It tells customers, "You can *expect* this business to strive to accomplish something significant for your benefit." It says several things to employees: "This is a vision in which each and every one of you has a part; this is what we are counting on you to deliver each and every day; and this is what you can count on others to produce as well." It says to shareholders, "This is how you can expect your money to be invested, and these are the standards of performance to which all of the business's employees and managers can be held accountable." Above all, the mission has a sense of elevation and transcendent purpose because it establishes high standards on which a particular kind of *relationship,* a value relationship, will be developed in which mutual benefit and shared prosperity is genuinely envisioned and strived for.[3]

I have never seen a mission process fail to help energize and focus an organization. The extent to which it does so depends on how well the mission translates into standards of performance and day-to-day guides to action for everyone in the company. Next, we tell a story about a group of young salespeople who got together to make some money, only to find out they had inadvertently created a business. I choose this story because it dramatically illustrates that a group of people can make a lot of money without declaring an explicit mission, or even creating a business. However, they can't create anything of value over the long term, without both of these. The mission and the business are created together to enable many people to work together, adding specialization, new talents and insights into what customers and stakeholders require.

THE CONIFER GROUP, LTD. FORMS A BUSINESS

In three years, the five partners of Conifer Group, Ltd. (CGL) had parlayed some up-front cash and credit card loans into a $20 million-plus enterprise. In that time they went from being five salespeople in telephone headsets, peddling refurbished computer gear out of a living room, to an operation that employed 30 people including salaried professionals, commissioned sales representatives and hourly production/administrative staff.

The partners were accomplished, successful salespeople. All of them lived on the phones, thrived on making cold calls, closing deals. They weren't "techies" who were out to make a name for themselves with a new computer breakthrough; they were salespeople. Still, they realized their operation was at a crossroads. The used computer equipment market was becoming less viable as new hardware prices plummeted; they were feeling pressures from the equipment makers who were none too happy that potential customers were being deflected into used gear. They either had to create more "value-add" in their offerings or take the money and run. And that latter choice was real. They had made a lot of money; they were obligated to no one. Why not just take the money and run?

They decided to hang together and create a business, and there were many reasons that made this the right decision. They enjoyed creating a business and felt a measure of responsibility to the employees' families; they had found a niche in the fast-paced computer industry that excited them; their quality of attention and quick turnaround was really needed in the marketplace; they were good at what they did; and they had made friends in the marketplace and had obligations to these customers as well as to their employees. These were not shallow people. They were young people of substance with a deep desire to do well by those with whom they worked.

While they wanted to stay in business, they soon found out that this decision put them at the beginning of a long and difficult road and entailed a level of thought, depth of commitment and ability to learn and accept risk that none of them had ever contemplated. If you asked each of them what the business would be doing in a year, three years or five years, you would hardly get an answer. The partners, never a cohesive group, quarreled over everything. They were five distinctive—and in the case of two of them, diametrically opposite—personalities. There was always second-guessing; and there was always finger pointing and accusations as to who didn't do what was expected, as well as the hue and cry about the rules constantly changing. Goals, roles, responsibilities, accountability were all words that were being hurled at each other like spears and stones. Nothing was moving forward.

Panic was setting in. Their markets were changing; used equipment was getting harder to locate and more expensive. New directions had to be plotted and agreed upon, but there was no way to make a decision. Since there were no defined operational roles among the partners—they were all owners and salespeople—they were constantly making and remaking the same decisions over and over, resulting in different outcomes from one day to the next. There was no budget, so there was no way to know what funds were available for investment. On top of this, sales were leveling off. There was no way the company could operate in the same cash-rich, cavalier way that it had, yet the partners were incapable of organizing themselves.

It will be useful to introduce the players. Kent started the business. Youthful in appearance and manner, he had charisma to spare and boundless energy to back it up. He liked people and always tried to be the host who helped people to be friends or buddies, or at least to get along. He liked a loose organization that would more resemble a fraternity than a corporation. He envisioned himself as being a customer's savior, not just a provider of equipment. Kent had dreams about the company growing and setting a new style of service and personalized treatment in what had been a cold, "take it or leave it" industry.

Mitchell, Kent's older brother, was the consummate salesman. Prior to coming to CGL, he had sold bonds. He was comfortable pacing the floor in his headset, staring into space or making quick notes on scraps of paper as he talked. He loved hitting the buttons opposite the blinking lights, moving from call to call, opening, moving and closing deals. His drawn-out, sonorous, Midwestern, slangy style of speech put you at ease, and the clear pleasure he derived from solving your problem with the equipment made you feel like he was your older brother, too. He was the "voice of the people" in the company.

At the time of these events, the confusion and dissension among the partners frustrated Mitchell to no end. He spent too much of his time talking people out of their anger at gaffs in shipping or bugs in the equipment and not enough time selling. He tired of the "priority of the week" and "hot product of the day" syndrome that derailed the company at every turn. He wanted change and he wanted it NOW! Still, for all his impatience and for all his equal share in the company's ownership, he didn't feel ready or able to spearhead change on his own.

Joe was one source of major friction within the group. Joe exuded a commanding presence. If he had resided in the vicinity of the other four partners, he probably could have been an effective spur to action. Instead, while everyone else lived in Boston, Massachusetts, he operated from a house on a beach in Hawaii. Instead of patiently working with the group, moving them ahead on issues or using his skills to pull them together, he dropped bombs: new hires unbeknownst to anyone else; a new product that just had to be the next CGL project; new financing schemes.

No one would ever accuse Joe of using his remote outpost in paradise as a hideaway or cover for indolence. He was always in a whirlwind of activity. The problem was, Joe never focused nor stayed with anything for very long. If he had a mere intuition and sent it out over e-mail, he was done with it, assuming it was accepted, acted upon and completed in a single breath. Needless to say, that never happened. But then he was also inconsistent with his own ideas. He'd give a directive to one person and it would change by the time he got to the next person.

The pace of change in the company also frustrated Joe, but for reasons that were quite different than those of his partners. He didn't mind the conflict, as long as it provided an opening for his ideas to get heard; too often, only he heard his own ideas. For him, everything was patently obvious. It left him in a quandary every time things came out differently than he had envisioned them.

Then there was Beau. He charged into life. Beau shot from the hip with a hair-triggered temper and deadly aim at a person's pride and confidence. Beau's ideas usually hit the mark, and he always acted with indisputably right intent and integrity, but his temper and brusque manner completely disabled, infuriated and turned off his fellow partners as well as key employees.

Still, more than any of the others, he was the partner who could analyze and conceive of long-range plans and complicated operations. At the time of our introduction into the project, his conceptual and analytical style didn't have a fertile field on which to operate in the chaotic world of CGL. A company that could not decide what it did could not take advantage of his skills at conceiving and maintaining processes and operations. Beau, a highly emotional person, often felt as though he were being pushed away or out of the inner partner circle and, to a large extent, he was right. While tending to view things in the extreme, he rightly observed that, in fact, the partners didn't know what to do with him.

Paul, the fifth partner, the technical "guru" of the group, relished being asked for advice. Soft spoken, easy to laugh, never aggressive or attacking, always ready to share a joke or a laugh, people liked him. He exuded the sincerity of a sweet kid that deeply cared about doing things right, but he rarely took the time or had the inclination to follow through on his own. He would passionately argue that something needed to be done, but acknowledged that he wasn't the one to get it done. He didn't block things, and he helped motivate the others; he just couldn't get things done himself. Paul badly needed the group to come together to help him focus, relax, gain recognition for mutually agreed upon accomplishments.

CREATING THE MISSION: "YOU GOTTA HAVE HEART"

The process of stating the mission of CGL took more than three months of work, for myself and two colleagues from Mage. We looked at some of the basic operations of the company and assessed them for their productivity, their capacity to grow and change. We assessed several of the people and identified a few who could be counted on for assuming larger roles in management. The partners each took responsibility for studying and making recommendations for different areas: Kent for purchasing and production; Mitchell for sales and customer service; Paul for technology and a new management information system; Beau for a general market plan; and Joe for long-term, future ideas and financing options.

We started to talk about the business in terms of its being a complex organization, rather than a mere collection of people. We divided up responsibilities, operations and commitments in ways that made sense for what the business had to accomplish if it was going to produce results for its customers. We laid out areas in which some of the partners would be individually responsible, and others in which they would be collectively responsible. We also established mechanisms for making day-to-day decisions and another forum for company-wide reviews of operations. Later, we would establish a format for monthly strategic reviews.

Besides these company-wide efforts, we also provided the partners with individual coaching. The coaching had several components: teaching some basic management techniques, helping the partners see what kinds of roles they could adopt and carry through with consistency and focus, helping clear the path of debris left from past squabbles. The coaching helped the partners elevate themselves to executive-level decision-making. We still did not feel that any of them would be able to be accepted as a full-fledged CEO (that would happen more than a year later), so we tried to maintain a more egalitarian, team approach for the time being. We wanted each of them to feel they could each act autonomously, and at the same time have the confidence that the mission was being fulfilled in the process by their own decisions as well as by those their fellow partners were making. This was crucial to all our efforts.

With this group, the company could move forward only when there existed the conviction that they could work, build and accomplish something together without having to check, double check and second guess each other. We worked hard to elicit from each of the partners a pledge to improve his contribution to the team by addressing one behavior that others felt would be of greatest help to the group. All of these were preparatory for an intensive two-and-a-half-day retreat during which we pulled all of the pieces together into a real, functioning, ground-breaking mission.

The Retreat

The setting was a beautiful resort in Newport, Rhode Island, in June. The weather epitomized the best of early summer in New England. Hot, bright sun, cut with cool ocean breezes and sometimes a patch of fog rolling in. But we saw none of it. For the whole two-and-a-half days we were locked in a windowless conference room hammering away at our objective, crafting the mission statement.

No one person was allowed to dominate the group. The process assured that everyone—the quiet, contemplative personalities such as Beau, Paul and Mitchell, as well as the gregarious types who love to hear the sound of their own voice such as Kent and Joe—was heard. The discussion digressed to points about operations, positions, organization, the future—and we were sure to allow time for this. We made sure everyone spoke up, we wrote their comments down on sheets of chart paper and hung them on the walls all over the room. With quotations, diagrams, notes and numbers pasted on every square inch of wall space, we were literally immersed in people's thoughts, concerns, desires and convictions.

Our mission-creating process consisted of asking the participants to answer four questions:

1. What does your company make possible for your customers (internal or external) to do in their daily work or personal lives?

This is the "value" question. Usually we spend a great deal of time on this question, which generates a lot of discussion and interaction. Although the most abstract, it is the answer to this question that distinguishes this company from all others. To help jog people's minds on this rather strange, even presumptuous question, we ask them to recall some of these more down-to-earth experiences:

- What do customers and vendors thank you for?
- What has changed for them as a result of your company's products or services?

• How do they feel when your company has succeeded for them?
• What would your customers be missing if they couldn't rely on your efforts?

We feel that this is the key question. It states exactly what the company is committed to accomplish for people. This question helps decision makers look beyond their fixation on a product or service to understand what their actions mean to others. This is the meaning that creates value for customers and motivation for employees.

2. *What does your company do to make this happen?*

We are not looking for a shopping list of products or services here. Our intent is to use this question to focus everyone in the company on the range of actions they perform that engage their customers—from planning and researching, to selling and educating them, to actually performing a service and getting paid for it.

In answering this question we also want to bring out "the pain" of the work. If the work a company performs was easy, natural or universally habitual, no one would pay for having it done. People pay for products or services when they can't do it themselves or hadn't even thought of doing it. Usually, providing that "something" involves work, maybe pain or stress. Every mission statement should make clear what that work, stress and pain is. It acknowledges and enshrines what everyone in the company knows is difficult, and what everyone in the company, ultimately, is getting paid to do.

The remaining two questions are inward-directed, focusing decision makers on their company's culture and expectations for performance. They amplify the values already set down by stating how they will be put into effect.

3. *What resources do you bring to bear in order to enable your customers to do these things?*

This question reflects on the organization and how it will be developed, shaped and changed over time. In the case of the CGL partners, the statement led to a discussion of how profits would be used and what the investment priorities would be in the future. It is used as an occasion to highlight how employees are valued, trained and challenged. Often the use of technology or R&D and other investments are mentioned.

4. *What is your company willing to change and how is it prepared to grow, including its philosophy about using profits, to ensure that your customers, as well as your employees, shareholders and community, will be served well?*

This question provides an opportunity to reflect on the company's strategic values: how is this company going to look toward the future; what can employees and customers expect and hold senior managers accountable for in terms of innovation and growth?

Not surprisingly, this question is often the hardest to answer. It requires a degree of honesty that some managers find unsettling. "We want to sell the company (or go public) and make a lot of money," some say with resignation. That is the wrong answer. To their consternation, I frankly urge managers that think this way to consider moving on, become a stock trader, or sell out quickly, while their company still has value. As we have said above, successful strategic organizations have a vision about what they want to change in the world. Setting down a commitment to invest in the future of the company's value—to owners, employees and customers—is not at all onerous when you are expecting others to pay their hard-earned money for what you are providing.

Creating a mission is the process of putting in words what the company's collective heart and soul is determined to make happen in the world, in service and commitment to others for the long haul. Nothing less will do.

The Process

Answering the first question took most of the morning. This lively discussion encompassed the most vital and compelling aspect of the statement. In a dramatic and inspiring way, the group developed a vision that took the best of what the company had been so far and conceived how it could move in stages to provide more service, consulting, contract support—all of which had higher profitability and an infinitely long life line for the company. Beau superbly articulated what those services accomplished for other people. Kent passionately described how he wanted CGL's customers to feel and respond after having dealt with the company. Mitchell emphasized his need for creating real, lasting relationships with customers, something that would be rock solid for both parties. Joe and Paul expressed the need to keep focused on what the people in the company could really do and what the partners could really afford—the voices of practical, bottom line wisdom.

After picking through every nuance and subtlety of the business's relationships to its customers—the Conifer style of discussion—we decided to divide up the remaining three questions among the five partners and have them produce drafts of the answers. When each team presented their proposals to the whole group, it was inspiring to see the reactions of the others. Clearly, this group had become far more united in their outlook over the course of the exercise. The comments were about wording and ordering, not about the substance of what they wrote. The group was finding its core, and finding the advocates for different facets of the business.

Kent and Joe were acknowledged as the most articulate and passionate presenters of the mission. Paul was the technical visionary. He would be relied upon to keep the company current and assure that the company was able to deliver the level of quality customers expected. Mitchell was director of sales and customer service. He not only knew how to sell, he was the one who articulated the vision of what a sale obligated the company to perform for its customers. He, too, was passionate about how this company should commit itself to the customer. And Beau had carved out his niche. He was unquestionably the operations chief, conceiving and developing all the internal structure and process that would enable the company to succeed.

The mission came out this way:

The Conifer Group Ltd. provides network computer solutions that blend products and services with knowledgeable installation and implementation. Our goal is to integrate the best technology and make the systems work.

Our top priorities are our customer's success and enhancing their competitive advantage. We are committed to providing comprehensive, forward thinking solutions to their current and ongoing challenges. Through our honesty and commitment, customers know they have gained a partner who can be depended upon to act in their best interests.

Because we are unwilling to compromise our customers' continued confidence in us, we are open to innovative opportunities, despite the calculated risks that are sometimes involved. We feel it is our responsibility to achieve sound profits, which will be reinvested in continuous education, innovation, research and development, new products, services and tools.

In order to meet and exceed our customers' expectations, we take a comprehensive approach to optimize solutions and continuously evaluate the solutions we provide. To do this, communications is key. We must continually develop our ability to listen, understand and respond to our customers.

As an organization, the Conifer Group is only as good as its people. We build upon the individual and collective talents of our employees. We work together to create an environment of support that fosters personal growth, team-oriented problem solving and above all, a commitment to each other to better service our customers today and into the future.

As the partners of CGL discovered, creating a mission for a new company entails much more than putting words on paper. While I have never seen companies fall apart as a result of going through a mission creating process, I have always seen great changes in balance of power, in organization, in partner agreements. In the course of a mission-creating process, they have ended up baring their business-related souls. The process creates change: people decide either to stay or leave, and people change their roles and make demands on others.

For the CGL, creating a mission demanded that everyone go into their hearts and see what they were willing to do to make things happen for others—customers, other shareholders, employees, the community. The statement, "making the systems work," is a bold, simple declaration that easily translates into a commitment to quality and performance. It is a declaration that its actions matter in the world and they will accomplish it or go down trying to do it. As I often say to clients, if you don't feel that your business has something special to offer, if you feel that you make or offer something that is a "me too," or that your company is a "wannabe," please, quit now, get out of business before someone that does offer something special, and knows how to sell it, eats your business for lunch.

The statement also makes clear that the CGL is willing to take on the pain it takes to make the systems work. By being "unwilling to compromise," and being "open to innovative opportunities, despite the calculated risks that are sometimes involved," they commit themselves to stirring up their organization so that their customers can use their systems to do what it takes to succeed on their own mission. The statement to "continually develop our ability to listen, understand and respond to our customers" reinforces the idea that no bureaucratic habits or internal barriers will be allowed to get in the way of making those customers' systems work.

THE SUCCESSFUL MISSION-CREATING PROCESS

Decision makers are rightly anxious about creating a mission statement. They often ask: "Will it open old wounds? How much time will it take? Who has to be involved? How can we take time from getting the work done?"

There is no single, best way to create a mission statement. At Mage, we have successfully conducted processes that took one or two days during off-site retreats and those that took months of weekly meetings with different groups in a large company. The single key ingredient to a successful mission process is to involve the company's effective leaders and communicators in the process. By "effective," I mean the people that have the credibility to make a statement about commitment to the company and have it believed—not just the ones with the big titles. Generally, we craft a draft statement with a smaller group of these leading communicators (they are often senior and junior managers but also often include representatives from nonmanagerial ranks), then have these people take the drafts back to their departments for comment and review. Then a very small group, or even a single person, revises the draft to accommodate the comments gathered from around the company.

This approach allows for a knowledgeable, credible and far-reaching discussion of the company's real situation during the drafting stage. It assures everyone that they have a voice in the process and can also raise issues that the draft either overemphasizes or neglects and then makes sure a finished product is presented. We have used other approaches as well, such as a company-wide solicitation of ideas, before the process goes into drafting. The important thing is to have a process that gets the work done in a reasonable amount of time, with sufficient opportunities for meaningful input from as many people as possible.

To evaluate whether or not we have created a compelling mission, we assess what we have written against ten questions:

1. A mission is about service to others, making the world a better place, enriching lives. Is this mission written as a direct, heart-felt declaration of what we intend to do or die trying?

2. Does this mission inspire others—our owners, employees, customers—appealing to the heart and feelings and not just the head?

3. Does this mission set out a framework for what everyone in the company must do? Is this a clear statement of what is actually going on, each and every day, in the lives of everyone in the company?

4. Does this mission show the pain that it will take to succeed at our work?

5. Is it jargon-free, written in plain language, a person-to-person communication?

6. Would I want to work to accomplish this mission?

7. Does it provide a clear basis for setting priorities, making tough decisions and changing what needs to be improved?

8. Does it make clear how we will move toward the future, and does it set an expectation for change?

9. Have we given as many people as possible an opportunity to contribute to this mission statement?

10. Have we created a process by which the mission is reviewed and updated, as needed?

And We're Not Done Yet

To do it right, the process does take time. And, even after the mission statement itself has been crafted, there is much more that needs to be done to have it become a viable management tool. Keep in mind that our purpose is not merely to get inspiring words down on paper. The investment in money, time and energy is only worth it if we assure that each step along the way creates something new in the way of greater organizational vitality and responsiveness. Thus, we need to put into place a kind of orientation to each person's work that is different from what is expected in traditional, mechanistic organizations. We must set up positions in which each person in the company is able to take responsibility for some part in the company's success and profits, and not just for efficiency in executing tasks in a process. So far, we have stated the values that give work its human content and context. And we have stated what the company's intentions are in regard to its customers and other stakeholders with its actions. But these are still just words. We can't stop here. It isn't good enough to have people simply feel good about the company for a day or two or have glowing words in which to describe their work.

In our view, there are few things that a business does (and even these are becoming more rare as automation and robotics advance) that can be reduced to mere process. And improving processes rarely leads to the kinds of organizations that can simultaneously sustain performance and invigorate its people. Workers at all levels of a company are now called upon to use judgment and discretion in resolving problems and situations in ways that carry the company forward. This can either be exciting to people or it can cause untold stress and anxiety. The remaining chapters put in place multi-dimensional "attractors," standards and expectations so they can meet this demand with confidence.

The premise of what follows is that a business creates value by establishing and maintaining *relationships* with customers and others around change and novelty. A company, then, has to put forward the kind of competence that will give people the confidence to move forward and experiment with the way they do things. With this confidence, they are willing to invest their money (customers), time and energy (managers and employees) and investments (shareholders). These relationships are what command the attention of people's strategic hearts and so lead to organizations that succeed by leading them and others to new horizons.

We have a ways to go to complete our work in creating a strategic organization. In the next chapter, we will to turn to the work of crafting an "Arrow of Value." With this process, we transform the words of the mission into the actions that each person in the company will perform each and every day to make it a reality in people's lives. In Chapter 8 we will round out this process by creating the Areas of Responsibility and Critical Success Factors that define the way each person in the organization participates in and contributes to that mission.

NOTES

1. Lao-tzu, *Tao te Ching* (64), trans. Stephen Mitchell (New York: HarperPerennial, 1988).

2. Admittedly, the term "value" here is unfortunate, since it confuses what we mean by "values" as described in the last chapter. Nevertheless, that is the terminology we inherit. In this case, "value" pertains to the priority a customer assigns to a business's product or service as indicated by the price he or she is willing to pay. It is related to the term "values," as used in the last chapter, in so far as that term also denotes a process in which a person evaluates and selects from options in the environment that lead to consequences in terms of behavior and responses from that behavior. Both terms point to a process in which choices, made in an external world have a direct bearing on the behaviors and expectations one adopts for one's self (or business).

3. See Michael H. Shenkman, *Value and Strategy: Competing Successfully in the Nineties* (New York: Quorum Books, 1992), for a full discussion of the "value relationship."

Chapter 4

Mission (II): Action and the Arrow of Value

One day, long ago, a young man walking down a road came upon a laborer fiercely pounding away at a stone with a hammer and chisel. The lad asked the worker, who looked frustrated and angry, "What are you doing?" The laborer answered, in a pained voice, "I am shaping this stone and it is backbreaking work." The youth continued his journey and soon came upon another man chipping away at a similar stone, who looked neither particularly angry nor happy. "What are you doing?" he asked. "I am shaping a stone for a building." The young man went on and before long came to a third worker chipping away at a stone, but this worker was singing happily as he worked. "What are you doing?" The worker smiled and replied, "I am building a cathedral."

—*Fortune*[1]

ACTIONS THAT CREATE VALUE FOR CUSTOMERS

Creating a mission statement accomplished a great deal for the partners of CGL. They had agreed on a unified strategy for the company and, just as important for this group, they acknowledged each other's contributions to the firm's leadership. The partners were energized with a sense of purpose and expansiveness about their work and the prospects for their company as well.

But too often we see our clients spend a weekend, clad in shorts and open-collared shirts, going about the collegial and uplifting exercise of creating an inspiring mission statement, only to come into the office on Monday morning and resume their old, familiar, mechanistic habits of operating. It's a dizzying descent from the heights of the lofty and impassioned intentions set out in the mission statement to the mundane, routine, boiled-down jobs assigned to employees. In successful, growing companies, however, the work of passion does not stop with creating a mission. To the contrary, the mission only provides a company's managers, employees and other stakeholders with a license for accomplishing something that matters, and maybe even something great. The real passion comes when people engage customers and affect their lives. Everyone in the company needs to think about those actions that, each and every day, create what has been promised to their customers.

Too often, business decision makers get enmeshed in the intrigues and intricacies of running their companies. They concentrate on where people fit on the organizational chart and lose sight of the actions on which customers depend. Keeping focused on value-creating actions makes for successful businesses. The living, complex systems that grow and thrive all around us provide important insights on this issue. In nature, each aspect of a living system's being is molded to perform some important, life-giving and life-enhancing action. An organism never loses touch with its environment. Its senses are inextricably intertwined with some aspect of its world; each organ and system performs in a way that adapts materials from that environment to its immediate, life-perpetuating use. During the course of many generations, it has honed all its systems so they can perform certain actions with grace, speed and precision. Likewise, the business organization's actions need to be done with effectiveness, grace and precision each and every day to make the mission come alive in the world that the customer experiences. To help decision makers shift their thinking away from preoccupations with the standard organizational chart—with its hierarchy and departmentalization—we created the "Arrow of Value."

The Arrow of Value is a foundation on which everyone in the company builds a sense of how to contribute to the mission in a way that creates value for the customer. The arrow lists, in a temporal sequence, the "core actions" people in a company must perform each and every day to deliver that value. Core actions are defined as *the actions that are repeated each and every day, so as to have a direct impact on what your company wants its customers to experience in using its products and services.* All personnel assignments, groupings and functional teaming keys off of this sequential listing of change-creating, customer-affecting actions. From correlating personnel with the direct, value-producing actions in which they are engaged, people coordinate across departmental boundaries or through any hierarchical ranking in order to focus on what is most important to accomplish.

We use the image of an arrow because it evokes the idea of a progression of events through real time. It also reinforces the idea that once energy and resources have been expended in that progression, they cannot be recovered. At the beginning of a production process, investors and decision makers put in place a structure and process capable of creating value. The subsequent actions either culminate in greater value for customers and thus increased returns—profits—for the company or a loss. When the resources have been spent, the funds expended, materials used, hours taken, are gone. Given the time pressures

Figure 4.1
Conifer Group's Core Actions

| Analyze products and technology trends for opportunities | Identify, contact, sell to potential customers | Identify, qualify customer needs; match to budgets | Assemble, integrate and test systems solutions | Implement solutions, assuring that the systems work | Assure customer support, service and satisfaction |

under which a business works, any loss is a dear one. To succeed, each step along the way must produce something concrete upon which the next step builds, ultimately culminating in all the actions having their intended impact on customers' lives, accomplishing something concrete and deliverable and creating value.

In our work with clients, we use the Arrow of Value instead of the traditional organizational chart—a time-worn tool that may provide a handy snapshot of who reports to whom, who's on top and who's not. We find it to be of minimal utility in building a successful company, since it doesn't give any useful information about *how the company really creates value and how it has deployed resources to create significant customer experiences of satisfaction.* By contrast, the Arrow of Value focuses on the business's *value-creating actions,* that is, *the actions that make a difference in the way your customer is able to do or experience that aspect of life your products and services affect.* Understanding these actions—seeing if they need to be changed and understanding why they are the appropriate actions to be taken—is the crucial management mandate for the growing organization, not giving out titles and fiefdoms of authority. The business is fully presented and understood in its organic unity as it grows, changes, shifts responsibilities develops new ones and lets old ones go, as it increases its capabilities in a demanding environment.

Here is how CGL translated its mission process into one that unified and focused everyone on creating a whole new company.

BUILDING THE NEW COMPANY AT CONIFER

Creating the Architecture of Charts

The Monday after the retreat, the partners of CGL were faced with the daunting task of transforming their company. We started with the simplest of questions: *What will CGL have to do to be able to fulfill its mission?* This is the basic question that the Arrow of Value answers. Using the answers to this question we created a sequential listing of the company's core actions (see Figure 4.1).

The partners then began to develop their organizational structure. Rather than think in terms of departments, we thought about the kinds of actions that needed to be done and the kinds of *working groups* that would best suit the actions (see Figure 4.2). These working groups may or may not be departments, but they are clusters of people who are actually involved on a day-to-day basis in performing these actions. Then we looked at who among the partners and other working groups would be directly involved in implementing these actions. We used this information to fill in the far left column. In each sector where an individual or group contributed or participated in an action, we put in a "loading factor," a number of 1 to 5, signifying how involved each person was in a particular action. A bar was placed in the field created by the matrix, the field was filled with a loading of 5 and a thin line represented a 1, etc.

This process created what we call the "Top Chart," the most generalized description of what actions everyone in the company performs. For people managing these processes, these descriptions are often too general to be useful in terms of making assignments for responsibilities or evaluations. So, for several of the actions, we started to create detail arrows. A detail arrow further elaborates on an action in a way that makes it possible to name individuals involved in groups or shows how an action is performed for the purposes of analysis and evaluation. By way of example, the action "Integrate and Assemble Systems as Ordered" is detailed in Figure 4.3. These core actions elaborate on the company's commitment to integrating systems that specifically fit a customer's needs and assure that "the systems worked" as promised in the mission statement. The complete Arrow of Value chart for these core actions is shown in Figure A.1.

Several other of the core actions were further detailed as well. We don't need to show them here.

The important points we are making in this stage of process are these:

- Work to get clarity about the core actions that have the most impact on your customers' experiences of the products and services your company is offering. These actions will not be esoteric; to the contrary, they will be obvious. These actions are usually performed every day, with each and every customer interaction in which your people are engaged. These actions constitute your "Top Arrow," or the company-wide Arrow of Value.

- Make sure the entire set of arrows in the architecture name the essential steps that you must cover in order to be successful and that everyone involved in the action is named, either at the top or at the detail level of the charts.

- Administrative support, top, non-line management functions or other non-value creating actions are not broken out on the arrow. They may appear as "Areas of Responsibility" within each or several of these actions and therefore will have "Critical Success Factors (CSFs)" associated with them. The purpose of this exercise is to clear away any possible distraction from succeeding in accomplishing these core actions each and every day.

Figure 4.2
Conifer Group Arrow of Value

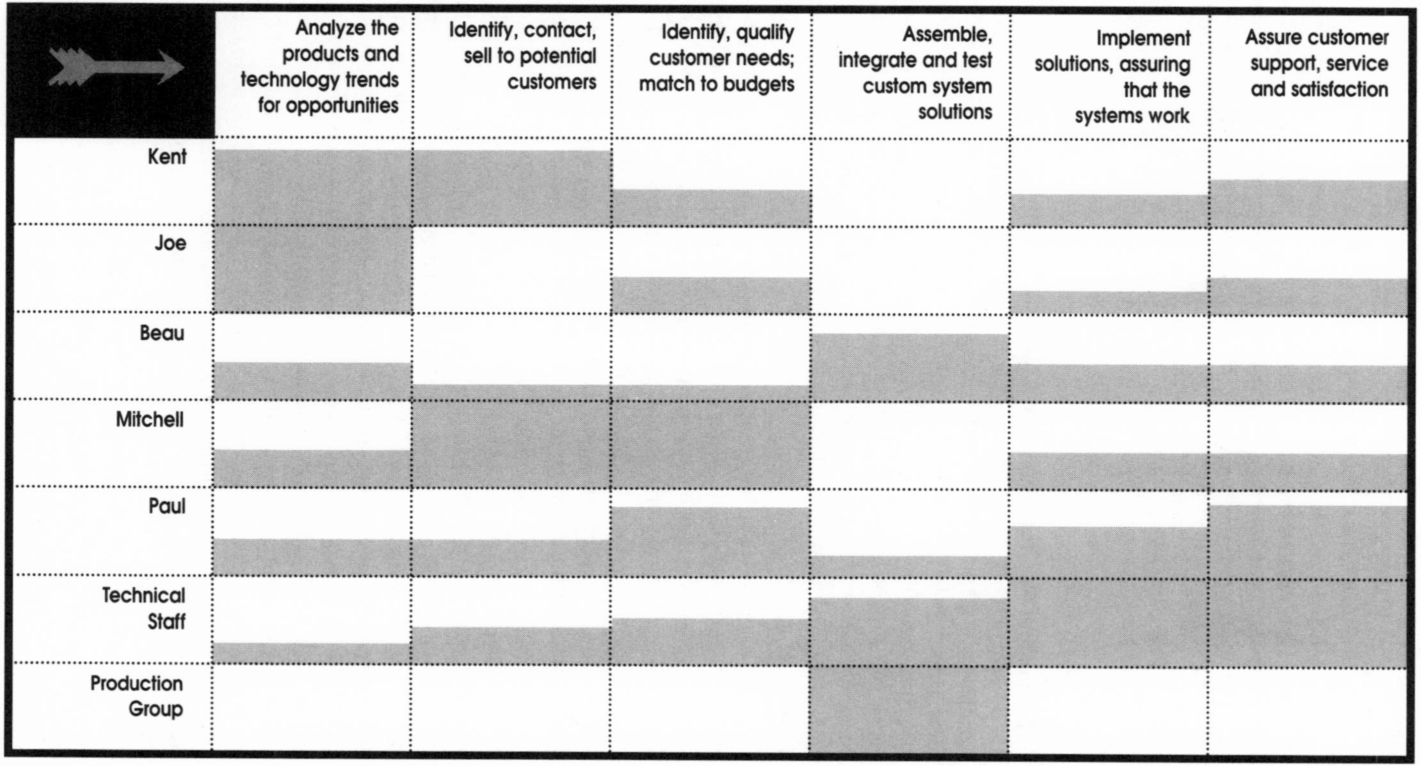

	Analyze the products and technology trends for opportunities	Identify, contact, sell to potential customers	Identify, qualify customer needs; match to budgets	Assemble, integrate and test custom system solutions	Implement solutions, assuring that the systems work	Assure customer support, service and satisfaction
Kent	■	■				
Joe	■		■		■	■
Beau	■					■
Mitchell		■	■	■		
Paul	■	■	■		■	■
Technical Staff	■	■	■	■		
Production Group				■		

Figure 4.3
Detail Arrow of Value

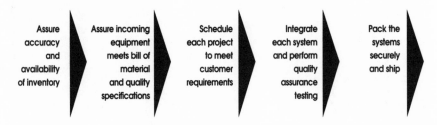

Taking the Process into the Company

Our goal was to create a spirited company, growing in capability and complexity, so the next step was even more crucial. Each partner sat down with people in the company and asked them to take responsibility, management and leadership responsibility for actions. They asked these people to conceive in detail what it would take to fulfill the mission of the new company. In this way, each necessary action was detailed according to a tree of dependent and more detailed actions.

Individually, each of these people created his or her own operations' Arrow of Value. Working together, they created mission statements for these operations—stating how the operation contributed to the mission—and envisioning the kinds of resources and groupings of resources it would take to do the job. Each group leader then worked with the line workers to define the operation, note the core activities that would be necessary to fulfill that operation and show the interrelationship between the various inter- and intra-group functions.

For everyone, this was a new way of thinking. Most of these young people who populated CGL at the time had never thought an operation through, no less organized others to accomplish it. They were the easy ones to work with. Those who were habitually ensconced in the traditional organizational chart and ''management by objectives'' kind of authoritarian thinking were the most difficult to enlist in the process. The experience actually became an introduction to managing in the new world of business: stay focused on the mission and pay attention to each and every action it takes to accomplish it.

Out of this process, however, flowed the whole organizational structure. After the actions were blocked out and individuals assigned to each action, managers met with the individuals assigned to the task. Each of these individuals then created descriptions of their respective areas of responsibility and their CSFs. These are performance-related descriptions that we'll discuss in detail in Chapter 8. In general, though, the ''Area of Responsibility'' summarizes how a person generally contributes to creating value for the customer (internal or external). A CSF describes what specific and positive things happen in the course of performing these actions and indicate how the mission is being accomplished and if the actions are succeeding as intended.

Looking at the Process

This process took several months. There were many interactions of arrows and descriptions; there were meetings and long discussions about how resources were to be allocated. All of these were fruitful, progress-making discussions that knit the new company together. By using a computer program (Mage now provides such a program to its clients), they had a database of what each person in the company was responsible for doing and how that person's success would be evaluated against the mission. They also had a tool by which to analyze whether or not they were focusing on the right actions; and, by looking at the CSFs associated with those actions, they could evaluate whether or not they were properly gauging the success of these actions. The Arrow of Value thus linked the most important aspects of the company's organization to the company's mission and strategy:

- All actions tie directly to what the company intends to make happen for the customer.
- All personnel and groups of people (departments or informal operational groups) define their responsibilities in terms of these core actions.
- All personnel clearly see who else is involved with them in accomplishing an action, regardless of departmental affiliation or ranking. This eliminates the temptation to set up "turfs" and instead fosters "natural teams" who share responsibility for their actions.
- Success is determined by evaluating the actual effects the actions have versus what they are intended to have on the customer, and not on any subjective criterion of a remote and detached manager.
- If changes need to be made, everyone has a clear, detailed map of who will be involved in making these changes.
- It may be worthwhile to note that this process is also used to define short-term projects and initiatives to create internal improvements.

CREATING AN ARROW OF VALUE

Now, we will briefly review the steps you can use in creating an Arrow of Value so you can begin to implement this useful analytical tool.

Step One: Define and List the Company's Core Actions

The *core actions* listed in the Arrow of Value are steps that are absolutely necessary to fulfill the mission. Here are some of the important steps that go into sorting out which of the many tasks performed in the company are core actions.

1. Start by thinking through in detail about what it is that your company wants to happen in the lives of each and every customer as a result of them buying and using your product or service. Then think about what that engagement with the customer will entail. Even if it is not done face-to-face or if there are retailers or wholesalers to deal with, these actions still contribute to the success or failure of that engagement and comprise the "core actions" of the Arrow of Value.

2. A core action has a *direct effect on customers' experiences.* This criterion differentiates a core action from the kinds of supporting (but necessary) actions that people perform in the company. (These actions are accounted for by means of the subtables that detail some of the actions performed for "internal customers"—other employees—who work more directly with the customer.)

3. A core action has a definite, concrete result that affects a customer's experience of the product or service. It is either a measurable outcome or a deliverable that others use in the course of their work toward fulfilling the mission.

4. These actions are always being done by someone in the company each and every day. They are not occasional actions or actions done to fill in or compensate for something that has not been done properly.

Generally, the kinds of actions we see across the top of an arrow fall into a few distinct kinds of groups. The first grouping considers what the company needs to have in place in order to carry on a transaction with customers. That may consist of some special knowledge, expertise or market awareness; it may consist of product inventory on hand. Sometimes it involves all of the above. Creating that knowledge base and/or purchasing that inventory comprise the first actions on the arrow. Here are a few examples of the kinds of actions we see quite often and how they satisfy our defining criteria:

Action	Result	Effect on the Customer
Research the market.	Analysis and report.	Determines the production decisions that follow.
Analyze the customer's situation.	Analysis and report.	Determines the production and design decisions that follow.

Next, think of how you contact customers and how you work directly and how you conduct your transactions with them. These are the next steps along the arrow. Examples of this are:

Action	Result	Effect on Customer
Conduct direct mail.	Qualified leads.	Customer awareness and access to the product.
Follow-up on referrals.	Call tracking records.	Perception and delivery of service.
Install the equipment.	Installed equipment on site.	Service delivered.

Next, it is important to consider how these actions are realized as revenue. This may seem like an internal function, thus violating our suggestion of sticking to aspects that affect customers' experiences of producing value. But getting the bill, having the bill understood and having a fair, firm and flexible collections process is a crucial part of the experience customers have of a company, and so is a crucial aspect of the relationships every company builds with its customers. Another reason this is important is that it is a time-consuming and important part of any business, and it is one that can be quite difficult for some service businesses, and even product-based businesses, that have a large built-in service component (which is more and more the case these days). It has to be accounted for in how the company spends its time and also how resources are allocated. Thus invoicing, billing and fee determination are important to show on the arrow.

Finally, it is important to put down those actions your company performs to ensure quality and customer satisfaction. An example of this kind of action is:

Action	**Result**	**Effect on Customer**
Conduct customer survey/audit.	Survey or report.	Better and more knowledgeable service, support and development.

Step Two: Individuals, Groups and the Division of Responsibilities

Next, we need to look at how your company has organized and grouped its actions. On a company level, this usually means that departments are involved with these actions. On a departmental level, this usually means divisions or individuals. These groups or individuals are listed down the left side of the chart, designating rows.

Where in the listing you place an individual or a group can signify different things depending on what it is you want to depict in the chart. We usually try to list people or groups according to their entrance into the process, rather than any kind of hierarchical listing. Actually, the nonproducing managers may not even show up on a departmental chart (but would show up on the company-wide chart).

As we mentioned, an Area of Responsibility is defined for each person or group in the table; and CSFs are created for each sector in the table that is filled in. This aspect of the Arrow of Value is described in Chapter 8. It is important to remember that all of the steps are crucial to making the process of creating a dynamic organization a success.

Step Three: Loading

Once the columns (actions) and rows (individuals) are set, you are ready to display the "loading" each individual carries in a given task. Along the row, create a bar of varying thickness under the action in which that person or group is involved. Each of the bars in each field vary in thickness depending on the quantity and quality of the time a person or group spends in the particular action.

We use increments of 1 to 5 to designate the level of involvement: 1 indicating low involvement, 5 indicating high involvement. To help better characterize what is meant by "levels of involvement," I have adapted a useful scheme for describing roles and relationships vis-à-vis tasks that was devised by Lee Bolman and Terrence Deal.[2] They use four groupings of roles and relationships: responsibility, approval, consult and inform. I make a few changes to this useful characterization of roles. I assign the level-designating numbers and apply each of these categories this way:

5 = Performance. The person or group is charged with executing this aspect of the relationship, carrying out a complete core action or set of core actions.

4 = Responsibility and Approval. The person or group is responsible for these actions and approves the materials and resources required to fulfill the action but rarely gets directly involved in performance. This person or group has responsibility for providing resources and a structural framework for the action, has to monitor their appropriate use and is always mindful of the action and concerned about its successful execution.

3 = Critical Contribution. This person or group contributes some vital element to the action but does not have primary responsibility for performing or completing it. Still, the action could not be properly completed without this person's involvement.

2 = Consult. The person or group has sufficient authority such that when asked for advice and guidance, they can affect the way the action is performed henceforward.

1 = Inform. This person or group is merely kept abreast of what is transpiring in the action and will not likely have the authority to change an action. Generally, these people need information in order to perform other actions.

Step Four: Detailing Actions with Action Details

Next, you will need to detail some (but not necessarily all) of the broad actions described at the company level. To do this, we create a "detail" of the action, a subset of actions that comprise the larger-in-scope action that the company as a whole takes on. Each action can have one or more "details" depending on how people and actions are grouped. The detailing of the actions stops, however, at the point when the described actions are invisible to customers and only pertain to internal requirements for processing flow. Usually these kinds of actions end up being used as Critical Success Factors (see Chapter 8).

A "detail" delineates a higher level, more generalized core action; it does not describe a functional group. These latter descriptions are covered in "areas of responsibilities." An action can have more than one subset; and a working group can have subsets that cut all the way across the "parent" Arrow of Value. For instance, in the case of CGL, the production group performs functions that need to be listed because each step is critical to successful delivery of a functional system that "works" as the mission promises. This group therefore has a "detail" arrow.

USING THE MISSION AND ARROW OF VALUE: SOME FREQUENTLY ASKED QUESTIONS

To further clarify how to make use of this productive organizing tool, I have provided these answers to our clients' frequently asked questions.

1. Why aren't there the usual goals and objectives?

When creating "Arrows of Value," some things with which clients are familiar seem to be missing. Where are the "objectives and goals," for instance? It is true—these shibboleths of strategic planning are gone from our program. In their place we have put a strict and consistent concentration on *actions*. We feel we have enunciated the goals for the company and its working groups and individuals through the values and mission. The values make clear how actions are chosen from among the many options that are available; and the mission makes clear what actions the company chooses are intended to change in the worlds of the people it affects. Now, let's get to work.

The individuals and groups who have to perform what are identified as the company's core actions are more than capable of determining the intermediate steps that comprise them. When it is necessary to be more specific about what an action or a detail of an action needs to accomplish, these can easily be accommodated in the CSFs. What is different in our process, however, is that people are held accountable for the action, which gives them a significant role in fulfilling the mission, not a supporting role or "process objective" that distances them from what the company is ultimately trying to accomplish.

The advantage of using core actions over the usual application of "goals and objectives" is when using core actions and CSFs (as we'll see in Chapter 8), the people performing the action get to evaluate their effectiveness themselves. The outcomes or objectives are for their use in improving and improvising, in order to accomplish what the mission requires, in a way that the company's values allow. Using core actions as their guide, people performing the actions get quick, maybe instantaneous, feedback as to whether or not they are accomplishing what was intended by the actions.

Another important difference between using core actions over goals and objectives is that the evaluation made can be qualitative as well as quantitative. Since objectives are not measured or looked at on a situation-to-situation basis, they tend to be quantitative in nature. They aggregate a pattern of many actions into a single, monolithic result that is supposed to indicate what is happening on a moment-by-moment basis. No numbers can ever really tell whether or not the company's mission to create lasting, meaningful change is really happening.

A salesman, for instance, can know that he is accomplishing the mission if the customer says to him, "I can't buy this from you, but I like what you're offering, so here's someone to contact and use my name." The numbers would show a negative result, since there was no sale. But the salesman was actually successful in winning an ally, an immediate referral and the respect of someone who may give more. The quantitative objective was not met, but the qualitative evaluation of the core action was met and surpassed. Quantitative criteria can be used in evaluating core actions, and any company has quantitative minimums that have to be met—whether they be in terms of quality standards or income, revenue and profits baselines or break-evens. In the long run, however, a viable, growing business would surely want that qualitative result of building allies and a wide referral network over a short-term, pressure-induced sale.

The Arrow of Value process and core actions don't eliminate goals and objectives, but they do transpose them to a status that makes the actions people perform the primary focus of attention. In so doing, managers and line employees have more freedom in creating meaningful, insightful and immediate cues to the success of those actions.

2. Isn't it crucial to create a single, unified vision for everyone in the company?

We concentrate our attention on gaining agreement on what core actions will make a difference in people's lives and that all employees agree on how they will collaborate in executing those actions. We want people in the company having conversations about those actions: deciding and evaluating if they are effective or ineffective in accomplishing the mission; discussing the priority of one action over another; and determining the timing, costs and risks of taking one action or another.

We find these conversations are enriched by each person's vision of what the company is trying to accomplish and his or her appreciation of its value. If idiosyncratic ideas are sending some people's actions off the mark, adjustments may need to be made. But even in this case, managers should enter into these conversations with some degree of openness. The idea and vision that motivates one person may also have merit not previously realized, acknowledged or incorporated into the company or detail Arrows of Value. The conversation is not about whether a particular vision is right or wrong, but whether or not the actions being performed do, in fact, accomplish a worthwhile vision for that person. The result is a honing of the actions toward a more focused result and a greater appreciation of what the line worker is trying to accomplish. The "Strategic Heart" is enriched, not diminished or discouraged.

3. What is the difference in your mind between a "Working Group" and our "Departments?"

The Arrow of Value program is not primarily concerned with how the work is departmentalized. There are certain standard groupings of people in a company: technicians, customer service representatives, marketers, salespeople, financial and accounting people, manufacturing people and so on. These are useful groupings because people who have similar outlooks and skills can be mutually supporting and coordinate a specialized flow of detailed actions that are done each day. However, these departments are not secluded fiefdoms in a strategic organization. There are no hard lines around the boxes that separate one department from another.

I prefer to think of these as working groups because that idea connotes a more informal association of like-minded and like-talented people who can be deployed as needed by the company as it grows and changes. A software technician may be assigned to a marketing group for a year to help create a database, even though that person may "report" to the VP of technology. This is not a "matrix" of one person having divided loyalties. This person's CSFs for a year are based on the results achieved for the marketing group's project of creating this data base. The technology manager will review and evaluate that performance just as she would any other person in her group. It's just that this one person is assigned to an internal technical project.

The idea is that the actions take precedence over the structure or, to put it another way, the *strategy is the structure.* The Arrow of Value enables decision makers to move resources around the company as the demands of the market and the growth of the company dictate. Confusion may result for a time, but this can be cleared up by reviewing the chart, clarifying how the CSFs are created for the new position and how they will be evaluated and then making sure all the people that comprise this person's natural team are apprised of the change and understand what needs to be done.

So, by all means, have your departments, but don't let those boxes on the chart become walls and barriers to getting the most valuable things accomplished for your company.

4. Is all this detail necessary?

I have two answers to this question. First, of course it is. I can't count the number of hours I have spent in conference rooms poring over the numbers, the details of quarterly budgets, hearing explanations and justifications of one line item after another. Yet when it comes to assessing the impact of a company's most important resource, its people, to develop descriptions of core actions and CSFs, people complain that it constitutes overload. I think not. These discussions often bring out misconceptions that people have about others' work, or they provoke statements of appreciation that people had never heard before. They also assure people that the work they really do will be recognized, improved upon and rewarded. As we will discuss in detail in Chapter 8, this painstaking process is the core of organizational management.

The second part of my answer is a bit more sympathetic. There is a lot of information here, and that can be daunting. For this information to be useful, it must be put into a computerized organizational database. Creating that database (as is the case in creating any database) is arduous at first, but once it is up and running people will be able to freely access just the information they want at a given point in time. They can call up all the people involved in an action to see whether or not that action is covered properly; or they can access just one person's file and see just those actions for which they are responsible. In addition, this database can be adapted to use as a work flow plan, as a deliverable schedule or a personnel improvement and evaluation format.

As much of the information should be public and generally available as possible, helping to foster communications between people by keeping their attention on the work, not personal or minor issues. And finally, with this information in a database it can be modified and updated as needed so it will always be current as the company changes and grows. The updating is easy.

So yes, this work has to be done, in detail. This, after all, is the company's organizational and human resource balance sheet.

LOOKING AHEAD

As we will see, taken together, the Arrow of Value approach to crafting an organizational design focuses people on doing the most valuable things toward accomplishing the mission. It provides managers with flexible tools that can be tailored specifically to make sure actions at any level of the organization are accomplishing the desired changes as declared in the mission. The conversations that take place around evaluation issues are about whether or not these actions are having the desired result, not about whether or not the objectives are being met. The conversations stay strictly focused on what each person and group of people in the organization are trying to accomplish in their customers' lives.

The next steps that need to be explained, in terms of the basic elements of the process, are CSFs and areas of responsibility. If you wish to fill in the component of this program right away, feel free to go directly to Chapter 8. In general, an area of responsibility summarizes all the actions a person or group is responsible for along the arrow. CSFs enumerate the ways people can identify whether or not they are succeeding in accomplishing what those actions intend. But before we get to that part of creating a strategic organization, we need to look once again at the kind of structure and leadership we are asking people to work in and respond to. We also need to understand the quality of experience we want the organization and its leaders to support and encourage if we are to fully appreciate the full range of talents and energies people can bring to the process of creating a strategic organization.

NOTES

1. "Executive Life," *Fortune,* December 26, 1994, p. 196.
2. Lee G. Bolman and Terrence E. Deal, *Reframing Organizations: Artistry, Choice,*

Leadership (San Francisco: Jossey-Bass, 1991), pp. 112–114. For one, I add the category "performance"; then I combine responsibility and approval, since these usually go hand in hand in business situations; and finally, I add the role of "critical contribution."

Chapter 5

Choice

Even though you try to put people under some control, it is impossible.
You cannot do it. The best way to control people is to encourage them
to be mischievous. Then they will be in control in its widest sense. . . .
First let them do what they want, and watch them. This is the best policy.
To ignore them is not good; that is the worst policy. The second worst
is trying to control them. The best one is to watch them, just to watch
them, without trying to control them.
                            —Shunru Suzuki, *Zen Mind, Beginner's Mind*[1]

THE "NEAR CHAOS" ORGANIZATION

When Mage consultants start their work with young managers, we often find
them to be obsessed with control—controlling processes, departments, budgets
and, most of all, people. Their obsession isn't entirely inappropriate in many
organizations. In traditionally hierarchical companies, the accusation of being
"too soft" can be the kiss of death. Accordingly, they go to just about any
length to demonstrate that they are "in control." The effects of this behavior
on an organization are quite predictable. When one manager exerts control,
someone else does not have control. The result is energy-draining, productivity-
killing politics. For the control types, no business seems to be too large to
attempt to dominate; no situation presents too insignificant an occasion to demonstrate who is in control. Control is their way of life, and politics is their milieu.
What a waste of time, talent and energy.

The organization that succumbs to the control and command mentality is a
depressing place in which to work. It takes on the limited abilities and perspectives of a controlling manager instead of blending, multiplying and amplifying

the talents and energies of everyone. Every organization has politics, and there is such a thing as "good politics." But obsessive control only breeds corrosive politics. And yet, while the political players in an organization can do far more damage than any competitor, and we all know that politics and control diminish an organization's ability to grow, few consultants and still fewer senior managers are willing to combat bad politics and overbearing control with the same fervor they take on a competitor. Politics are accepted as a "fact of life," the "price of getting bigger."

Complexity and the Growing Business

In contrast to this behavior, the best managers of growing organizations learn to succeed without exerting obsessive control. They are distinguished from the run-of-the-mill manager that thwarts growth because they have found that by overly controlling people they diminish their own effectiveness and that of the organization. You can be sure, no one individual can ever be as productive, imaginative and creative as a group of people who collaborate together in a well-organized business.

Successful managers control people and decisions, but they do so *selectively.* They realize that growing companies are high-energy places in which ideas are generated faster than there are programs to implement them. There is always more work to do than hours in which to do it. No one person, no matter how well placed, can honestly say he or she has a complete grasp on what is going on throughout the company from moment to moment, day to day, week to week. This kind of environment can scare the timid and completely frustrate those who need to have things "under control." Happily, the science of complex systems points to a new way to think about fast-paced organizational change and growth. It has a great deal to say about how order emerges out of high-energy, deeply challenging situations. In fact, it is in just such high-energy environments, those like we experience in successful businesses every day, where this science has the most to teach us.

So far, we have used the science of complexity to elucidate how the business relates *outwardly* to its environment. From the idea of an "attractor," we have seen how a company's values enable it to adapt to change and grow while maintaining its seminal core of values about the world. Then we have seen that a business grows and changes by inextricably linking its intentions and actions with the needs, perspectives and attention its customers and markets are requesting. In the form of the mission and Arrow of Value, we have set the company on a course of first discerning what it is that people want the business to provide in their lives and then setting each person in the business on a course to work with others, day in and day out, to provide that for them.

Now we take an *introspective* turn and look to the new science of complexity to see what light it can shed on the internal workings of the growing business.

The key insight that complexity offers is that, as we stated in the first chapter, *development toward higher organization only ensues under "near chaos" conditions.* This characteristic of self-organizing systems has been studied extensively in the last few years. Ilya Prigogine won the Nobel Prize for establishing much of the physics and creating the most widely used framework for understanding near chaos situations and their importance in the development of complex systems.

Chaos and Complexity

Prigogine analyzes what happens when energy is applied to materials at varying rates of intensity and for varying lengths of time (in more technical terms, these states describe the "thermodynamic" conditions of the material) and divides the results into three categories. In the first, a material's mass overwhelms the amount of energy being applied to it. In this instance, the material is "at equilibrium." We see materials in equilibrium all around us in the form of rocks, for instance. These materials do not adapt to conditions around them. Rain, wind, heat or cold over eons of time eventually wear them down to materials of less and less mass. On the other end of the spectrum, there is the condition of being "nonlinear" or completely chaotic and beyond the pale of any possible organization. Explosions or riots in the street are examples of this condition. This state results when the energy being applied to a system overwhelms the structural integrity of the material or organization. In between these two conditions is the level of excitation that is called "far from equilibrium," or "near chaos." A "far from equilibrium" condition occurs when something is subjected to sustained energy, in just the right amount, for an extended period of time.

Within this "threshold" or range, the energy is raising the level of excitement in the system to just the right level so it is "alive." All elements of the system are in motion (molecules move more rapidly, fields become more active), yet the bonds between these elements are sufficiently robust to prevent the system from being blown apart. The result is that the system remains in a state that is highly agitated and active; far from equilibrium but still intact and self-contained—albeit, straining to keep itself together.

According to Prigogine, if this energy bombardment persists, the system is "[compelled] to evolve toward a new regime that may be qualitatively quite different from the stationary states corresponding to [stability,]"[2] And, what is just as significant, when molecules (and atoms and subatomic particles) are in a state of being far from equilibrium, they are able to "sense" things around them. The organized system evolves by adding the elements and forms of organization that will elevate it to a new level of capability, one that is equal to the task of withstanding the specific and irrepressible forces that are impinging on it.

From Control to Choice

The science of complexity is telling us that an essential quality of being alive is living in a state of high excitation that stresses the status quo and yet does not imperil its long-term integrity. Since this model holds true for any complex, dynamic system, it certainly holds true for business organizations. Businesses are subject to constant streams of energy in the form of demands made from many different sources: from customers comes the pressure of increased orders and increased demands for improvements and innovation; from the markets, a new entrant enters the fray or a technology threatens to eclipse a product or service; from the inside, a new CEO or owner comes on the scene who wants to change things. There is no shortage of energy impinging on the business's organization.

It is natural for people in the business to respond to these pressures by resisting change and trying to control the situation—no one wants to change, after all. But when the persistence of the outside energies renders it impossible to maintain the *status quo,* the business has to "evolve toward a new regime," whether it likes it or not. Controls that enforced the old way of doing things also have to give way.

That does not mean control disappears. As we have seen, the business organization has forged many important bonds that keep it together. It has its values that act as "attractors," controlling and sorting out the many stimuli in the environment in order to arrive at appropriate responses. Then, it has its firmly rooted intentions and spine of core actions that coordinate and focus its actions each day. These attractors and actions provide powerful conceptual constraints that keep people, groups, teams and departments from flying off into oblivion.

A complex system such as a business has many attractors that act "hierarchically." The organization's values unify and integrate all aspects of the business at a very high level. Managers also act as attractors. Some managers unify and coordinate single operations, while others coordinate many similar and related operations. Still others, a company's senior decision makers, hold the company together as a whole by embodying the company's high-level, values and mission. Theoretically, there is no limit to the level of organization that can be achieved, provided there is a significant enough attractor to integrate the existing structures.

Managing in Chaos

The outstanding managers with whom we have worked understand that the organization exists in the first place so as to be able to respond meaningfully to changes and forces in the environment. If it is going to do this, there has to be a high level of excitation, possibly bordering on chaos, in the company. Trying to control the flow of ideas, concerns, issues and experimentation is tantamount to letting the organization wither on the vine. If the organization is to be productive, it needs to grow, and so egos need to get out of the way.

Successful decision makers also realize that the people closest to the action and the customers are in the best position to understand the demands being made and are thus in the best position to determine what responses need to be. The organization provides a framework of focus, intention (mission) and values, so that these people can break new ground with meaningful decisions. Organizations become what Robert Burgelman calls "opportunity structures,"[3] where top-down controls give way so that the organization's real mission—to meet, exceed and anticipate customer and competitive demands—can be met with new ideas, initiative and actions.

In place of exerting control, outstanding executives like Harry Kaufman, whose story we tell below, engender *choice*. They actively create situations that require everyone in the organization to generate options. Then they create processes and structures that enable people to collaborate in order to capture and implement those ideas. There is certainly an element of control in this formula— everyone is not just running wild. But the control is exerted selectively and carefully, by artfully crafting solutions from among options generated by the people doing the work. Rather than controlling individual initiative by denial, refusal and rejection, these leaders rely on their employees' own sense of the company's values and mission to guide them and self-select from among the options. The leader's job becomes one of assuring that people who offer values- and mission-supportive ideas and options see their creativity put into practice in the business's operations.

This is not a matter of "empowerment." Empowerment means giving power to people who are presumed, in advance, not to have it. In the science of complexity, each component of the organization has power to do its part, or the organization dies. Employees are now called upon to exercise the power their positions entail and *make choices* that respect the company's "attractors," and so make reasonable, constructive responses to changing conditions.

Harry is a perfect example of the leader who carries a mission forward within the bounds of values and with awareness of which company assets can provide the best leverage into the future. Encouraging an organization's people to make choices is among the hardest and most demanding of managerial attitudes to maintain; and keeping this stance and attitude alive in a company's culture is among the most emotionally absorbing and time-consuming tasks an executive has to undertake. Leaders constantly have to cajole the control types in the organization into a wider appreciation of their responsibilities as choosers and creators. But the effort is worth it. Politics have a harder time taking root. Those who try to maintain their control and defend the *status quo* sound off-key, self-serving and out of line. No matter how hard they try, the controlling personalities can't cloak their parochial demands under the mantle of a larger purpose. It doesn't work, because things change too fast and require too many people working together to make adjustments. People have to pitch in, not pitch their own causes to others.

It is hard, sometimes discouraging work; sometimes apparently good people have to be replaced because they can't let go. But the benefits to the organization are so outstanding, they more than compensate everyone who sticks with it for their efforts.

HARRY KAUFMAN: MOVING BEYOND CONTROL

At the time of this story, Harry was president and GM of a growing company in the burgeoning wireless communications field. In his mid-forties, tall, graying around the temples, he exuded the image of a CEO. It just so happened that Harry also had the confidence, insight and wisdom to back up that image. From the start of our engagement, it was clear that we were dealing with an accomplished, broad-minded and seasoned executive.

In our initial assessment, the team from Mage determined that Eastern Wireless Corporation was among the best operating companies we had ever seen. We read some of the company literature, its values statement and mission statement. We were impressed with what we saw. From these statements, we saw that Harry fully grasped what an organization's values and mission need to express. Harry really intended to serve customers, to break down bureaucratic barriers in the company, to allow for and encourage an employee's individual and team-spirited initiatives. People did their jobs effectively and efficiently. Everyone we talked to, up and down and across the organization, understood the mission and could recite the three-word condensation of it with passion and energy. Profit margins were good. The company was expanding, and there was plenty of opportunity for everyone to grow and advance in their careers.

So why did Harry call in the consultants from Mage? I learned, over the years, that Harry was never satisfied with leading only a smooth-running, machine-like business. He worked on a different set of priorities. He really believed that working in this company, in this field, at this time in the industry's history was fun. At our initial meeting he explained, "I just don't understand why people aren't more excited. The elevators are jammed at five o'clock. It's like they can't wait to get out of here. People talk about 'us' versus 'them.' I don't get it. There's no us and them, there's only one company here. Why do people feel that way?"

People weren't engaged, he felt. He was concerned about complacency and that when tough times hit, the employees wouldn't have the heart to deal with them. He was dissatisfied, it turned out, for all the right reasons. "Will these people rise to the occasion, be creative and take initiative or will they wait around for someone to tell them what to do? We can't afford that in this business," he wondered out loud to us.

In our investigation, we found that Harry did indeed have cause for concern (not alarm, to be sure, but concern). While many employees knew this was a good company, brimming with lots of opportunity for advancement and exciting careers, some felt that working here was just a matter of doing a job, not something in which to invest emotional, heartfelt energy. They were, as Harry expected, detached from everything around them except for the tasks, equipment and processes that impinged within the narrow definitions of their jobs; they were always waiting for someone to tell them what to do. If a printer was down in the area, they waited for someone else to fix it; if a process seemed inefficient or even useless, no one did anything to change it. And they were satisfied to take home a pay check and the raises offered to them.

This was not the kind of company Harry was trying to build. "I remember the early days of the business when we worked out of the trunk of our cars. If there wasn't a way to fix a problem, we invented something new that would. I know that a bigger, more bureaucratic company can't be as spontaneous, but it doesn't have to be dull either, does it?" In Harry's mind, everyone had enough responsibility for important things built into their positions so they could invent and create solutions to improve their work. Of course there are limits, but Harry felt there were plenty of choices and opportunities such that people could enjoy their work if they chose to exercise them.

The problem, we decided, started at the top with Harry himself. The company's potential for spirit, enthusiasm and engagement was being strangled by the fall-out from a decision Harry made two years earlier when he took over the general manager position. Harry was dealing with very powerful personalities on his senior management staff. Each of the four VPs were highly competent and extremely effective in their areas of expertise. However, two of them, Ned and Darlene, couldn't see any way of working other than competing against the other two VPs, Sal and Carol (about whom we have more to say in this chapter and in Chapter 9). Harry knew that politics created by the incessant rivalries among these executives could hamstring the company. Facing this situation, he had made a Faustian bargain. He felt that over time he could change the behavior of Ned and Darlene, but in the meantime he had to erect and maintain much stricter boundaries between their areas of operation than he liked. He had to insist, at least for the time being, that each VP kept his or her energies strictly focused within their own areas; and that put Harry in the position of making decisions that he would have preferred be reached by means of collaborative discussion. Still, in the interim, the company could succeed and operate smoothly by his acting as an honest broker between the competing factions.

However, the competition between Ned and Darlene didn't abate. There was little give-and-take or interaction between departments and people's roles were tightly restricted. The strict boundaries restricted and diminished the energy levels throughout the organization, subverting the very enthusiasm Harry was trying to protect. He was surprised to hear this assessment, but he didn't disagree with it and asked us to proceed with suggestions for making changes.

Our recommendation was to counterbalance the strict controls at the top by creating more free-flowing opportunities for innovation at the line level. If the

VPs wouldn't cooperate, our theory went, then with Harry's imprimatur, the employees would cooperate and collaborate on their own. Harry and we decided to instigate what were called "Idea Teams." The model for our recommendation was home grown. Carol Listner, one of the two, nonpolitical VPs and a highly creative and effective manager, had created Idea Teams in her department. They made recommendations for improving service, internal processes and increasing revenues. The teams were highly autonomous. They met privately every two weeks and prepared suggestions and recommendations that either line managers or Carol would fix.

The next logical step, we felt, was to provide everyone in the company with this outlet. Idea Teams in each of the four management areas met autonomously and prepared recommendations. The advantage of grouping people into Idea Teams (or quality teams without the bureaucracy) was that the ideas would be thought through and would reflect a department-wide consensus as to their relative priority. Made up exclusively of line level people, these teams would present innovations to their managers who would have the authority to approve many of them on the spot. If high level executive approval was necessary, the idea would be presented to Harry and the four VPs simultaneously. No VP could veto the idea unilaterally without Harry's knowledge and no idea could be approved over someone's head. The intent was to implement these ideas wherever possible—sooner or later, in one form or another—and not reject them.

To say it precipitated friction in Ned's department is putting it mildly. Ned insisted on attending the meetings of his Idea Team and prescribing deadlines for them. The Idea Team members staged a mini-rebellion. They literally threw him out of their meeting and told him that they were determined to work on their own schedule. It worked. Ned backed off his aggressive oversight and agreed to accept the team's agenda and time frame.

The program succeeded in all dimensions. One objective was to spark employee involvement. These line people met on lunch hours and before and after work; one group worked on their presentation of ideas over the weekend at one of their houses. (All non-exempt employees were fully paid for this time.) But most important, the program sparked the practice of line people generating options for solving problems on the spot, with as little red tape, bureaucracy or politics as possible. In general, the first six months of the program produced hundreds of ideas, most of which were implemented on the spot. Twenty-seven ideas were presented to the senior management team, and all of them were implemented.

People were proud of what was accomplished. "When I walk by and see those new printers," said one participant in the program, "I know that my idea put them there." Another group came up with an idea for a company fair at which each department would have a booth or exhibit to display what it did for the company. This was important, the team felt, because the company was growing so fast that there were so many new people and organizational changes it was impossible to keep up. This idea was turned into the year's kick-off event and was a tremendous success.

After this round of ideas was thoroughly worked through, new teams were created. Henceforward the teams' personnel rotated out one-by-one over the course of four to six months, so everyone who wanted to serve on the teams would get a chance. Of course, anyone in the department could submit ideas to the group and knew that there was a stable, open-minded process in place that would consider the ideas and implement them if at all possible. Over the next two years, the teams continued, even after Harry was promoted and reassigned. No extrinsic rewards were offered for work on the teams. While people were paid for any overtime they put in, that was hardly any reason to be a part of the Idea Team. Participating had its own rewards: accomplishing something for the company, showing how well a person could solve problems and think up ideas, and making something happen that would have practical, helpful results every day.

In essence, the Idea Team program formalized the concept of "choice." Conversations about where investments needed to be made and improvements implemented were going on at all levels of the company, all the time. The teams generated choices that the line managers and then the VPs had to acknowledge. The message from Harry was, "You can't play politics with the good ideas that people care about." It wasn't a perfect antidote to the VPs quarreling but succeeded in invigorating the spirit of a growing company.

CLEARING THE WAY FOR LEADERSHIP

There are politics in any organization, but there are good politics and bad politics. Good politics are the efforts people make to involve the right people in a project or an issue at the right time and in the right way. Good politics help people expand the horizons of their contributions to the company's progress and challenges.

In larger organizations, good politics take more time. In the crush of events and pressures, it may seem impossible to cover all the bases and deal with all the people that need to be involved in a decision or action. But the essence of leading a high-energy, strategic organization is to use technology and organizational innovation to involve the right people in a timely, open and constructive way. Optimally, people in different departments at all levels talk and share concerns, ideas and progress reports. When the lines of communication are open and freely flowing, when people are involved together to create and execute initiatives, and investing in practicing good politics up front actually ends up taking less time than to make up for bad politics after the mistakes have been made.

Unfortunately, people are most familiar with bad politics. The causes of this malady are clear and unmistakable. They come down to obsession with control: people trying to use whatever leverage their position affords for personal control, advantage or power in the hierarchy. It is never anything more than that. When employees view their efforts as going solely to feather someone else's nest, this behavior saps individual initiative. It also saps the business's drive to expand its capability as an organization. Time and energy are expended needlessly to accommodate internal and individual needs and not to expand the organization's comprehension and responsiveness to its challenges.

Leadership: the Magic Bullet?

In the literature on change, "leadership" is portrayed as the magic bullet that slays the dragon of bad politics. Where there is leadership, the truism states, change can happen in the right way, for the right reasons, at the right cost, within the right time frame. These writers have it backwards. Leaders usually arise when they are necessary, but they are only necessary when people are asked to generate choices that enable the organization to change and grow. A stymied organization cannot be roused by a leader to act strategically, energetically and creatively. It is within strategically dynamic organizations that leaders are sought.

Every day, a growing businesses industry encounters situations never experienced before. Under the pressures of time and scarce resources, everyone needs to create new ways to work and integrate new people and/or systems into the process. Everyone is continually involved in generating choices that have to be made in response to the new, pressing and unanticipated demands made by new customers using a new technology. These issues cannot merely be managed; the choices the workers generated for decision often require leadership for forays into new and uncharted waters. That's when a company demands leaders. Good leaders aren't sufficient for invigorating an unfocused, bureaucratic organization, and bad politics can stifle the appearance of promising leaders even in good companies. In growing organizations, more leadership is demanded than what any one CEO could provide. The Idea Teams created multiple settings in which the leadership throughout the organization could be recognized, tapped and developed.

Complexity and Leadership

Strategic organizations operate at "near chaos" energy levels because people are generating choices in response to the demands of customers, markets and competitors. These people are driving, sensing and responding to all the input that is coming at them. The company's hierarchy of attractors keeps them together. At the highest level, people respond to the incoming energy on the basis of the company's values, selecting out certain actions from the many options that present themselves. Then, at the next level, their decisions are focused by the company's mission that spells out what it intends to have happen as a result of its actions. To resolve the remaining ambiguities that always accompany situations of change, people go to their leaders for a sense of what is most urgent or most appropriate to do as the terrain changes and the winds shift before their eyes.

Leaders act as "attractors" who order the near chaos that comes from acting strategically and creating change. They don't and can't supply the energy that drives organizations, and they can't produce all the ideas that shape an organization's responses to its challenges. People go to leaders with the choices they have generated in response to change. Leaders then shape that energy into a response around which people can first cluster, then organize, amplifying their individual talents into a new, emergent capability of great scope.

Leaders aren't only found at the "top" of a company. In growing organizations they arise at every level. They may not have fancy titles, but they are the ones who embrace the need for decisions and take up the task of seeing them through, fighting the battles, convincing and persuading others to also engage in the decision creating process. People choose whether or not decisions are needed each and every moment of their working lives. In successful, growing businesses where politics are contained, or are of the "good politics" variety, choices and needs are pushed to the fore. Leaders are called into action by an act of recognition: people recognize that certain people enhance their own abilities to bring about solutions to problems and shape them into opportunities for collective decision making and action. By the catalytic "attracting" agency of these leaders, the collective acts of everyone in the company build upon each another and thus amount to something greater than what they could accomplish alone.

SUMMING UP AND MOVING ON

The science of complexity has provided us with a new framework for guiding an organization's growth and for managing the initiative its members offer in response to challenges. Each of these insights adds to our ability to see an organization as a platform for multiplying the talents and energies its people offer. There is, in today's business world, no other reason to create large organizations other than to capitalize on this ability to amplify many people's concerted efforts. In the end, no structure, statement, concept or analysis has any use if it does not serve to release the energy people bring to their work; that is, no structure is effective if it doesn't nourish the organization's "strategic heart."

Complexity has shown us why this is the case. An organization is dying if its constituent members aren't excited and energized, fully sensing and interacting with their environment. This new science has also given us the basis to create valuable organizational tools and models that organize people without bureaucratizing and stifling people's energies. Harry's outlook on replacing control with choice brings us to complexity's most compelling lesson: highly structured, rigid and routinized companies are dying organizations. A complex system not only has to be a highly energized and excitable entity; to borrow Tom Peter's image, to grow, an organization actually thrives on chaos. Focused by its values and mission, grouped into the "natural teams" that execute the company's core actions, the company's structure is its strategy in motion, and nothing more.

The question before us as we move to Part II is: How do we keep people energized and "pumped up" in the face of continual upheaval and change? Anger, confusion and discouragement are as likely responses to this formula as a feeling of satisfaction. So, we have to turn our attention from the macro to the micro, so to speak, and see how flow, the new science of experience, informs us about managing, thriving and growing—hence chaotic—organization.

Mihaly Csikszentmihalyi's contention is that flow is nature's way of attracting people to the challenge of becoming more complex, individually and collectively. Flow, as he describes it, is an experience of "enjoyment," of timeless engagement in something that matters and something that actually changes us, in the process adding complexity and capability to ourselves as individuals and as a species. The manager's challenge, as we will see in Part II, is to provide the kinds of conditions for people that will transform their working time into flow experiences.

In so doing, we make another shift of attention. So far, we have taken the viewpoint of the organization's master builder, the CEO or founder, and built organizations from the ground up, so to speak. Now we move into the province of line managers—the managers who work with the people who confront customers, bend and shape materials, make the sales and process the paper flows. I am pleased to do this, because I think this is a group of people that is often overlooked.

In our work as management coaches, we find new line managers are often thrust into their positions with little guidance as to what they are supposed to accomplish. New middle managers are often terror-struck when suddenly confronted with the situation of having to create value in the company and yet not producing anything that is tangible or measurable. They usually think that their value will be proven if they just do the same jobs that they excelled at as a worker, but on a larger scale, or make others do it the same way they had done it, thus producing more of the things they once made. This is a prescription for failure, guaranteed. We suggest that a line manager's job is to engender flow in their workers' experiences on the job.

The work of Csikszentmihalyi and his colleagues points a way toward new roles and responsibilities for managers of growing companies. Using the tools and insights they provide, we can complete the picture only sketched out in the preceding chapters. Having flexible, dynamic organizational models is only the beginning. Our intent must be nothing less than to enrich the hearts of the people that get the work done and create strategic organizations that can do the hard work of changing and growing, no matter how strenuous the challenge.

NOTES

1. Shunru Suzuki, *Zen Mind, Beginner's Mind* (New York: Weatherhill, 1987), p. 32.

2. Ilya Prigogine and Isabelle Stengers, *Order Out of Chaos: Man's New Dialogue with Nature* (New York: Bantam Books, 1984), pp. 141–142, 190.

3. Robert A. Burgelman, "Corporate Entrepreneurship and Strategic Management: Insights from a Process Study," *Management Science* 29, no. 12 (December 1983): 1353.

Part II

Unleashing the Power of
High Performance

Chapter 6

Flow: From Work to Peak Performance

Ironically, most people who work experience a more enjoyable state of mind on the job than at home. At work it is usually clear what needs to be done, and there is clear information about how well one is doing. Yet few people would willingly work more and have less free, leisure time. . . . Generally unnoticed is the fact that the work we want to avoid is actually more satisfying than the free time we try to get more of.

—Mihaly Csikszentmihalyi, *The Evolving Self*[1]

TIME FOR A NEW IDEA

We are all familiar with the standard model of "productivity." That word translates into getting more "out of" the people while they're on the job. Thinking of businesses as assembly lines that combine human and mechanical devices leads to the mechanistic, "human engineering" methods that take pride in eliminating any wasted motion by cutting down the "human factor" (mistakes, down time, absences) involved in manufacturing. The thinking goes, the more machine-like people's actions can be, the greater the productivity. While there are some tasks that can still be appropriately managed under these antiquated rubrics, that work is probably a short time away from being automated.

The idea of productivity has changed. In most of the companies with which we work, people are being asked to perform at a higher level of intellect and judgment. Not only are the tasks people must perform more difficult, the results that are expected from their efforts are more consequential than the output once expected of the industrial assembly line worker. It is no longer a matter of getting more stuff out the door each hour, but having people decide, moment by moment, *what are the most valuable things they must be doing to succeed*

at accomplishing the mission. The stress created by these circumstances is sometimes overwhelming; when managers try to apply old-school, quantified standards to the work, people either cry, laugh or disappear. The task before decision
makers is how to keep people working and contributing under the stresses of
these far more complex, demands and not get burned out. There must be a new
way to manage and get the work done.

And there is. Just as scientists have developed a new, dynamic and vital model
of how matter combines to form ever more complex organizations, so too the
psychologist Mihaly Csikszentmihalyi and his colleagues see human performance in its dynamic, creative and evolutionary dimensions. Csikszentmihalyi
has explored those aspects of our experience that lie beyond the classical, mechanistic reductions of the human psyche that managers have relied upon for years.
His work opens up a dimension of understanding that more closely reflects the
way we really deal with ourselves and each other. He observes that human
psyches have evolved beyond simple stimulus-response mechanisms to the level
of possessing a capability that permits us to shape our actions and behaviors in
more individualistic, self-determined, creative ways.

This observation opens us up to ideas that we most cherish about our lives
as human beings: that we can grow and change and become better, more constructive, capable and compassionate people. This capability is what we call the
''self.'' He distinguishes his idea of the self from the outmoded, reductionist
approaches to psychology this way:

> The human organism cannot survive as a bundle of neural reflexes or even of stimulus-
> response learning pathways. In order to perform within the infinitely complex ecosystem
> to which it became adapted, it needed to establish autonomy from the genetically deter-
> mined instructions that had shaped its behavior through the long eons of its evolution.
>
> The system that has evolved to provide this autonomy is the self. The function of the
> self is to mediate between the genetic instructions that manifest themselves as ''instinc-
> tual drives'' and the cultural instructions that appear as norms and rules. The self must
> prioritize between these various behavioral instructions and select among them the ones
> it wants to endorse.[2]

Csikszentmihalyi is interested in how the self evolves and develops—increases in complexity and capability—by means of engaging with its world
through experiencing and meeting challenges to the status quo. He has identified
a facet of our experience that seems to be specifically designed to enhance and
expand the self. Furthermore, evolution seems to have ''selected for'' this capability by marking it with sensations of engagement and enjoyment, making
the experience both absorbing and liberating. He calls this quality of experience
''flow.''

Most of us have experienced this phenomenon at some time in our lives: that
sense of engagement in an activity that is so absorbing that we lose track of
time; though strenuously exerting ourselves either mentally, physically or both,

we are left with a sense of exhilaration, not exhaustion. Athletes talk about the "zone," for instance—a pitcher cannot help but throw strikes right by the batter or the basketball guard's jump shot can't help but rain down into the basket. Csikszentmihalyi took note of such experiences and wondered if there was more to them than mere pleasure, if this quality of experience wasn't also increasing our capabilities and expanding our horizons. His twenty years of research led him to this conclusion:

> The function of flow . . . seems to be to induce the organism to grow . . . [fulfilling] the potentialities of the organism, and then going beyond even those limits. The universality of flow might be accounted for by the fact that it is a connection evolution has built into our nervous system: Whenever we are fully functioning, involved in a challenging activity that requires all our skills, and more, we feel a sense of great exhilaration. Because of this, we want to repeat the experience. But to feel the same exhilaration again, it is necessary to take on a slightly greater challenge, and to develop slightly greater skills. So the complexity of adaptation increases, propelled forward by the enjoyment it provides. It is through the flow experience that evolution tricks us to evolve further.[3]

FLOW AND WORK

This well-grounded scientific research opens a clear path to making the work environment a place of human growth and development, rather than one of boredom, anxiety and/or apathy. The idea of "flow" clears away the remaining shreds of legitimacy for thinking mechanistically about how to manage people in their work. That people can learn and grow in the workplace has been demonstrated in extensive studies by Csikszentmihalyi and his collaborators.

In a study that compares the quality of flow and experience in work and leisure, Judith LeFevre confirmed that people spent more time in flow experiences at work than in leisure activities. It's not surprising that one might find this for the engineers and managers she studied, but this result also stood up for assembly line and clerical workers. It is true that they experienced flow less frequently on the job than did the managers and engineers, but they still experienced flow more frequently at work than they did during leisure activities. For both groups, LeFevre noted,

> When in leisure, they were rarely in flow, but rather spent their time in the apathy context. It is possible that the higher levels of concentration and activation in flow cannot be tolerated by most people for extended periods of time. In making the choice to spend their leisure time in the low-challenge, low-skill context rather than flow, the workers may be indicating their preference to rest from the demands of work, even at the cost of an overall reduction in the quality of experience.[4]

Not only can the workplace offer desirable experiences in people's lives, it can be the place where people perform at their peak, stretching their skills and expanding their personal and professional capabilities. When managers recognize that enjoying work is a core value, they openly acknowledge the fact that people really want a chance to grow in and through their work. Productivity, that key criterion of managerial accomplishment, results when people perform at their peaks of energy, concentration and skill. Thus it is not only desirable but good business and management practice to encourage people to experience flow in their work. When managers boil work down to boring and empty tasks, they are not making the workplace more productive, they are stifling the wellsprings of productivity, preventing any semblance of productivity from arising.

Csikszentmihalyi cites these as the clear benefits people get from their flow experiences:

Creativity. People feel they break new ground, open new vistas of understanding. Indeed they do. People are, in fact, creating new understandings and connections to the world around them and discovering new depths of self when they experience flow. The flood gates open, resistance due to fears, doubts or other impediments break down and performance gives rise to new thresholds of skill and hence greater improvement. Goals, previously unreachable, are achieved; and, what is just as important, all these added dimensions of competence and complexity are retained.

Peak Performance. People are not "hard wired" to their worlds. When people are engaged in their work, they are not merely miming prescribed responses but are thinking and deciding about their situations, responding to the nuances and details of what they are doing. When this kind of engagement triggers a flow experience, these responses are intensified. All senses and energies are concentrated and driving in one direction. Csikszentmihalyi speculates that flow seems to be the evolutionary mechanism by which consciousness counteracts *entropy,* the natural tendency of active systems to run down and settle into equilibrium. Other experiential states—boredom, anxiety, stress—create that "psychic entropy" in which we feel apathetic and disengaged, and our energy and enthusiasm is either dispersed or nowhere to be found. Flow is the experience of consciousness that pulls energy from all sources available in the organism, concentrating it, driving it toward a purpose, being completely connected and engaged with what is happening.

Loss of self-consciousness and altered sense of time. The ego is quiet and self-centered needs and gratifications are at bay. Something is going on that is larger than merely surviving, desiring, craving. The person is completely engrossed in the actions, thoughts, feelings and interactions that are occurring. Time flies when you're having fun (and when you're over 40 years old). That cliche expresses an essential truth about flow. No one in flow is a clock watcher. If a person in flow is competing against a deadline, that is experienced as a compression of time, not as an oppression of one's working conditions. Like competing runners, a person's concentration is not on the clock, but on pushing every muscle, every breath and swing of the arms and legs toward new levels of speed. Performance is an obsession.

Behaviorist "stimulus-response" models of motivation don't work when people experience flow in their work. A manager's reward for getting the job done on time will look very foolish and petty to someone so engaged. Rewards and "motivational techniques" are, in fact, petty as compared to enabling someone to experience flow in their work.

Self-Esteem. This elusive personal characteristic is reinforced and solidified in many people who experience flow. People who have a high sense of self-esteem are most likely to achieve excellence in whatever they do. Many of these people expect to succeed. This is not a false expectation based on grandiosity but an attitude where people are willing to go through the pain of trial and error to get there. Flow often occurs when high challenge is met with high skill—exactly the kind of condition that breeds self-esteem and that people with self-esteem seek out. When people successfully stretch their skills and meet greater challenges, self-esteem can rise or be confirmed, and this in itself can breed a heightened expectation of success.

Positive Reinforcement. When people experience flow in one arena of their lives, it builds a taste for the experience that is carried over into other aspects of their lives. The habit of seeking flow experiences in the workplace can spill over into other arenas, and vice versa. For instance, Csikszentmihalyi cites that executives who reported stressful situations at home or on the job or due to financial problems also reported more health problems; but if they experienced flow in the course of their work, the health problems somewhat diminished. In her study, LeFevre confirmed the finding that people who experienced flow in work were more likely to seek flow-engendering experiences in their leisure time. The phenomenon of flow is habit forming. When you experience it in one aspect of your life, you seek it in others; this creates a positive feedback loop that makes it more likely a person will seek out flow opportunities.

FLOW AND ENJOYMENT

People who enjoy flow are not "pleasure seekers" who bask in luxurious settings, striving to look good in their tans. Csikszentmihalyi makes an important distinction between pleasure and enjoyment. *Pleasure* is a feeling that arises when biologically or socially reinforced needs are met, when hunger is sated or when the sexual urge is satisfied. But this satisfaction only lasts until the next predetermined urge comes along. The satisfaction doesn't change the urge, it just signifies its temporary passing. *Enjoyment,* on the other hand, is the word associated with flow. All the characteristics we listed as describing flow apply to enjoyment. This is the experience of novelty, of the expansion of capabilities and opening up of new horizons. New experiences become alluring, new actions become possible, a new and expanded sense of self has been proven and validated.

But while flow does evoke feelings that are positive and exhilarating, it requires a great deal of energy and can also stir up anxiety. The challenges that lead to flow are demanding and the exertion to meet them is equally demanding and unforgiving. You can't stop half way up the mountain or slow down yards before the finish line. For some, this level of challenge can be unnerving. When they leave this demanding arena, they take refuge in unchallenging leisure activities or seek out the safer, less taxing havens of pleasure. That is why achieving flow, even under the most promising circumstances, is not automatic. A person's negative attitude about flow and the exertion it requires can create a limiting factor on whether or not one can actually realize flow.

The workplace offers the potential for experiencing flow's sense of enjoyment—but at a price. That price is the tension that comes with growth, strangeness and newness under the pressures of time, competition and limited resources. People are exploring new territory: there are new tools to learn, new tasks that have to be conceived, tested and made effective; there are new opportunities and ideas that need to be proposed and advocated. Someone is always unsettling something; there is no rest for the weary. All the senses are in play, emotions run high. There might be outbursts of anger or tears of joy, but there will not be a detached, "business as usual" apathy. Successful, dynamic businesses exude an atmosphere that is laced through and through with this kind of tension. If people are willing to enter this frame of mind, they have to trust those around them. Mistakes have to be tolerated, support has to be there when more time and resources are needed and honesty and appreciation have to be proven as genuine.

Flow can yield unimaginable rewards for businesses in terms of people performing at their peak. But if decision makers want to engender flow, managers have to act much differently than they have been in the past. Merely measuring outputs undermines any possibility of creating flow. Managers become "result producing coaches" as Harry Kaufman calls them: people who keep the end in mind but whose ultimate challenge is to keep others in the game, encouraged, seeing possibilities and believing in themselves.

FLOW BASICS

In Part II of *The Strategic Heart* we focus on what managers can do each day with each person to foster the conditions that can yield flow and peak performance. As we do this, we are laying out a new management regime. We leave behind the mechanistic assumptions about people's experience and the conditions that move them to succeed and grow and form a clear picture of just what it is mid-level managers do to engender flow in their companies. We will also look at concrete management situations and see how the tenets of creating flow can become the primary focus of the line managers' work.

There is never any guarantee that managerial efforts will result in an actual flow experience for a worker. From our observations, however, the efforts that go into creating conditions that are amenable to flow always produce benefits in productivity. There is always a gain in people's appreciation of the value of their work, its impact and their ownership of it. They always benefit from the awareness that someone is making the effort to have this work really amount to something for the worker as well as for the company's bottom line.

There are four basic conditions managers need to foster in order to create flow or at least to improve the real productivity people can bring to their work:

1. Concrete goals, manageable rules and a sense of potential control.

All people who perform tasks want at least the sense that they have the leeway to see it through, follow out the logic and the manipulations envisioned to their consummation. As we will see in Chapter 7, to do this means elevating the work to encompass larger objectives and not just a list of isolated tasks. Tasks must be embedded, or at least must lead to, in some meaningful conclusions and aims. Each task envisions the larger picture, and provides manageable steps along the way toward accomplishing the company's larger intentions as set out in the values and mission. The manager's role is to let the people doing the work make as many of the rules as possible or, failing that, completely justify the rules they can't make—making them meaningful within their understandings of their responsibilities.

Managing for flow means allowing workers to envision what the meaning of an action is—all purposeful actions that are done in a business had better have a meaning. The creative work of the manager is to build *intrinsic* rewards into the work rather than rely on superficial (and often perceived as arbitrary) extrinsic rewards. In other words, to award a bonus because a customer service representative takes 60 calls a day devalues that person's time and expenditure of energy, insight, understanding and compassion in exerting the skill necessary to fully and completely solve a customer's problems. An *intrinsic reward* acknowledges and recognizes how well that person solves problems for customers. That may be harder to measure, but that is why there are managers and not machines—these managers can figure out a way to recognize and reinforce the success-building qualities in people's work.

2. Opportunities to act decisively, matching abilities to the challenge.

People need to make choices about their work and feel they personally make a difference. People experience flow when actively engaged in a situation, when they feel they are central in determining its outcome. When a decision, action or skill is called for that is new, the actor doesn't stop to say, "I've never done that before," unless the situation is so far out of that person's skill and knowledge range he or she can't comprehend what is supposed to be done. Instead, the rhythm, the flow and press of events evokes a higher level of skill from the actor. The situation is changed, and so is the actor.

Managers engender flow when they nudge workers into making more challenging choices, while easing anxiety and fears of the consequences of failing. This might entail encouraging someone to take a course or it might mean turning over decisions to people who formerly didn't make those decisions. Another way to do this is to involve people in the planning of their operation. Have them determine the meaningful measurements of success—and partial success— and the milestones that signify progress or problems.

3. Concentration.

When workers feel that their work really counts, they spare no amount of attention, awareness, sensitivity in their effort. Everything matters too much to let up or get distracted. The work has a life of its own. Irrelevant stimuli disappear, worries and concerns are temporarily suspended. Action and awareness merge. The manager promoting flow fully grasps what this situation is demanding of the worker. Any worker who is going to experience flow in a situation is going to be stretching. The real managerial skill is understanding how that worker experiences that stretching. The manager's task is to help that worker over those gaps where knowledge and experience might fall a little short of what is needed. And this needs to be done without taking away that worker's initiative. That task, that success—partial or total—still has to belong to the worker at the end of the day.

Certainly, the chances to achieve this aspect of flow are far greater if people's work space is conductive to concentration. A planning process needs some continuity, so phones jangling off the hook with constant messages from the boss can disrupt this process. Performing an intricate manual task in the midst of intermittent pops and jolts disrupts this flow. A manager can easily foresee what kinds of physical circumstances will foster people's ability to achieve a flow experience and can try to get it for them.

4. Immediate feedback.

People in flow know how well they are doing. Sports often engender flow because someone is always keeping score or the nearest competitor is within close range. Achievement is measured in discrete events that give immediate feedback: a successful pass, a catch or a hit or a strike, yards gained, aces made. These are the enticements of flow. You either hold steady because you are doing well, or you dig deeper, look for more out of yourself to catch up or beat the deadline. A manager has to understand the experiences of the people doing the work and be there at the right times to recognize and acknowledge what is happening. It's not enough to give a pat on the back—or a reprimand—when the work is done or at yearly reviews when the work and the learning needed to succeed at it have long since gone cold.

The best time for feedback is while the experience is still fresh; and the best person to evaluate whether or not an action has succeeded is the person who is performing it. In Chapter 8 we introduce the idea of CSFs as a way to evaluate performance that operates like an instantaneous feedback loop by means of which people are able to recognize their own success and progress, whether or not a manager is present, involved or aware of what is happening at the moment. The role of the manager is to assure that an employee is being measured against the right CSFs and uses them to evaluate the work in progress.

MANAGING EMOTIONS

Engendering flow experiences in the workplace comes down to managers investing a tremendous amount of time and energy into the human side of production. People-focused management is not "soft" or "touchy-feely," as the denigrators want to say. While peak performance need not be—and peak performance cannot be—a matter of just driving harder, faster or even smarter to crank the stuff out in greater quantities, it can be measured and evaluated; it can be modified and improved. Managing for flow and peak performance is not a matter of coddling either. Flow depends on reaching goals, exerting oneself and even exceeding one's own expectations.

Working in situations where flow can happen necessarily puts people at risk of failure. And people do fail, even when they experience flow along the way. And if they succeed, it also exposes them to a sense of loss. They are no longer who they were, their friends might have to change, the work they once enjoyed may no longer satisfy. This means prodding a person on to succeed at a new level despite the losses incurred along the way. And this is why flow-engendering management is an emotional vocation. Cold rationality is fine for assessing the numbers, for looking at the facts, figuring out what happened yesterday or an hour ago. But it completely fails to grasp the essence of the growing business organization in which people stretch, go out on limbs, give up time and energy so as to create new ways for customers to see, act and experience the world. The emotionally focused and energized action of flow can propel people out of the ordinary and into the realm of excellence. But these energies need shepherding and nurturing to survive in a business context.

Of course, one basic requirement for developing the kind of strategic organization we envision is that its managers be able to encourage the business's growth—adding complexity, nuance and capability to what the business is able to do. These managers are able to capture and implement ideas, insights and actions that have a greater impact on customers' lives and, accordingly, can develop the means to handle the more difficult problems adding value entails. Knowing the actions needed to engender flow in each employee provides the concrete framework that can guide managers' daily operational decisions.

Dealing with emotions is always difficult. It isn't enough for managers to become "sensitive," playing with more and different head games that seem trendy or fashionable. The normal approach treats emotions as something to get out of the way. "Get back to rational, programmed, permitted tasks and things will take care of themselves," the thinking goes. We see this differently. As we all know, a business cannot afford to have its workers acting out in continuous temper tantrums; neither can it be the place for workers to bring their emotionally wrought personal issues to bear on their actions. We have identified four states of mind as being the key to engendering the kinds of emotions that lead to flow and organizational growth: responsibility, engagement, envisioning, aspiration. We will examine each of these mind-sets in the chapters that follow.

It was once thought that dealing with people's attitudes and states of mind comprised the "soft" side of management. One reason these issues were relegated to this denigrated status is that they didn't lead directly to tangible, hard results. But there was another reason this work took on these second-class connotations. There were no firm methods or signposts on which managers could rely to get consistent results from one person to the next. Csikszentmihalyi's work changes that. Now we do know what conditions we need to have the best chance of people performing at their peak. Now, there are not only motivational tools available to get better quantitative results (by improving processes for instance), but the science of flow points the way toward considering how to optimize these processes in a way that helps people enjoy and also learn from those processes. Not only do managers have tools to cut costs, but they now have tools to make judgments about whether the cuts will help people perform better or will degrade performance. Not only will managers enforce deadlines, but they will be better able to appreciate an individual's ability to get the most out of the time they put in on a project.

Successful management that is supportive and even enriching is no longer a matter of intuition, but of proven fact. Peak performance will most follow when people are allowed to work in certain ways. Flow won't happen all the time, every day—that doesn't happen to anyone. But managers now know what they have to do to have any shot at it. They can recognize when it does happen, appreciate the benefits (pointing out how to learn from the mistakes made along the way), and help that person to regain flow after it has passed. From this proven method, productivity and growth will ensue, and so will the numbers.

Creating conditions that support these constructive states of mind is hard work. There's nothing "soft" about the effort it takes to succeed in this kind of managerial discipline. But it is still quite true that this is not the work of the cunning mind—manipulating, measuring, controlling, predicting. Rather, this is the work of the "Strategic Heart"—encouraging, supporting, nurturing, disciplining with a mind toward accomplishing something new and possibly great in the world. It is a matter of making what is actually only possible seem real; it is a matter of making palpable to others what is only really imagined. The "Strategic Heart" is about doing this work. It is about changing managers' orientations from results to process, from things to people, from intellect to will and heart. It calls upon all of us to realize and act on the basis of this simple truth Gandhi used in describing how he pushed himself to the pinnacle of accomplishment:

I am an average man with less than an average ability. I admit that I am not sharp intellectually. But I don't mind. There is a limit to the development of the intellect, but none to that of the heart.[5]

NOTES

1. Mihaly Csikszentmihalyi, *The Evolving Self* (New York: HarperCollins, 1993), p. 33.

2. Mihaly Csikszentmihalyi and Isabella Selaga, eds., *Optimal Experience: Psychological Studies of Flow in Consciousness* (New York: Cambridge University Press, 1992), p. 17.

3. Ibid., p. 367.

4. Mihaly Csikszentmihalyi, "Flow and the Quality of Experience During Work and Leisure," in *Optimal Experience*, p. 317.

5. Howard Gardner, *Creating Minds* (New York: Basic Books, 1993), p. 313.

Chapter 7

Engage

When a person is able to organize his or her consciousness so as to experience flow as often as possible, the quality of life is inevitably going to improve, because . . . even the usually boring routines of work become purposeful and enjoyable.

In flow we are in control of our psychic energy, and everything we do adds order to consciousness.

—Mihaly Csikszentmihalyi, *Flow*[1]

BEYOND THE TASK MASTER

People in flow are engaged in their work. Ideas pop as new avenues for collaboration, experimentation and challenge take shape. Workers comment that they can't wait to get to work in the morning; and once there, they look up and suddenly it's six or seven o'clock—and they haven't even called their spouses. The work that results is often exceptional. That doesn't mean that more work gets done, or that it is done with zero defects. The work that is done when people are in flow is *qualitatively* better. It shows a depth of discernment and thoroughness that goes beyond the ordinary. Even if the work isn't quite right in some way or is off target somehow, it still has value because people have learned, new ideas were tried, possibilities were opened up, better communications and working relationships were established.

This doesn't happen accidently. It happens when decision makers purposely engender flow. In this chapter and the ones that follow, we focus on understanding the basic tenets of flow and describe ways to support flow experiences on the job. As we do this, we will help today's struggling line (or mid-level) managers reach a whole new conception of their roles in a business.

We focus on the roles and actions of the line manager, because the line manager, more than any other figure, has the opportunity to help workers realize the benefits of flow. Devoting our attention to changing the perspective and operating models of these line managers will be well worth it if we can truly provide them with fresh and effective tools for today's demands, not hand-me-down ideas from bygone eras.

Managers sincerely want their people to take initiative and fully engage the challenges offered by their work. I hear proud managers say, "My job is to let people know what has to be done and then get out of the way." In most mechanistic, "rational" work environments, that translates into announcing the work load at the beginning of the week and, on Friday morning, telling the people how far behind they are. Managers are surprised and perplexed when this "hands-off" approach leaves employees cold. They are shocked and hurt when this approach generates complaints of being out of touch. They become disillusioned with the "new management philosophies" that espouse treating workers with respect and communicating with them. Unfortunately, these responses only prove that no matter how "humanistic" and "understanding" the boss is, the old approaches to improving performance and effectiveness only assures that no one in that organization will have a chance at succeeding. The purpose of their new found "humanism" is defeated before it has a chance to see the light of day.

From the perspective of those who advocate fostering flow in the workplace, the reason for this is easy to see. In the mechanistic model, the managerial job translates into steps such as these:

- Define the problem.
- Create the solution.
- Break it down into small bite-sized tasks.
- Create the command structure and gather the tools needed to fix the problem.
- Assemble the implementation group.
- Delegate some of the tasks.
- Issue the orders.
- Watch ("Monitor") the project unfold: keeping deadlines, keeping people focused, measuring results.

This may be the "rational," "scientific" way, but the logic and progression of managing in strategic, growing organizations emanates from a completely different outlook. Our formulation of the manager's work is to create the conditions that engender flow, *concentrate on how people are likely to experience what they are being asked to do rather than on the minutiae of work processes.* Instead of listing the tasks and subtasks that people have to perform, focus on a completely different set of issues. Shift attention away from bearing down on the nuts and bolts of a project—its processes, deadlines and near-term costs— toward different questions that take the nature of human experience into account.

Harry Kaufman, the general manager we talked about in Chapter 5, described the line manager as a "results-producing coach." We couldn't agree more. The coach pays attention to the talents and temperaments of the players when they are practicing and helps to keep them engaged and positive as the challenge, competition and stress of the game unfolds. Likewise, line managers have to help employees execute with confidence, focus and enthusiasm. While the coach turns every engagement into a learning experience for the athlete, the coaching line manager turns every working day into an opportunity for challenge and growth for as many workers as possible. Besides being a very concrete and descriptive way to crystalize what the new managerial demands call for, the image also moves away from the idea that a successful manager has to be a charismatic leader who rides in on the white horse to save the day. Managing for achieving flow is about working with people day in, day out, leveraging their small accomplishments into larger gains, helping them stay engaged and enthusiastic in the face of setbacks.

The story we tell here dramatizes just this point. In one way, it is hardly the typical "success story." Phil Jefferies, a shy, bright and dedicated young man, was pulled out of a comfortable technical job in the government by his father-in-law and suddenly thrust into the position of assuming major management responsibilities in a family-owned, sales-driven distribution company. Phil was not the budding entrepreneur, nor was he likely to suddenly flower into an inspiring, charismatic leader. Because Phil's path to managerial success is hardly paved with the gold of charisma, his example demonstrates that engendering flow—achieving high performance from others and thus being a highly effective manager—is something that is within reach of many people. In place of heroics, Phil's story offers the perfect case study about line managers acting as "results-producing coaches."

The story also shows how Phil, even with his limited "people skills," did succeed at becoming an effective, flow-engendering manager. The case epitomizes how managers can, and do, learn an entirely new skill set that focuses on people and is not limited to processes alone. When they do this, they often get great results for everyone: the company gets great performance and quality outcomes; the workers feel, and genuinely are, more productive; and the manager gains recognition, respect and stature for all the right reasons.

PHIL JEFFERIES: LEARNING TO PUT PEOPLE FIRST

When he was approached by Gary, his father-in-law, to move to Boston, Phil had been a successful computer programmer for the United States government. Gary, then 57 years old, envisioned that Phil would learn the family business,

Atlantic Transmission—a large, independent and growing power transmission parts distributorship—and eventually take it over.

Even the most extroverted and vivacious of personalities might have found it difficult to fit into Atlantic's culture. The business had grown steadily and plod-dingly over the past twenty years. There were now eight branches spread across five states. The people that ran the branches had been with the company for more than a decade; few had college educations. The sales staff and sales man-ager, all long-term employees, felt they knew what the company needed far better than Phil.

Phil was in his early thirties when he arrived, and Atlantic had a work ethic that wouldn't quit. He'd be at work by seven in the morning, stay late every night, only to put in at least one day on the weekend. He was a shy man, awkward in his dealings with people. In meetings, he would slump down in the chair, looking fearful and ill at ease. He had a reputation of not listening to people and losing his temper when he heard bad news.

He immediately went to work on the computer system, revamping the inven-tory tracking system, adding accounting and reporting functions, all of which were necessary and important. Over the course of the next seven years, he became the primary advocate of computerized approaches to management. Whatever the problem, he wrote a program for it; if there were issues to inves-tigate, he'd generate a report. Conflicts arose as he imposed one system after another onto the tried and true manual practices of the company. He alienated dozens of people in one fell swoop as he tried to issue one authoritative edict after another. When questioned or meeting resistance, he exploded in anger; he couldn't explain himself, except in the most broad, abstract or bureaucratically authoritarian terms. In his own mind, Phil believed that he never acted with a sense of "entitlement." And, while he earnestly believed he was earning every bit of his heir-apparent status, he was not trying very hard to improve his skills in working with people. His reputation grew as someone who didn't deserve what he was having handed to him. This didn't seem to bother him, though. His criterion for success was how much could be done with the press of a computer key, not how happy people were or how well liked he was.

Gary was worried. If Phil wasn't able to take over the family business, it would have to be sold. Gary saw that as a loss for everyone in the company and, most especially, as a loss for his family. He asked Mage to assess whether or not Phil could lead the company.

When the team of Mage consultants came on the scene, Phil was about to implement a new inventory counting system. The value of the inventory was the baseline for the business's profitability, and it was fraught with holes, in-consistencies and poor management practices. Up until this point Atlantic had always counted the whole inventory all at once, one time, at the end of the fiscal year. That deficiency was compounded by other management complications. Atlantic divided its inventory among its regional branches so that customers could get what they needed as soon as possible. Inventory was thus increased or decreased at the discretion of each branch manager. Sometimes one branch manager could add or remove items from another branch's inventory. That put a lot of power and ease of action in the hands of each of the branch managers— a prerogative they coveted.

Phil wanted to change that for all of the right reasons. He wanted to install a cycle counting system in which a few bins of product would be counted every week—some bins of slow moving merchandise would be counted once per year, while faster moving items would be counted more often. It meant more than just smaller, more frequent counts, however. It also meant reorganizing the warehouses, setting up new computer systems and instituting uniform management programs in the fiercely independent branches. Inventory would be controlled more closely, taking away discretion from the branch managers and putting it in the hands of a new centralized purchasing department.

Phil was about to make these monumental changes in the old way: write up the procedure, put it into the computer, issue a memo, distribute it to the branch managers and set a deadline for the new system to be up and running. We stopped him cold in his tracks. We urged him to take a moment and think about the impact this change was going to have on everyone in the company. He was instituting monumental changes in behavior, authority and discretion for each and every person in the company; especially for the die-hard, independent branch managers.

Implementing a new inventory counting system was only 10 percent of the job; 90 percent of the work was getting each branch manager to be enthusiastic about it and to feel he or she had a stake in its continued, long-term success. The branch managers had to be partners in this venture. Phil's job, as an officer and a designated leader in the company, was to elicit the best possible performance from his people; and, for us that meant enlisting their participation in a way that would elicit the intensity and concentration of flow.

We wanted Phil to think about the people and their experience with the project. Instead of solving technical and operational problems, we focused his attention on the people he was going to work with to achieve his intentions. Rather than think about the tasks needed to transition to the system, we asked him to think about a different set of questions:

• Who is interested in this kind of problem?

• Has anyone spoken up about this kind of thing?

• What are the skill sets of these people? Do they need training?

Our idea was simply to make these people allies, bring them into the process early and have them help in its roll-out and implementation. To do this, we had to get Phil to move out from behind the computer and to work directly with the people who would make this project a success. If he focused on the people, they would take care of the process. The roll-out would take twice as long as Phil originally envisioned, but we bet that our approach would be worth the extra time up front by preventing resistance and dissension later.

Phil learned a whole new way of working. Instead of being the program writer and issuer of memo's, he became a convener by getting a group together at the test site that would think through the transition and the implementation, and that would also serve as exemplars—if they could do it, there could be no excuses—to others who might be more slow and/or reluctant to sign up for the program. He asked them, individually and collectively, to give their insights into the inventory problem and to suggest opportunities that existed for improving it.

Not only were the procedures written up, but a handbook of suggestions, anticipated problems and easy-to-follow instructions was coproduced by the stocking staff on the floor. At each step of the way, we encouraged Phil to get out from behind the computer and personally verify the accuracy of the counts to see that the bins were organized sensibly and that the numbering system would allow for flexibility and growth. To assure that there would be some "small successes" along the way, Phil set up a test site in the branch closest to his office. This would be the "laboratory" in which things would be tested and peer level trainers would be developed to act as advisors when the project was fully implemented.

All of the data gathered from this conversing, prototyping and querying was prepared for the program's roll-out at the company's quarterly office managers meeting. Phil, who was coached to have all the materials ready and overhead slides produced, prepared for this meeting as though it was the first meeting of his professional life. He worked closely with his test site team to anticipate the branch managers' concerns. Members of the test site team were then strategically scattered throughout the group during the meeting. This meeting would convincingly demonstrate that Phil was focused squarely on the people in the meeting, ready to help solve their problems and be able to act on their concerns. He made it clear that he and the new purchasing person—a former branch manager who was promoted to that new position—would be visiting the branches and spending time with everyone who needed help. The program would be phased in and would accommodate the different situations faced by each of the branches.

The meeting went superbly. Not only did Phil listen, he even wrote down each of the concerns raised on an easel pad for all to see. If the plan was attacked, he asked one of his planning and test groups to answer from their experience with that problem (both acknowledging the obstacle and providing a story from a peer about how it was overcome). Not once did he get defensive. The branch managers responded with interest. They offered many other observations about how inventory, purchasing, billing and pricing could be improved and better coordinated among the branches. Even the most skeptical of these seasoned pros came to the conclusion that this program was for real and could really help them in the long run. A hurdle had been cleared, but there was a long way to go. The managers felt less "imposed upon" by the change, but there was still a lot of skepticism about how well "management," meaning Phil, could pull this off.

The make-or-break steps were in the implementation. Phil lived up to his promises, visiting every site to help them get started in the project. He went out to the branches, showing his determination to roll up his sleeves. He convinced people that this was a time for pulling together and getting something done. When Phil visited the sites, he left the tie and jacket at home. He came in jeans and T-shirt ready to move gears, sprockets and bearings alongside his branch workers.

As of this writing, the program is completely implemented and cycle counting is to be used in this year's inventory audit. The managers are fully on board with the program. I personally accompanied Phil as he verified the counts and worked with the office managers on the kinds of processes and procedures that each branch needed to institute in order to improve the counts. Similar problems popped up at most of the branches—time pressures, not enough people, space shortages and, most of all, a lack of confidence in working with the computer. But there was no second-guessing or outright resistance. In fact, the subject of the meetings was about "how the company was changing." The project demonstrated the potential every one had for making meaningful, customer-supportive and profit-increasing change.

When the auditors came to certify the inventory, all the branches passed and one branch had no discrepancies. The carping about Phil changed from "we'll see . . ." to a sense of shared pride in the accomplishments that had been made. As a final note, the branch in which the system was prototyped has been ISO 9002 certified—a highly coveted achievement.

CRAFTING WORK FOR FLOW: THE RESULTS-PRODUCING COACH

By shifting his attention from mechanistic processes to the requirements of fostering positive experiences, Phil energized the project and brought it to its highest level of acceptance. He gave up his protected, comfortable status as the most knowledgeable technologist and computer guru and took the time to listen intently to the people his services were intended for, personifying an attitude and priority that encourages people to invest emotional energy and passion in their work. He became a partner in helping people welcome change and growth in the face of challenge. The project now looks as though it will succeed all across the company, in all of the branches.

Phil learned that line managers play the key role in enabling people to experience their work as an opportunity to grow personally and to advance the mission of the company. We emphasize to young managers how verbally convincing people of the value of a new program or of the necessity to change isn't enough. More often than not, people will nod their heads in agreement to the deluge of verbiage and, as soon as they get back to the privacy of their desks, they resume whatever habits and attitudes they were accustomed to. People have to discover the value of something on their own terms, in their own way, according to their own priorities and values. A manager guides, nudges, persuades people to perform at a high level by creating conditions in which the value of their work can become apparent on their own terms.

Won't a leader's charisma result in the high productivity decision makers desire? In some cases, charisma can carry the day and get short-term results. A charismatic leader can cast a spell that lasts for a while. He or she can spark workers' imaginations so that they feel the leader's goals are their own. But, without the hard work that goes with it, over time, and through the real struggles of successful production, these images fade. For line managers, leading the charge over the hill and saying "follow me" often ends in disappointment and shattered egos. The burning issue of whether or not leadership can be taught is a red herring. Line managers, charismatic or not, can always do the hard work of putting the basics of flow in place in the hopes that people can realize the experience for themselves.

There is no doubt that what we are proposing here is a new managerial imperative. Young managers often think their role is to act as a super-taskmaster, directly mirroring how they would have done the job. Instead of actually doing those tasks, now they delegate—supposedly the hallmark of the accomplished manager—by splitting the work they used to do among more people. This idea is wrong on several fronts.

First, this model pushes more and more people further away from the work that really produces something of value. Making tasks smaller, reducing them to more fragmented components, only adds costs. Even if the volume of production increases, growth by fragmentation does not increase capacity, it only increases the need for middle managers. But, it is wrong in another, far more significant way. A company, or even a department, can't merely grow *quantitatively*, so that ten people can be able do the same things only one or two people used to do the day before. Growing companies, departments and functions need to grow *qualitatively*. The line manager's responsibility becomes one of organizational interpreter and negotiator, rather than task master. They not only have to add *capacity* to the processes an organization uses, they also have to add to the *capability* of all the people performing those processes.

In the growing organization, managers help others work in a focused, balanced and coordinated way to enhance the business organization's ability and willingness to change. The new managers work with the hearts, the strategic insights and contributions of the people, and let them enumerate the specific tasks that will be needed. Figure 7.1 helps to explain what "results-producing coach." It provides a clear outline about what the manager in today's business world has to make happen each and every day and points to the actions that

Figure 7.1
Results-Producing Coach

Results Required Outcomes	Producing Manager's Action	Coach Manager's Role
Attention People are focused and effective	Organize work into large blocks of responsibilities that have meaningful outcomes	Create "occasions" and marshal resources for workers' growth and development
Recognition Critical success factors are understood and met	Ideas, innovations are captured, implemented	Understand and acknowledge each person's work, initiatives and milestones
Constancy People feel productive, informed, involved, listened to, valued, evaluated fairly	Negotiate for managerial latitude and appropriate situations that help working groups succeed.	Act as advocate and reasoned supporter of working group

help create flow, peak performance and growth for the worker and profits and productivity for the company:

As the chart indicates, there are three aspects to the role of Results-producing coach: (1) helping the workers sustain *attention* to the work; (2) making sure they have a sense of *recognition*, not just of the results, but a fuller recognition of the way they are approaching the work and the quality of attention they are applying to it; and (3) *constancy* amid change and hard times—that there is some sense of building and progress even as the company grows and changes. These conditions cannot be created by any amount of verbiage and inspiration. They require the hard work of a line manager who is aware of the worker's experience and is directing the resources of the company in a way that makes sure these conditions are sustained and respected.

Let's look at each of these aspects in some detail and see how following the prescriptions of the ''results-producing coach'' supports the necessary conditions for creating flow experiences in the workplace.

Attention. Following Csikszentmihalyi, we think of attention as expending ''psychic energy'' in order to gather, recognize and make use of information and placing it within a context that suggests appropriate actions. Attention directs energy toward the task at hand with a wide and full awareness of what is going on in the situation and how it fits into a context of experience, history and the business's values and mission.

Since attention expends energy, managers have to be able and willing to shepherd this scarce resource. We can appreciate this in our own lives. When we have a chance to concentrate on something, give it our focused attention, we are more effective. When we are constantly interrupted or distracted, we get frustrated and angry. We often just give up, feeling we are just dissipating precious psychic energy without getting anything in return. It takes undivided attention to really accomplish something, and this is especially the case at work.

Flow occurs when attention is focused on accomplishing something, and the mind orders itself. It is using past experiences to provide a sequence of successful actions and then carefully observing the outcomes. The mind operates in an orderly, effective way and is able to sustain this kind of engagement in an action over a long period of time. The worker modifies the next action. The actions become more focused, competent and effective as this learning process goes on, while the person becomes more skillful, knowledgeable and capable.

Attention is on the *sine qua non* of flow. When we are merely on automatic pilot, going through the rote motions, suppressing awareness of what is going on, there is no way we can learn or grow. Repetition, for instance, is a flow killer. Variety, progress, decision making and resolving difficulties are the characteristics of work that can command one's attention and engender flow. They keep the conscious mind engaged in the action, always measuring, comparing, even competing against the way things were done in the past. When we are attentive, aware of what is happening around us, and can juxtapose these events with what we already know, we can grow.

In Phil's case, his visits to the sites and constant check-ins with the branch managers aimed at creating ''occasions'' in which full and focused attention could be paid to learning new skills. Managers underestimate the importance of this simple action. Creating a situation in which people are paying full attention to the issues and objectives at hand is the starting point for any effective action. Phil's coaching role in these situations was to act as catalyst—focusing attention, giving priority to a project and helping people overcome whatever difficulties were blocking progress or their confidence in attacking their problem.

These actions certainly were necessary for establishing sufficient motivation to carve out the time and energy needed to support a flow experience. When Phil was present, the office managers were less likely to jump up to take the next phone call or chat with the next salesman to come in the door. The meetings were working sessions. Phil wanted these people to work in a concentrated way and achieve some kind of flow. He answered questions on the spot, which helped bring the challenges of such a massive reorganization and shifting of responsibilities into balance with the people's skills. Hopefully they would then replicate these conditions and working styles on their own in an effort to establish the new system. This wasn't accomplished on the first visit, to be sure. Phil had to return to each of the branches several times to go over the materials and reemphasize the priority of the program before the managers took him seriously. But, over the course of several months, the managers picked up the pace and the positive results started to accumulate.

Recognition. On the job, the gratitude one gets for making a difference one minute seems to evaporate the next. According to the late Andy Warhol, avant-garde artist, everyone gets fifteen minutes of fame; but in the workplace, appreciation rarely lasts that long. Get one thing done, and the next customer is on the phone with a new, unsettling demand. The issue is always, ''what are you doing for me now?'' There is no chance that flow will be established when workers expect that today's triumph won't mean anything tomorrow. These conditions sew the seeds for apathy, then burnout and, finally, cynicism. ''What's the point,'' the complaint goes. The sense of future and meaning have been gutted.

Flow is an experience in which there is a future. As a basic tenet of faith, a person in flow believes something is happening, being created or solved and that the effects from these actions will be visible and will matter. In the work situation, the time frame of this future can be short; but if flow is to be present, some sense of progress, development and accomplishment needs to be there. Recognition provides that sense of the future, and it is the line manager's job to make sure that recognition is forthcoming in a meaningful, timely and constructive way.

As you recall, feedback is one of the crucial building blocks of flow. Frequent feedback engages people in their experiences in a dynamic way. A worker can both be immersed in what is transpiring at the moment and change behavior and learn new skills in small, digestible increments. People get a reading of what is happening here and now, their accomplishments marked by concrete results. The person really cares about what is going on because changes are happening in two directions: something happens out there with what is being worked on and new skills and capabilities are being learned at the same time.

Managers have difficulty providing timely feedback for many reasons. Time pressures and competing demands all undermine their best intentions. But one major reason it is difficult to provide this in the workplace is that the actions that accomplish things are distributed among many people, and so are the successes. How do people know that they have contributed to saving a customer, adding one or reducing costs? The payoff from these events happen far in the future, have many other people involved and may or may not be visible on a case-by-case basis. Only the aggregated results show up in the income statement.

Unfortunately, the recognition that leads to flow has to take place immediately, and thus long before the final results are in. Recognition is not simply a matter of congratulating people for something that was done; it is not sufficient to pat a worker on the back for a job well done. Feedback that supports flow has to take account of the details and nuances of the work people are doing at this time, and so line managers have to recognize what people are experiencing and provide highly detailed, fine-grained feedback about that experience.

Recognition frames the efforts being made in a day; it creates a meaningful and timely "packet" of experience that connects each action to the future. Let's say a customer service rep calms down an irate customer by giving an excessive break on a bill. If the call were being monitored, a manager could immediately congratulate the rep for saving the customer and then provide coaching on how to succeed without giving away the store. The rep's experience would be intensely vivid, and the coaching—assuming it was positive and supportive— would be remembered. The rep would know that his or her efforts mattered and would also see that there are more nuances to the work to learn about. The rep would also know that the actions he or she performs now connect to something, to someone, and will carry forward to future improvements and the company's growth and success.

In Phil's case, his frequent visits to the branches were absolutely essential to the success of the project. The visits, as we have said, helped to establish a pattern of attention and priority to the program. But the visits also gave Phil— an irrepressibly optimistic person—a chance to recognize and appreciate what had been completed by the branch staff up to the time of his visit. No one was looking for or expecting pats on the back, since the job was not yet done. But they all wanted to be assured that their work amounted to something, that change was really under way. The visits put him in the role of being the motivating coach. He could see how people were responding to new tasks and assignments and could urge them on. He had time to pass on good ideas that had been tried and used successfully at other branches.

The feedback that engenders flow doesn't even have to be positive all the time. If, for example, I am enjoying a tennis game, I can still lose and be in flow if I am hitting the ball well. If my opponent says, "Nice shot" even once, I can get immediate enjoyment from the feel of the ball on the racket or the shot landing right where I intended it to go. At work, especially in a growing business organization, it's a little different. Here the feedback cues are not so clear. I may be doing as best as can be expected, but because the whole operation is new for the company, I could feel that I am failing. This is not conducive to creating flow; it is conducive to stress, headaches and the need to quit. As Csikszentmihalyi points out,

What makes [feedback] valuable is the symbolic message it contains: that I have succeeded in my goal. Such knowledge creates order in consciousness, and strengthens the structure of the self. Almost any kind of feedback can be enjoyable, provided it is logically related to a goal in which one has invested psychic energy.[2]

Constancy. If flow is to occur, people need to be able to work along with a consistent set of rules, over an extended period of time; and the rules have to make sense within the larger mission. Managers often work toward achieving *consistency,* meaning the work fits within what has gone before and goes on elsewhere in the company. In many situations, consistency becomes a straitjacket that diminishes initiative and insight into the work that needs to be done. To engender flow requires a different outlook on managing work, one that we call *constancy.* Constancy is an attitude and orientation to the work that allows for variation and experimentation in working methods. The idea of constancy is to manage so that the core actions are held constant over time. They are executed in a way that fulfills the mission, and yet the workers themselves determine what that "way" is (i.e., they determine the set of discrete tasks).

Consistency has been called "the hobgoblin of little minds." There is some truth to that. Consistency, after all, can be enforced by forms and written procedures. Constancy, in contrast, can only be maintained by a continual negotiation of requirements, rules and resources that both the organization and the workers need. Most managers are tempted to be either overly rigid or "soft" (a result of being worn down by the incessant press for attention). But the successful managers learn to maintain balance through it all. Constancy can only be provided in the workplace when line managers assure that amid all the swirl and hustle of the daily routine, there is something that is clearly set out as a path, as a route on which there can be acknowledged progress and the chance for success. A sizeable amount of a person's time and energy is going into a situation where there is a beginning and an end and the effort required will not be interfered with or complicated. It is easy to envision these people saying, "Yeah, I can get into this. It makes sense. It'll amount to something."

By meeting with the branch managers prior to undertaking the cycle counting initiative, Phil was acting in the way that leads to constancy, while foregoing consistency. By asking for their input in terms of how to conduct the transition and introduction of the system, he ensured that the managers understood what the initiatives' basic specifications were and made sure that the time frames and resources would be available. He assured constancy by taking on the role of facilitator and broker, negotiating with his peers for the branch managers' requirements so that the program could be fully and successfully accomplished.

The group set up their own milestones for feedback: drawing up maps of the bins into which the inventory would go, setting aside a day for training on the computer, and planning a period of time—set at their schedule, within a 90-day time period—when the move would be made.

To this project-based kind of constancy we also need to add another dimension—constancy through hard times. Nothing does more to demoralize a company and undermine its ability to engender peak performance than knee-jerk layoffs or other peremptory cutbacks. The impression this gives is that the company is weak, the leaders are fearful and that the work they are performing is not really worth that much after all. These impressions are prescriptions for disengagement and, ultimately, lead to a complete inability of the company to adapt to changing conditions and competitive pressures. The company that exhibits constancy through hard times opens wide avenues for people's patience and trust, especially when being on the edge of chaos frays nerves and tests tempers. Constancy creates the opportunity for change; managers guide people along the pathway this kind of constancy has opened.

HANDS-ON MANAGING THAT ISN'T BEAN COUNTING

So, it turns out that a line manager engenders flow by being completely involved, not hands-off. But there is a decidedly significant difference between what we envision the manager doing and what the time-worn model of managing prescribes. As the next chapter will show, using the Arrow of Value and CSFs as a guide, workers are completely capable of performing many of the monitoring and measuring management functions once thought to be the manager's province.

What workers are not capable of doing on their own is keeping their focus on their work. In today's demanding working environments, the temptation is for decision makers to assign many divergent tasks to the same people—to keep a branch running to the satisfaction of customers and, at the same time, completely overhauling the inventory system. While justified by pressures to change and cost economies (and these are powerful justifications, to be sure), the challenge before line managers is rather to use their positions with other managers and working groups to make sure the organization supports the work that needs to be done.

This effort has to go in two directions. First, the line manager has to act on their "organizational values," assuring choice, innovation and readiness (see chapter 10). Then, they must assure that the conditions are right, as often as possible, for people to do the most valuable work that needs to be done. This means wheeling and dealing with their superiors to get the time and resources people will need to succeed in the new venture. This lays the groundwork for achieving flow by allowing the initiative to be pursued with some measure of constancy over time. When there is some assurance that there will be an accomplishment in the future, learning and recognition can take place.

In the other direction, line managers have to pay attention to what the workers are doing in the course of their efforts from day to day. Rather than insist that workers do things the way the managers once did, line managers have to assure that workers have a chance to learn new and better ways to do things. The work that is done should be conceived in such a way that learning is involved in many of the tasks and that workers stretch their talents in ways that make them more capable and more responsible for achieving the mission.

In a strategic organization, there can never be any question of whether or not people have to stretch and grow. The line managers' primary mandate is to assure that the intentions of that organization to drive change in customers' lives and in the marketplace can be met. Managers often spur high turnover, and thus failure, by using a rigid, bureaucratic, "do it my way or else" approach. Instead, they can become coaches, encouraging and actually helping each of their workers grow into the new demands. For workers to take on that kind of challenge requires the vigilant attention and in-depth understanding of line managers. The tools of flow give the manager firm guidelines and signposts for employing that option and acting as results-producing coaches.

For instance, "Why are you pushing me?" a worker might ask. A coach has an answer that makes that extra effort worth something, frames the effort into a challenge that can be measured and appreciated for what is accomplished. "I don't see what this will accomplish," another might object. A coach can point out why an action is necessary in a way that makes that action compelling and meaningful to that person, as well as a personal goal and milestone of growth. "I just can't get this to work!" another might exclaim in discouragement. The coach finds a way to keep that person in the game, offering an insight, reshaping the task in some way, providing the right assistance to get that person engaged once again.

This way promises success by nurturing the "Strategic Heart," that attitude evidenced by the experienced, high performing people who have a sense of responsibility to the mission, an expectation of excitement in their actions and a feeling of loyalty to the people and the organization that have helped them grow.

NOTES

1. Mihaly Csikszentmihalyi, *Flow* (New York: HarperCollins, 1990), p. 40.
2. Ibid., p. 57.

Chapter 8

Responsibility (Not Jobs)

Today's organization is rapidly being transformed from a structure built out of jobs into a field or work needing to be done. . . . Jobs are no longer socially adaptive. That is why they are going the way of the dinosaur.
—William Bridges, "The End of the Job"[1]

THE JOB IS OVER

So far, we have seen how the strategic company maintains its growth and success by having a meaningful impact on its customers' lives. The strategic company operates according to a declared set of meaningful values that resonate with its customers; it is focused on a mission to create an experience of import. With this framework established, the growing company puts people to work, performing day in and day out to make its mission come to fruition and profitability.

But as any experienced manager knows, it is a long way between the words and charts put on pages and executing the plan in everyday, real life. The greatest plan seems to break down somewhere between completing it and the worker's desk or work station. We have already examined part of the process of designing the work that leads to growth in Chapter 4, when we introduced the Arrow of Value. There we focused on understanding the core actions that everyone in the company must perform successfully to create value for customers. Now we must consider more closely what it is we are asking people to do in their working lives.

In most companies today, when people are put to work, they are assigned jobs. Here is where the plan breaks down. It is not that people don't do their jobs well, but rather how well they can actually do is limited by their jobs.

Distilling and reducing value-creating work into the narrow confines of jobs limits not only what workers do but lessens whatever chance of success a company can have in meeting its mission, customer demands and competition. While going largely unnoticed by decision makers and consultants alike, the strictures imposed by the job structure of work prevent a company from reacting nimbly to changes in markets. Jobs reinforce rigid mind-sets that limit skills and erect turf boundaries around even trivial tasks. Getting beyond the job structures of work is the single most important step decision makers can make in transforming their mechanistic companies into strategic organizations. Decision makers that end jobs move their businesses beyond merely making things to enabling people to fully engage with their customers and, within the limits defined by the values and resources (rather than job descriptions), do whatever is necessary to create value.

This one factor differentiates the growing, strategic organization from the stagnant, mechanistic (and doomed) business. When a company grows, it not only serves more customers, it also has to meet a widening range of more diverse, more sophisticated and evolving demands. To meet these demands people have to expand their contributions in two directions: First, they have to take on more responsibilities to meet increasing customer demands. Second, in order to do that, they must stretch in an inward direction by broadening and deepening their own skills and talents. In other words, not only does a growing company have to add *capacity*—the muscle to crank out more stuff—it also has to increase its *capability*—the ability to do things differently, with greater variety and insight into customers' situations. People cannot add to their own capabilities, no less to that of the company as a whole, when performing even their best work in the context of a job.

Moving beyond the job is another way of asking that crucial managerial question: How do we get people to respond to the challenge of growing in ability, contribution and commitment? I suggest we look within ourselves for the answer. When do we put aside our own momentary comfort and pitch in to do something we have never done before? When do we take risks and push ourselves beyond our predefined limits? We really dig in and do our best when the work has some meaning for us, when it is challenging, and when it really calls for our particular contribution, participation and talents.

Managers that seek commitment from their people and that little extra effort first have to consider what they are asking people to do. Is this work worth their attention and energy? As we continually point out to decision makers, the company exists solely in order to have an impact on people. If the company has to do something worthwhile for customers, why should anyone in the company have to perform tasks that are less than meaningful and worthwhile? Of course their work should be meaningful and important. For people to be willing to stretch and grow, they must be intrinsically, viscerally connected to the results of their work.

Assigning Responsibility, Not Jobs

Yet, after the exciting work on the mission is done, people go back to their desks to do their jobs, while managers look over their shoulders to make sure they do things right. Who, then, is taking responsibility for what is happening with the customer? What happened to that exciting and challenging work set down in the mission and values? It gets lost in the triviality of narrowly pre-scribed jobs. The further people are distanced from the effects of their actions on the lives of customers, the less willing or able they will be to grow and learn from their work. When bound up in the confines of their jobs, people are eval-uated on how efficiently they perform a few closely defined tasks. To grow or expand their capabilities, they either have to ask for permission to rework things, to be promoted, to be moved to a new position, or to await a larger organiza-tional "reengineering" effort. All these steps cause anxieties and, possibly, un-savory political problems. These are the barriers that kill individual initiative to grow. What managers forget—or are afraid—to put into their plan for organ-izing work is *responsibility*. Getting beyond the job means asking the business's workers, managers, vendors and partners to take responsibility for a part of the relationships the business creates in the course of fulfilling its mission.

Having people take responsibility for fulfilling a part of the company's mis-sion opens the door to the flow experience and thus has the potential of un-leashing the power of peak performance and productivity. Flow cannot occur in jobs. A worker cannot act decisively and creatively in a job when actions have to be cleared with a superior or have to reinforce a prescribed set of rules. A worker cannot have a sense of self-direction or growth when success means behaving properly—like an obedient child. The managerial plaint, "Just do your job," is the death knell of flow. In contrast, peak performance thrives on flow; and organizations grow in capability and complexity when its workers are able and willing to achieve flow. As we continue in our presentation of the new model of organization and work, it will become clearer why the job must go and why it is the most difficult step business decision makers must take.

In the successful growing organizations we see, workers organize the core actions they have been assigned (the actions spelled out in Chapter 4) into manageable "areas of responsibility." They cluster tasks into a range of deci-sion-making actions that enable people to meaningfully engage with the custo-mer's (internal or external) experiences with the business's products and services. This applies to groups that serve internal customers as well as those who serve the cash-paying customers. Since an accounting department, for in-stance, would probably serve internal customers most often, people would share responsibility for all the ways financial information is made available to people within the company, making sure the reporting was meaningful, usable, timely.

As for working with external customers, a customer service representative's area of responsibility, for example, would have sufficient decision-making dis-cretion so that customers are immediately provided with meaningful help and support. A person on an assembly line would have the decision-making authority to stop the line if something was not done properly. It is incumbent on the manager to understand how that person works and help improve his or her ability to meet the requirements of the mission on his or her terms. Managers do this by acting as results-producing coaches, helping people stick with their responsibility for the mission until they find their own way to succeed. The tool we use to guide managers in this effort is called the "Critical Success Factor" (CSF). A CSF enables managers and workers to share in the question: *How do I know I am performing this action (one of the core actions in the Arrow of Value) in a way that satisfies the mission?*

Rather than having a job description, for instance, people have a list of CSFs (that are summarized by their "area of responsibility"). The CSFs keep in front of people the purpose of the action by helping them keep in touch with *the immediate and concrete responses that indicate whether or not their effort had the intended effect.* A CSF, for instance, might be: "The customer feels his problem has been solved" or "The customer has been directed promptly and introduced properly to the most effective person to handle that problem." When people take responsibility, they measure their own effectiveness and craft their own sets of tasks that enable them to fulfill a responsibility. Their responsibility is their own—their own field of play and action in which they can and want to grow and excel. Responsibility means just that—the ability to respond fully and openly to a situation that demands a certain outcome. The purpose of the action is reinforced in the CSF, and the evaluation of the success of that action is clearly related to what the mission intends to accomplish for each and every customer.

Using CSFs provides managers with a framework for coaching each individual on how to improve skills and thus be more effective. Rather than focusing on point-by-point task measurements, CSFs lay out the areas of responsibility that the manager and the worker share in order to accomplish the mission. An area of mutual concern is opened so that the tasks become secondary to the ultimate responsibility. Tasks can be changed, the outcomes can be tested to see how relevant they are and the person's experience in performing these tasks can be discussed without fear of judgment or reprisal.

In this chapter's story, we return to the Purchasing and Receiving Department (PRD) of Barry's Sales. Delineating the company's values (as we described in Chapter 2) created a better atmosphere in which cooperation could develop, but the people still needed to develop a new approach to their work. We needed to instill a way of working that would include an acceptance of the necessity, inevitability and benefits of the growth-driven change they were experiencing. They had to break free of their attachment to their jobs. The company was growing too fast, in every way imaginable, for people to be locked into that kind of a strait jacket. The tasks they did yesterday might change tomorrow when new stores are opened, computerization is expanded and new people are added to the department. We coached the group to take responsibility for making the company's mission come alive, not just for their prescribed jobs.

BARRY'S SALES REVISITED: MOVING BEYOND THE JOB DESCRIPTION

As we recall from Chapter 2, the people in the Purchasing and Receiving Department of Barry's Sales rarely saw a customer. They implemented all aspects of purchasing operations from rush order forms from the stores to invoices and packing slips from vendors. Yet these people were hardly paperpushers. They had to check that the merchandise ordered from all over the world arrived at the right place, on time, that the stores were stocked (but not overloaded) with the right merchandise; that merchandise returns were tracked all the way back to the vendor; and that any repeated problems were straightened out. The work was demanding. The volume grew every year, and the necessity to pay attention to the most minute details never went away.

Many people in the group had been there for years. Their jobs had stayed constant for long periods of time. Change had been slow in coming for many years. New technology was introduced slowly and growth was constant, but not explosive. Then, all of this changed as the company grew explosively. Not only were new stores opened, they were much larger than any the company had operated in the past. As customers were added from new regions, the product line had to diversify, while the demands for service and individualized attention intensified. New technology was added continually, and a dedicated Systems Group was created. Day by day the old ways gave way to new processes; these, in turn were constantly modified and streamlined. Fortunately, there were no lost jobs, because the growth was so demanding. The technology automated many of the routine paper shuffling, but management also demanded more by adding new product lines and vendors and by increasing pace and coordination of deliveries to new store locations.

As the pressures increased and new people, including new managers, were added, the people in the PRD became defensive. They focused more and more on guarding their turf; in the face of change they defended their old and familiar methods and practices. By the time Mage started its work, people in the department were clawing at one another. They looked over the shoulders of their peers to be sure they were doing as much work as everyone else—"carrying their load." If someone was overheard on the telephone talking about personal things, he or she was marked for criticism. As we pointed out, the new manager who was hired—with his systems experience and expertise—was isolated from the group.

The antagonism radiated out beyond the department's partitions and stung people company-wide, since the PRD worked with all departments. It worked with store managers on stocking and ordering issues, with accounting on invoices and returns; and with the warehouse on deliveries. They touched the lives of everyone in the company. But whenever these other departments offered suggestions about doing things differently, the PRD members raised hell. The ideas weren't only dismissed, those who made suggestions were often vilified.

Our work on defining and identifying with the company's values helped to soften some of the hard edges. Because the value the group held in greatest esteem was Barry Sales's reputation for service, they all awakened to the idea that their work was an intrinsic part of that service. Because they chose the lack of teamwork and communication as the biggest barriers to realizing this value, they started to look at how cooperative and communicative they were. They all realized they had a lot of work to do.

Continuing the weekly group meetings, we shifted attention to the actions each person performed—individual Arrows of Value, in other words. We asked them to focus on the question: What do your actions accomplish for your customers—internal and external? That is: What do people thank you for? What do people experience when they deal with you? What has changed for them? What are they counting on you—and only you—to do for them in those moments when you are working with them?

They responded with stories about things they did every day that truly helped customers or helped fellow employees succeed in their dealings with customers. Danielle told the story about how a customer wanted a couch upholstered in a fabric that Barry's didn't carry but a competitor did. She had to call the manufacturer and convince him to special order this fabric. They all liked the fabric after all, and both Barry's and the manufacturer started to offer this line of material. Everyone learned and gained from the customer's demand.

Michelle told the story about how her work has saved time for delivery truck drivers. She has had to work hard to schedule these trucks' arrivals so they don't wait for a loading dock to open up. This has been hard enough—dealing with hundreds of deliveries each week. She has also had to cope with a constant flow of special situations: deliveries that had to be postponed or rushed, bumping someone else out of the queue. Although she now had to deal with a lot of frustration, most people have appreciated that she was saving the drivers time and doing her best for the customer.

Betty told stories about tracking returns and how she had to help vendors who had repeated problems get their work up to par. Then there were the tribulations of working with offshore vendors whose work habits were not as disciplined as most U.S. manufacturers. She constantly had to cajole them or juggle multiple vendors to keep a steady supply of merchandise stocked and on the stores' shelves. She was always negotiating and dealing with shipping companies and U.S. Customs to get the merchandise in on time.

The acts of telling these stories and having them heard by peers transforms mere work into real accomplishments—recognized and appreciated by everyone. By thinking about all that they do to make their customers' lives a little better, for a greater or lesser amount of time, employees realize that their work is not a matter of filling in forms. Their work truly makes very important things happen in the right ways for everyone concerned. Although they did not deal directly with the final customers, the people in PRD made it possible for everyone who does deal with customers directly to be successful.

Although the people in the PRD didn't see the difference between "areas of responsibilities" and job descriptions at first, this difference became readily apparent as we progressed. Their job descriptions included the forms they filled out and the vendors with whom they dealt. In contrast, their "areas of responsibility" described what their customers (mostly internal in this case) experienced as a result of their actions, what they had to do to accomplish this and what support they needed to assure that these actions can continue successfully in the future. As each story unfolded, significant shifts in perspectives took hold for everyone in the group: *the tasks they performed weren't the point, they were just the tools. What really matters is fulfilling the responsibility they have for the end result with the customer.*

Clearly, an area of responsibility is not a job. A person's success in fulfilling the mission is not dependent on doing one or another job right. A machine does a job right. When people work within an area of responsibility, their work requires their judgment and balance in responding and making needed adjustments so that the right things happen for the customer. Let the tools change and let in the good ideas and suggestions that could make these things better for others, as well as themselves. Nothing was being taken away by their ideas; in fact, every suggestion offered was a form of recognition for and engagement with what they did for the company. They realized that the important thing was to focus on the results: the satisfaction of the customer, the good service provided by vendors and the ability of the company to respond and learn from customer demands. They were key people in making Barry's Sales the outstanding company it was. Making that company an outstanding place for everyone that came into contact with it was their responsibility, no matter what jobs they did along the way.

FOCUSING ON RESPONSIBILITY

In growing businesses, people are assigned an area of responsibility so they can have an impact on some complete aspect (or several aspects) of the company's critical relationships with customers. They perform actions, or a group of actions, that help to make those relationships both successful in the customers' eyes and profitable for the company. Each position marks a range of actions that intend to have a beneficial outcome for customers and/or other important company stakeholders. A person who occupies that position carves out an "area of responsibility" to assure that the right things happen in the course of the business's daily work.

In terms of the Arrow of Value chart, an area of responsibility summarizes the core actions to which a person has been assigned (across the row with that person's name on it). People are assigned to one or several of the core actions that the company has to accomplish in order to fulfill the mission, and then the people themselves define what tasks or operations can be utilized that satisfy this assignment. The focus for each person is not the prescribed tasks by means of which an action is accomplished but the action itself. An area or responsibility requires that each person complete the core action in a way that accords with the company's values, meets the requirements of the customer and accomplishes the intent of the mission. Within their areas of responsibility, people can continuously experiment, create efficiencies or add new tasks based on their immediate insights. And, most importantly, they can learn how and why improvements and innovations are necessary; and they can learn on their own terms, making these lessons immediate, powerful and meaningful.

This approach to the work, maps onto the requirements for flow, as you have probably noticed. The situation is always challenging, because customer demands are always being made. The core action, values and mission constitute concrete but highly generalized rules because they require specific outcomes that are significant to the company; they can be modified to accord with the talents of each person. Defining this area integrates many tasks into a field of action that promotes concentration and focus where feedback is immediate (and will be reinforced by CSFs).

To create a description of an area of responsibility, we ask five questions.

1. What do your actions accomplish for your customers—internal and external?
2. What are the things you do—tasks and jobs—that make up your work?
3. With whom do you most frequently interact in order to perform your work successfully?
4. What resources (space, equipment, management) do you need to accomplish your work?
5. How do you envision this position changing and evolving over the course of the next year, three years and five years?

1. What do your actions accomplish for your customers—internal and external?

As we see in our story, answering the first question in creating areas of responsibility focuses people on the kinds of real-life responses each action is intended to elicit when accomplishing the mission. There are many ways to elicit those responses. An area of responsibility marks out the set of tasks and jobs that are needed to be successful within the parameters of the company's values and mission.

Now, let's look at the other questions in turn and see how they open up opportunities to increase people's access to a flow experience and peak performance and how they also add to a company's complexity, its ability to grow, change and respond.

2. What are the things you do—tasks and jobs—that make up your work?

This question covers the information contained in the typical job description. But here, the tasks and jobs are neither fixed nor are the sum total of the tasks and jobs equal to the whole position. In an area of responsibility, the tasks and jobs are enumerated so that they can be analyzed for their appropriateness to the larger responsibility as described in answering the first question. As long as the company's mission remains the same, someone will have to take up this responsibility, but the tasks can be changed at any time.

As we were developing this list with the PRD, we asked people who had been with the company for a long time to recall whether these were the same tasks they had performed three years ago. To a person, they all recalled how differently they now do each and every task. The addition of computers, the fact that there were more stores and salespeople to deal with and the advent of so much foreign buying had all made it necessary to change these tasks. The point was made: this task list was merely what they would constantly be improving, innovating and changing.

3. With whom do you most frequently interact to perform your work successfully?

In the case of the PRD, Barry's dedication to service and responsiveness demanded that the right inventory of stock, in proper quantities, be available at all times to keep the showrooms viable and competitive. Since no one person is responsible for all aspects of this key component of competitive success, people have to work together, pitch in to fill gaps and do whatever else is necessary to keep things flowing. By using the Arrow of Value, it was easy to see who relied upon whom to help complete an action.

It turns out the people in the PRD were truly at the hub of the company. They worked with all departments in one way or another. If they made a change in the way they worked, everyone was affected; if others changed the way they worked, the PRD was affected. They saw that part of their responsibilities, therefore, was to keep in constant communication with other groups and departments in the company. Rounds of meetings with these groups were set up to keep everyone apprised of changes and innovations. The new manager of the PRD spent much of his day acting as facilitator and broker, wheeling and dealing with other departments to keep everyone working in sync as the amount and pace of change accelerated.

4. What resources (space, equipment, management) do you need to accomplish your work?

This question opens a manager to consideration of what it takes to get flow into people's work. Do the tools allow people to focus on what they are trying to accomplish, or do they constantly have to stop their work, change tools, ask for information, put up with interruptions? If people cannot achieve flow in their work, I don't think it is possible to put in the longer hours either. As Csikszentmihalyi points out, these disruptions cause "psychic entropy," a wearing down of energy and initiative. A manager's job is to assure that people can achieve flow, and the right tools are a baseline requirement for this.

As for "management resources," people on the line of fire also have to assess the kind of management that will help them fulfill their responsibilities. As you recall, from Chapter 2, when Terry assigned the wrong kind of manager to the PRD group, the people staged a rebellion. The last thing they needed was a heavy-handed, systems-minded task master. The problem in the group was not efficiency or coordination. These people knew their jobs and each other cold. The management resource they needed was a communicator, a facilitator of change and a negotiator to work with other departments to coordinate change. When the new manager provided those resources, the department started to hum.

People with responsibility do need managers but—it may be shocking to hear—managers cannot merely assume proprietary authority over a worker's areas of responsibility. In truth, the person on the line is making the moment-by-moment decisions and has the greatest opportunity to determine what the impact of the engagement will be. It is incumbent on managers to assure that this person is fully vested with the authority, values, will and enthusiasm to make the right decisions. Managers need to know from the real expert, the line worker, how this position will grow and develop—how to continue to pay attention to these relationships as the company grows and changes.

The ultimate management resource here is the manager who fosters opportunities in which a flow experience can develop. By ensuring that people can succeed at fulfilling their responsibilities, this manager opens up the opportunity for people to perform their task differently, better and more effectively. When people are devising how these changes are being made and thinking of ways to do things better, they are engaged in more than just their tasks: they are fulfilling their own sense of pride and accomplishment; they are growing and extending their reach into the nuances of their responsibilities. This is the kind of experiential terrain on which flow can develop.

5. How do you envision this position changing and evolving over the course of the next year, three years and five years?

This question is never asked in job descriptions. Successful organizations build outward from their existing skills. But this can't be done in a hurry, by buying new talent and turning on a switch. People can adapt their skills gradually to new situations—especially ones they themselves have identified. They know what parts of their actions need to be modified. It is exciting and stimulating to be able to make these changes. This is one of the primary tenets of flow as well. But people must be encouraged and supported in making these changes, so they are welcomed as increasing their value to the progress and growth of the company.

CRITICAL SUCCESS FACTORS

A machine's output is relatively easy to measure: number of units, speed and cost of production. Measuring the in-process progress of a growing organization is another matter, and far a more difficult one. The whole intent of using areas of responsibility to define work is to get away from the quantitative, repetitious, volume-oriented degradations to the value of a person's work. But how do you evaluate a person's effort and willingness to take responsibility for achieving the intent and spirit of the mission? Evaluating qualitative contributions to the mission is difficult, but it is not impossible either. For instance, how do you quantify the value of Michelle's scheduling excellence? How does the fact that the deliverer's time is not wasted translate into numbers for Barry's furniture? First, the reason Michelle is doing this work is because relationships with vendors and their delivery drivers is important. To keep the merchandise coming in, you need to keep the people that get it there happy and not cost them precious time and money. So, one way to measure Michelle's success is to notice if vendors are satisfied with the receiving process at Barry's.

This example points to vendor satisfaction as being what we call a "Critical Success Factor" (CSF) for Michelle's work. While a quantitative measurement may not be possible in the short term, each person can note the kinds of experiences he or she wants to create in interactions with others that are affected by his or her actions—and the right responses mark success for these actions. In the long term, however, even these assessments can be translated into quantitative measurements. In the case of Michelle, a vendor who keeps costs low because Barry's helps him keep costs low is a direct translation to the bottom line attributable to her efforts.

The most important way to create CSFs is to answer the following questions (a complete listing of CSFs for the scheduler in the Conifer Group's Production Department is provided in the Appendix):

How do I know I am performing a core action (described in the Arrow of Value) in a way that fulfills the mission? In our Arrow of Value process, wherever a field intersects an action column and an individual or group row, that field must have a CSF associated with it. With Arrows of Value charted to the most appropriate level of detail—to a level where each person can recognize what his or her contribution is and how that contribution links up with others— the CSFs are powerful tools for communicating to each person quickly and with certainty how well they are doing.

Each action along the Arrow of Value changes something or affects some aspect of the relationship between the company and its customers or prospective customers. Each of these changes will be signified by some kind of behavior that is noticeable and memorable (or, it may be that the change in behavior results in a lack of a negative, detracting or cost-producing behavior). It is these qualitative (or quantitative) changes that are noted in the CSF. A CSF states unequivocally, clearly and concretely what kind of response is anticipated by these actions. Some CSF's can be quantitative outcomes (a percentage increase in efficiency), but they can also be strictly qualitative (people are satisfied or pleased by the result of an action).

CSFs evaluate not only the amount of output, but also the worker's experience of producing that output. The usual evaluation schemes measure abstractions like "output per hour," "professionalism" or "team spirit." What do these things mean on a day-to-day basis? Frankly, in many situations I have encountered, they mean nothing to the person being evaluated. These shibboleths of the evaluation form only signal that a detached and otherwise preoccupied manager doesn't want to understand the detail of a person's work and settles for making generalized criticisms, rather than working to help that person blend individual talents with the actions required for success. CSFs, however, evaluate the experiences each of the workers have in the course of fulfilling their responsibilities in accomplishing the mission.

What are the vivid and immediate cues and feedback signals people will key in on so as to know if their action has succeeded? CSFs point explicitly to success, not to failure. Quantitative, mechanistic evaluations operate on the premise of failure. They define a benchmark that has to be reached, by hook or by crook. The premise is: If you don't make it, you have failed. If you haven't failed, the manager has little to do. A contest of egos ("I know I've done my job well" versus "You didn't do the job the way I wanted it done") is a foregone conclusion. CSFs explicitly enumerate those customer (internal or external) responses that signal success. A worker's actions either succeed or the worker is expected to modify these actions in order to achieve success. The limits are defined by the company's mission, values and available resources, not the manager's definition of the job. The manager offers observations and suggestions and points out other specific reactions the worker can seek to elicit. No egos are involved—just doing the work successfully.

The process allows both the worker and the manager to ask, How do I do my best? Do I have the temperament and personality to handle this kind of situation? Michelle was quite adept at working with the truckers but was not necessarily the one best suited to deal with foreign suppliers and cultural and language differences. The process also opens up qualitative conversations about ways to improve performance and what new skills are worth learning.

In this way, CSFs are designed to support flow by providing cues to managers on how to evaluate, coach and guide employees. But evaluational signals provide the most effective feedback when they come from those being affected most directly by a person's actions. For example, I recently worked with a woman who was a hard-nosed manager, to put it mildly. Her abrasive style was creating stress and dissension in her department and was detracting from the many other valuable skills she offered her company. A typical evaluation might have cited her "interpersonal skills" and marked this as an area for improvement. This criticism stops at the negative comment. Except for devaluing her overall performance, what does it accomplish? What cues does it provide so that she can improve on her own or with a manager's coaching?

To help her improve, we created a CSF in which we stipulated that when people left her office, they should feel positive about the meeting. Of course, there was no way to measure this instruction immediately. In the short term, however, we wanted her to concentrate on the immediate experience she was creating for others during that moment and to focus on making it as constructive for all parties as possible. In the longer term, that CSF is quite assessable by having conversations with her employees and by noting the department's overall morale.

YOU CANNOT DEMAND COMMITMENT, BUT YOU CAN EARN IT

Regardless of what the work is, assigning people areas of responsibility instead of jobs can transform their good will into a commitment to the company. Every manager wants this elusive quality—a sense of commitment—from workers. But I suggest that this is a lot to expect from anyone. Commitment is something that is freely given, it cannot be required or mandated. It is given when a person feels that there is in place an equal and mutual process of action, recognition and growth on the part of two parties. Commitment will follow, as we have seen over and over again in our work, when people take responsibility and are taken seriously for doing so.

Commitment is also inextricably linked to flow. When do people form and hold to commitments? When there is a clear and compelling mutual benefit to be derived. Commitment is self-serving, but it is not selfish. Commitment fully encompasses a giving up of one's narrow, ego-driven desires so that something larger takes place. But this giving over of the narrow and parochial is offered with the intent of really accomplishing something larger. People expect to grow within a commitment, to become more than they were before. Flow is the human experience within which that growth and accomplishment happens.

Businesses cannot make long-term promises of life-time employment. What can they offer to engender the kind of commitment it takes to put a successful product or service on the market? They can offer two things: first the opportunity to create *value* for people, and thus do something worthwhile; and second, they can offer the opportunity to experience flow. Offering people the chance to learn, grow and contribute to the communities they care about is the only true, viable and mutually rewarding link a business has to its employees' and managers' commitment.

In Chapter 9 we talk about how "envisioning" one's work in completeness and depth is a necessary element to achieving flow. Yet, there can be no envisioning in a job. A job is set within strict organizational and process boundaries. For a person to envision beyond this infringes on someone else's turf or tugs at someone else's control. Our model calls on decision makers to make the difficult step of letting go of control in favor of acting out a vision, a set of values and a mission. This is a steep order.

When talking about "aspiration" in Chapter 10, we show the benefits that accrue when each person experiences the possibility of professional and personal growth in his or her work. A job is work within walls. When they work within areas of responsibility, people will not see walls; instead, they will experience how effective they can be in the face of a challenge, and they will welcome the next one. Their work will cultivate the habit of experiencing growth and change, to the betterment of everyone concerned. Our model calls for business decision makers to see over their own walls, open up to what the collective talents of people performing at their peak have to offer and help them aspire to accomplish greatness for themselves, the business and its stakeholders.

When people are set free from jobs, there will be surprises—not a welcome prospect for many managers. But to the true masters of business organization, those surprises are the stuff of excitement and vitality. In the next two chapters, we will see how these masters step out of the way and let their people release their energies into the flow of excellence.

NOTE

1. William Bridges, "The End of the Job," *Fortune*, September 19, 1994.

Chapter 9

Envision

I think most of us are looking for a calling, not a job. Most of us, like the assembly line worker, have jobs that are too small for our spirit. Jobs are not big enough for people.

Studs Terkel, *Working*[1]

TEAMS: THE TERRAIN OF FLOW

Since managers routinely envision the broad responsibilities that contribute to the company's success, they may also expect that the "big picture" is grasped by their workers as well, framing and driving their sense of challenge and excitement. But as managers soon discover, translating the grand vision of the values and mission into an individual's high performance is no easy task. In this chapter, we will see how well-managed and well-led teams help people achieve high performance by providing a context that is conducive to flow.

We look to teams as a context for flow because it is hard to sustain big ideas by ourselves. Ideas become compellingly alive when people form groups around them and display dedication. In groups, people reinforce disciplines around these ideas, create rituals and test themselves and each other against them. The great ideas a business sets out to accomplish also need this kind of collective awareness.

In a business, we see this kind of interaction when teams emerge out of operating groups. When teams form, people combine their talents to work together with an awareness that the company's values and mission give *meaning* to their work. People on a team believe that responsibilities need to be carried out with excellence if the company is going to succeed in its mission. They don't just polish off a list of tasks. Everyone on the team cares about all aspects of what it sets out to accomplish. They jointly monitor its progress and significance, its effect on individuals and the team members, and so together share in the joy of its success.

Types of Working Groups

There are many very useful and productive ways to bring people together in the workplace. When managers think of organizing people into working groups, they first think of creating *departments*. Departments generally perform operations that the company needs day in and day out, even though the tasks that comprise these operations may change from day to day. People who work together in a department share many things: they usually have similar talents (people in accounting departments usually have a facility with numbers, while the people in marketing are likely to be good at making analytical or synthetic judgments about the trends and implications of those numbers) and they perform tasks that are similar to, or are on a continuum of commonality with, one another's tasks. Every business organization needs these departments in order to assure that essential disciplines are in place. But there are many other kinds of groupings of people businesses use in order to do the wide range of tasks, projects and programs that make for a successful operation.

Task forces and *committees* are often formed to examine special issues that face the company, and they comprise people from many different departments who combine their perspectives and expertise in order to make recommendations that others will carry out. Then there are other *clusters* of people who meet, make recommendations and/or decide important issues. For instance, there are executive groups, where senior executives keep each other abreast of the initiatives in their respective areas; management forums, in which appropriate groupings of people are gathered to hear about innovations or discuss organizational issues and perspective; and employee forums, in which workers are informed about company developments, benefits and policies and are asked for input on specific issues.

What Makes Teams Different

All of these groupings are useful, but just because more than three people show up at a certain place at a certain time to have a meeting does not mean they are teams. A "team" can emerge out of any of these functional groupings, but none of these groupings will necessarily coalesce into a team. The differences between teams and working groups don't jump out and hit you over the head. On the face of it, a team still operates under the same conditions that the other functional groupings in the business do. Teams are formed with exactly the same managers in place, and they comprise exactly the same people that are in the departments, committees and forums that existed before teams were formed. But inside the teams, everything is different. Teams enable each team member to *envision* what their work is about at a deeper, more significant level than they can when they organized into discrete task-performing jobs.

The work is not done to meet some abstract number; neither is it being done solely to meet someone else's goals. When working on a team, the goals are close at hand, as near and as pressing as the next conversation with a team member. People are able to accomplish everything that needs to be done, from investigating honestly and in-depth what the situation really is, to devising and implementing an appropriate response to it. Yet, by the same token, the goals are of manageable dimensions. The work isn't fragmented in an artificial, mechanistic sequence; rather, it is shared as an integrated whole, in which many people are involved.

The team counts on all its members not for just a piece of the job, but for each member's contribution to accomplishing the whole job. No one works in isolation. People on the team care about more than the end result; they also care about how well members are able to stay with the whole team before, during and after doing their part. When the team doesn't succeed, they want to stay together to do it right the next time. When people work on teams, they create an internal world of actions, standards, expectations and camaraderie that carries with it a balance between a meaningful challenge and a chance to succeed at meeting it—a sense that each of their talents is understood, has a place and so has a chance to be expressed (and recognized) to the fullest.

Teams and Flow

When work is infused with that special sense of challenge, ownership and completeness, efforts become opportunities for the creation of flow. If managers are to derive the maximum benefit from teams, they need to be aware of the kind of experience they are coaching the team members to have. To press the team to work faster or to divert them from what matters to them will utterly dash their effectiveness. By realizing that the team's "micro-world" can act as an incubator of flow, and thus optimal performance and accomplishment, the manager can act appropriately, with patience and a good ear.

Managers also need to fully understand the risks they run in creating teams. Flow creates a sense of autonomy, personal accomplishment, a sense of owning a piece of the mission. Teams and control do not mix. By appreciating the energies and focus unleashed by teams in which flow occurs, managers have a chance to witness an amazing phenomenon: potential realized, excitement and dedication fulfilled. It just won't have the manager's name on it. We'll discuss these risks at length later in the chapter.

By quickly reviewing the major requirements for establishing flow and comparing them with the team experience, we can see why the team experience matches up so well with the requirements for establishing flow:

• Flow requires concrete goals. A team turns the values and mission of the company into concrete goals that the team sets out to accomplish.

- Flow requires a sense of potential control and offers opportunities to act decisively. Team members work in an environment of trust. They have been given a challenge and they know they are being counted on to meet it. They're on the team to do the whole job—everything it takes to succeed—and they guard that prerogative fiercely.

- Flow requires concentration on the actions at hand. Teams reinforce an atmosphere that helps everyone limit distractions and maintain focus. The priorities are clear, the goals known, the time frame set. Other team members "run interference" if necessary.

- Flow requires immediate feedback so that actions can be modified and improved. This is a crucial element that teams provide. As we'll discuss in more detail later, teams provide not only immediate feedback, but meaningful feedback. The team members intimately know what each person is trying to achieve and will find ways to help that person along. People are supported, not merely judged.

Of course, many of the activities that are known to optimize flow experiences, such as rock climbing or writing, are not conducive to teamwork at all. But in a business context, it is hard for flow to occur outside of a team environment. The goals of the business are too big, too complicated, for one person to accomplish alone, and the pull of distractions and conflicting priorities are too constant for flow to occur "naturally" on a single or solitary basis. And the pace is too demanding for a single person to be able to concentrate long enough on one thing to possibly trigger an enduring flow experience. For flow to occur in a business setting, people need the reinforcement and/or protection of the convened, sanctioned, goal-driven team.

In this story, we will see how a team was created out of a dysfunctional department. This is no "reengineering" project where the department's processes were reworked by a cadre of "experts," forced on the others and then monitored for presumed efficiencies. The program changed the attitude, spirit and working hearts of all the people in the department.

CREATING THE TEAM

The Collections Department of Eastern Wireless Corporation (Harry Kaufman's company that we visited in Chapter 5) was renowned as "the dungeon." Fifteen collectors sat in cubicles tucked away in the back of the building. No one ever walked by the department. The collectors might as well have been chained to their desks (by their headsets) since they were required to meet a quota of outbound calls each day. It was lonely work: you could see your neighbors but not talk to any of them because they were on the phones, staring at their terminals, digging up customer information or writing tickler notes. Their hours were long, and they were always shorthanded.

It's hard to know which came first, the reputation or the actuality, but in fact, the people conducted themselves like convicts. They constantly complained. They conspired to figure out new and imaginative ways to "beat the system." Any of these problems might concern a manager, but they were particularly upsetting to the managers at Eastern Wireless since Harry Kaufman had put so much effort into instilling new models of leadership and demonstrating respect for employees. The collectors' behavior and resistance to the "progressive" changes were puzzling and disturbing.

Mage was approached to look into the problem by both Carrie Listner, the Division Vice President, and the Business Services Group Manager, Mac Ellery (who reported to Carrie). These people just "didn't get it," Mac told me. "The rest of the company is pulling together, fostering contribution and team spirit, and this group is lagging behind, backbiting and trying to beat the system."

Carrie and Mac focused their consternation on the department's supervisor, Norma Jeannette. She had great heart and ability but she exhibited little in the way of tact or subtlety. She ruled with an iron fist, acting like a domineering warden over a brood of disgruntled delinquents. No matter how appropriate that behavior might have been at this point, something had to change.

We interviewed each of the collectors extensively over the course of a couple of weeks. Individually and collectively, we found them to be deeply thoughtful and quite amenable to self-sacrifice under the right conditions. These people had a firm belief in discipline and fair play and most displayed a great deal of maturity in how they saw their responsibilities. Still, their jobs ground them down. Not only did their work suffer from a great deal of repetition, it also produced a lot of stress. They frequently dealt with tense situations and had to juggle highly sensitive decisions that directly affected a customer's individual financial well-being with the company's bottom line and its potential for continuing a relationship with this customer.

We came back with findings that surprised Carrie and Mac. First, moving Norma would have been completely self-defeating and disruptive. The group was fiercely loyal to her. They felt that she had grown a lot over the years and was really making progress, and they were as much involved and took as much pride in her progress as she did. They were not at all concerned about what appeared to "outsiders" as her heavy-handedness. They viewed her as "one of them" and counted her success as an accomplishment of their own.

The next finding really surprised Carrie and Mac, however. The people in the Collections Department, we said, did not need a new manager. We felt these people were outstanding candidates for working in self-managing teams.

"What?" they asked.

Neither Carrie nor Mac could picture how these people, negative and unwieldy as they were, could manage themselves. The one person in the management group who really embraced the idea was Norma. It seems that she, as well as the collectors, had been put in a situation that stifled her spirits and underestimated what she was capable of contributing. She immediately started showing up at department meetings with books on building high performance teams. She demonstrated to us that she had a firm, almost intuitive grasp of how this could be done. The idea was out of the bottle and could not be put back in.

Over the course of several months, we inched toward the changeover. First, we had to convince Carrie and Mac that this was worth doing (there was no need to convince Norma, and Harry Kaufman encouraged his managers to innovate methods that involve people in making decisions). Then we had to allay fears. And that list of fears changed constantly from day to day. So-and-so isn't responsible; these two will never get along; Norma hasn't had any training in this; other department supervisors feared they were going to be laid off because self-managing teams were being installed. The fears were legitimate, but eventually Carrie and Mac realized if the department was going to improve, they would have to take a chance, a leap of faith, one way or the other. Only when these highly emotional issues were dispensed with, could we start to work with the group. Eventually, they came to the conclusion that of the alternatives—go with our recommendation or make wholesale personnel changes—our suggestion seemed more palatable.

Planning the Change

Once we got rolling. Mage worked closely with Norma, suggesting ways to augment the reading she was doing, observing her conduct meetings and providing coaching on her managerial approach. During the process, she did not manage in a domineering or controlling way, and she developed into a superb team builder and coach. She played the pivotal role in energizing and focusing the collectors on making the transition. Norma instituted weekly evening meeting for the group—rotating coverage so that over a month's time, everyone could attend the meetings. The meeting time was used to get the group to start talking with each other about their work and to start seeing that their suggestions would be taken seriously. She also started to introduce some team-building exercises: group problem solving, information sharing and the like. These exercises were intended to see whether the group could, in fact, behave as a team before the switch was announced or made.

In the background, Mage worked with Carrie and Mac to institute some basic rules about the teams:

- Create a broad, mission-based charge for the group to accomplish and let them do whatever it takes to succeed.

- Put no more than eight on a team.

- Create no formal competition between teams (competition that was sanctioned or rewarded by the managers).

- Periodically, infuse the team with new members (trainees) and/or start new teams as the department grew. Try to balance continuity of the teams without them getting stale.

- Allow time for at least weekly team planning meetings.

- Set formal evaluations based on departmental performance, not on the team or the individual (informal, friendly competition was inevitable and not harmful when managed closely).

• Arrange the seating to foster continual intra-team conversation.

Individuals were then assigned to prospective teams. Norma and Mac initially selected who would be on each team by observing various talents and personalities throughout the course of the exercises. Later, as the teams rotated, the groups would be more self-selected (creating an effective mechanism for both identifying top performers and weeding out slackers). The supervisory relationships were discussed and realigned. Each team would select its own "senior rep" who would convene meetings, record work assignments and be a communications clearinghouse. This role would be rotated or could remain constant, depending on the wishes of the group. Norma would have more of a coaching job than a watchdog role, and she would take on a greater role in recruiting (at this time the department was expanding at a rate of a new person each month). A new seating plan was devised.

Taking Charge

Delegates from the Collections Department worked for several weeks with the company's computer department. They changed the screens that could be called up on their terminals so they could get more customer history and added space for notes to be recorded. This helped them treat each situation in greater depth and make more informed decisions with the customer. They also devised a more flexible and self-directed means of creating weekly call lists. Only new names were arbitrarily assigned to one of the teams. Once a name was assigned, it stayed with the team for the duration of the collection process. Instead of the people being names on a list to call, they became "cases" for the team. Difficult and long-term cases were handled with continuity. Conversations about how to resolve a case could occur each week among the group so the best solution could be arrived at and maintained until all the funds were collected.

When the transition actually occurred, all that was left to do was to physically rearrange the cubicles and move people around into their new locations. They came in early that Monday morning, in casual dress, and packed up, moved in, got settled. The real impact of the moving day was symbolic, being physically engaged in a process of rearranging and settling in.

The process was up and running without a hitch. Every Monday morning the teams met to decide roles—who would make initial calls, who had what follow-up calls to make, who would be the landing place for incoming calls, what would be the escalation path. Except for continuing case assignments, most roles were rotated on a voluntary basis. The group tried to spread different kinds of jobs around so that the team had within it all the experience necessary to do all of the work.

The groups of collectors readily coalesced into teams. They knew each other well, they all knew their work inside and out, and management was not telling them how to get their work done. With the new information at their disposal, their range of decision-making (creating payment plans for customers and preventing the need to terminate service) was expanded. Cases were discussed and approaches to some of the more touchy problems were suggested. They moved cases around to people who were more compatible with a certain customer or had more experience with a certain kind of problem. They focused on two goals: retaining good customers and collecting outstanding charges from those who had to be terminated. Their goal was no longer to merely reduce the company's exposure to bad debt, but to do everything possible to create better customers, and more loyal ones, through demonstrated concern, polite and professional discipline and consistency.

Two years after the teams had been instituted, we went back to visit the group. All the original team members had moved on. Carrie left the company to take a consulting position, and Norma was promoted to a position in the parent company's corporate headquarters. Harry Kaufman had long since been promoted and moved on to a new assignment. Only Mac was still there. Now, despite all these changes, the process works exactly as we envisioned it more than two years ago. And the results have been rewarding for all involved. Ideas do flow; turnover is not an issue (the average tenure in the position is fourteen to eighteen months). People successfully move into telemarketing, sales, accounting and other departments throughout the company.

TEAMS: CREATING FLOW FROM JOBS

Teams translate the larger values and mission into "do-able" challenges and thus render them amenable to flow. Managers can capitalize on this opportunity to achieve peak performance from people by creating and fostering teams with these tenets in mind:

Team Members Choose Their Own Goals

In their useful book *The Wisdom of Teams*, Katzenbach and Smith report one successful team member's passion for the experience:

"In my mind," says Dave Burns, "the key word to this team was 'shared.' We shared everything. There was a complete openness among us. And the biggest thing that we shared was an objective and a strategy that we had put together jointly. That was our benchmark each day. Were we doing things in support of our plan?"[2]

For flow to occur, people have to have a sense of completeness in their work. As Csikszentmihalyi points out:

One of the basic differences between a person [who is experiencing flow and one who is not] is that the former knows that it is she who has *chosen whatever goal she is pursuing*. What she does is not random, nor is it the result of outside determining forces. This fact results in two seemingly opposite outcomes. On the one hand, having a feeling of *ownership* of her decisions, the person is more strongly dedicated to her goals. Her actions are reliable and internally controlled. On the other hand, knowing them to be her own, she can *more easily modify her goals* whenever the reasons for preserving them no longer make sense. In that respect, [a person's] behavior is both more consistent and more flexible. . . . [It] implies the ability to *sustain involvement*.[3] [Italics mine.]

This doesn't mean that teams go off and reinvent the company day after day. The Collections Department did not choose their own goals out of the blue. The department existed to perform a certain function. But the collections team did *reframe* those goals in their own way. Instead of collecting overdue bills, they worked to retain good customers and lower the company's exposure to bad debt. This "mental" shift enriched their experience with each customer. Their work went from being a narrowly defined series of negative tasks, measured by the numbers—call minimums and dollar quotas—to constructively helping the company's customers solve problems in mutually beneficial ways.

In the case of the Collections Department, the group's goal was clearly understood. But, that may not be the case for task forces or other kinds of cross-functional groupings. A manager has to exercise judgment and care in mapping out the charge given to such groups. On the one hand, the mandate has to be broad enough so that the group has an opportunity to formulate its own goals or solutions to the problem. On the other hand, the group can't be left to flounder in this stage or all will be lost. Formulating the goals are a crucial step for the group.

A sound method for guiding a group toward evolving into a team is to have them begin their work by intensely focusing on analyzing the problem. Keep to these simple rules: investigate honestly; don't presume a solution; describe the problem fully and completely. Normally, preliminary work will be divided up according to what interests or bothers the team members the most, so each segment of the work will start to have its champion. Plus, out of this kind of intense, unbiased analysis, solutions usually present themselves. From these insights, meaningful and significant goals can be created.

Teams Convert Vision into Action

Teams rise up out of other kinds of groups when the team's members set their own methods and standards. When teams manage the work that they actually do each and every day, they have a chance to create their own environment, perpetuate or modify it and see it contribute consistently and powerfully to the company's mission. This environment is vividly real because it is created by the network of understandings created in the heat of battle, so to speak—in conversations, arguments and experiments tried and failed that happen moment to moment with the people in the next cubicle or on the telephone.

As reported by one of the collectors a few months after the teams were formed,

Every Monday morning we start out by getting together to look at the week's work. We decide how it will be done; who will take on what roles; who needs to be trained in this or that and who will do the training and when. There's always new things going on, and we are always reorganizing. It's our work; it's ours to divide up; it's to succeed with or fail because of.

This is a critical step in creating flow. Not only are tasks performed, but new personal and interpersonal capabilities are unleashed. People find that the same tasks have a different meaning, a different scope of goals and intent. Their abilities are thus valued and needed and, at the same time, they can envision new modifications that will take their abilities into new responsibilities and opportunities. For the collectors, this meant each one of them had a role in solving more difficult and potentially more interesting, situations—proactively, in the form of discussions about cases pending. Over time, people were put in more and more challenging situations.

There is little for managers to do but to let events take their course. In the case of the Collections Department, once they formed into viable, self-managing teams, there was no longer any system to cheat, no arbitrary measurements to conspire against. They worked among themselves to find better ways to work at agreed upon goals. The collectors shared their respective ''motivations,'' the things that got them going, that helped them ''gear into'' the work. They helped each other find ways to excel, feel good about their work, learn and grow from it—they encouraged opportunities for each other to realize flow experiences. The quality of doing the work, not just the output, became the primary focus of attention.

Continuous, Timely Feedback

People can be put together to perform a variety of important organizational tasks—some temporary, others quite permanent. But in whatever context they are used, teams only form when people commit to getting something done that is of importance to them and when they experience the excitement of incremental, but real, progress toward their goals. They don't merely tally up the results at the end of the day. Team members are involved with each other throughout the work process. While its members hold each other accountable for each and every contribution they make, they also offer recognition. After all, they offer each other the deepest understanding of what the members' intentions and objectives are; and there is also the stick close at hand—as close as the look or leer of one's peer at the next meeting.

These actions fulfill another major requirement for establishing flow—that there be immediate and meaningful feedback. The team members that stay with the program become high performers, experiencing flow themselves and creating it for others. For the people in the Collections Department, that feedback loop didn't have to be printouts of their calls from the CMS (Call Management System—"the Big Brother spy," as one member called it). It could be a matter of a knowing look, a roll of the eyes, a pat on the back. All are knowing and instantaneously meaningful acts of recognition. But now, instead of being codes passed between prisoners in "the dungeon," as it once had been, the recognition was geared to support the mission and the team at every turn. The behaviors that were being reinforced were constructive and career-creating, as opposed to rebellious and dead end.

Teams also become the fertile ground of perpetual professional development. In the Collections Department, new hires were always assigned to an existing team. They learned quickly from their peers what was expected. Since roles and tasks were regularly rotated, they were coached on a task as their time came up. Their talents and shortcomings were observed by many people moment by moment. These new people learned their jobs quickly. Also, as teams experimented with different techniques and methods, they were incubators for innovation. All team members learned about innovating, creating new capabilities and growing in their jobs.

Teams Emphasize Work's Intrinsic Rewards

With all of this said, however, the property that most marks self-managing teams as the ideal contexts for creating flow is that within the team, *motivation becomes intrinsic to the work itself.* As we have said, whatever the company's hierarchy, these teams develop their own standards for excellence and their own means for recognizing that excellence.

To Eastern Wireless management, the only motivating measure was lowering the percentage of bad debt. For the members of the collections team, that measurement was abstract, distant and strictly financial, not relating or speaking in any meaningful way to the work that each of them could accomplish or have some discretion over. Because the team acted according to its vision of what needs to be accomplished, their means of recognition became more qualitative, immediate and timely than any external, motivating system could provide. The team focused on what they intimately knew as the operational and situational decision skills that were called on to get that result. They rewarded each other for what was most meaningful—fulfilling their vision of how the job needed to be done and seeing that vision get the results that management and the company genuinely needed.

The team's goals and the company's goals were in sync. Management saw the numbers and measured them against capital requirements and their needs for investment. However the team saw the operation in its full relational sense on a one-on-one, customer-by-customer basis. They were the ones who knew how to manage the relationships. And that's what they did. No team member can "experience" the numbers. They can each only experience the effect and outcomes of each call.

Team members can judge each other on how well they contribute to the goal and act within the standards for performance from one call to the next. They are the ones that are best qualified to know if a collector did everything possible to keep a customer and, at the same time, ensure payment. The team recognizes the effort, wisdom and innovativeness that each of them produces on the spot, from call to call. The team is able to reward what the people actually do, not just what someone else—manager, shareholder—gets. The fact is that no perspective from the outside has the same meaning, import and weight as the recognition that is offered graciously from one who is doing the same thing. It will be difficult for a detached manager to fully appreciate what it takes to envision what a change will mean and make possible.

Since each and every task is a learning experience with immediate feedback and a chance for change and growth, the team experience can be a hard one for many people. The crucible of challenges the team takes on sorts out the wheat from the chaff. High performers will be rewarded by invitations to be on other teams, while those who don't measure up are left behind. This is the best early warning system for personnel problems—and opportunities—a manager can have. Using teams, managers see who the people select as their leaders, workers and cheerleaders. There is no more accurate and unambiguous evaluation system than what peers on a team provide.

FROM TEAMS TO HIGH-PERFORMING COMPANIES: RISKS AND REWARDS

When teams are active and performing, managers give up control of day-to-day decision-making. This can be a bitter pill for some managers to swallow. In our work, the biggest barriers to transforming ordinary working groups into effective, flow-engendering teams are erected by the managers' overwhelming need for control. When the managers at Eastern Wireless were considering our proposal, Mac came to me expressing his reservations: "If these people manage themselves, what will I do?"

His boss, Carrie, had other reservations around control issues; that is, that things would get out of hand, that performance wouldn't be measured, that people wouldn't pay proper attention to professional development. Their concerns, at one level were justified. Some of the tasks that mark traditional management authority go out the window with self-managing teams. The team members make work assignments, assign their own roles and so put each other in line for new assignments or promotions.

But when I went back to visit two years later, I asked Mac, who was still the group manager, about his initial reservations. He hardly remembered having any reservations at all. With two years' experience under his belt, he said, "It's great. I don't manage them at all. I am a communicator and a facilitator. I keep them informed about what the corporate goals are and I keep them in sync with what other departments in the company are doing. I'm like an ambassador for them to the other departments. My role is completely constructive." The team's success had allowed him to elevate his own contribution and understanding of his role as a manager.

The moral of the story: When using self-managing teams, managers must be prepared to give them a wide berth. Teams and control just don't mix. Any group that is controlled, is necessarily being relegated to more isolated jobs and task fulfilling. For teams to form out of any kind of working group, the company's leadership must be willing to change, even eliminate, control-oriented operating assumptions and models. Katzenbach and Smith make the observation:

Each team must find its own path to its own unique performance challenge.... This discipline, and the performance focus at its heart, provide the essential compass to potential teams that must navigate through all the risks inherent in moving up the team performance curve. Joining a team is a career risk, giving up individual control is a performance risk, acknowledging personal responsibility for needed change is a self-esteem risk, allowing others to lead is an institutional risk, and abandoning hierarchical command and control is a stability risk. Taking such risks makes sense only if it unleashes a team's capabilities in pursuit of performance. Only then can people avail themselves of the wisdom of teams.[4]

This doesn't mean teams operate without limits or without managerial intervention and involvement. To the contrary, effective managers shepherd teams toward the highest levels of autonomy, while assuring that their efforts remain integrated within the larger company. Sometimes managers do have to say, "No," because teams can become insular, their ideas sounding wonderful to them, and are deaf to other influences in the company. But managers can also find ways to say, "Yes, if we do it this way" or "Yes, if we can involve these people."

The manager, in other words, connects the team's work and spirit to their appropriate outlets. The team changes and elevates the manager's role. Instead of being a monitor and a task master—the most elemental and limited form management can assume—the team's demands raise the role of the manager to being a facilitator, negotiator and path-breaker, using the organization's resources to realize the maximum benefit from the team's efforts. This feeds back into the team, further motivating them by validating the import of their work and, in turn, paves the way to take on the next challenge.

Teams Are Hard to Stop

Once they get rolling, the team's members are spirited, enthused, empowered. The organization has to have a place for that energy. Decision makers have to be sure that these people, with their new outlook and heightened expectations about their work lives, will have a place to go. Teams are high-stake ventures for an organization. The members have a vision and have no intent other than to get something done. That means changing the behavior of the organization, not just in this one instance, but henceforward.

Teams change the members' impressions about the organization. In planning their work, the team members dissect the organization—its history, performance, leadership, systems, processes and culture. All of these things come out on the table. Stories are told, secrets and rumors are aired. Teams usually undergo an intense process of discovery that sometimes changes people's sense of affiliation with the company. A truly empowered team has the potential to change that sense of affiliation for the better. A team that is constricted or whose mandate is changed after the fact will often serve to weaken that sense of affiliation even more.

Teams also create insiders and outsiders in an organization. This can be as dangerous as it is productive—a real potential downside risk. The insiders are the ones on the team, and the outsiders are the ones involved in the problem or situation the team is addressing. No matter what a team does, it is also making changes for someone. As the teams change, they can broaden the impact company-wide in a reasonable and equitable manner. If only a single department or a single group's behaviors are being affected, a cautionary note is warranted. The effects of the team's efforts can be worn down by the friction around them. If this happens, cynicism about the company is not far behind. Any diminution of their assignment or limitation on what they are doing will result in profound disappointment and possible loss of trust.

Once teams have been put into place, there's no going back.

Why Risk a Team Experience at All?

There is no other way for today's business organizations to succeed. The way teams enrich the experience of working for their members by encouraging conditions that foster flow provides the single most important and reliable "motivational tool" available to managers today.

Here are obvious problems managers have to face in building and sustaining businesses today and the reasons that team experiences provide a solution to these problems:

1. Today's businesses cannot guarantee lifetime employment. Job security is a thing of the past, and yet businesses need continuity in their work force and need to benefit from the bank of accumulated knowledge their workers can provide. If people are experiencing personal growth, in the form of flow experience or in the context of meeting significant, meaningful challenges, they will often stay with a company. When people respond to the lure of challenge, excitement and growth, they evince the "Strategic Heart" that defines a company's success. Teams provide the kind of intensely vital experience of challenge and

growth that make the work experience worthwhile for however long a person is employed.

2. Today's businesses have to constantly reorganize and retool, and sometimes re- and depopulate their staffs to meet tides and shifts in market conditions. Thinking about an organization in terms of teams rather than departments, the managers can create seamless and fluid streams of production. With no rigid departments and hierarchies, people can move to wherever "the action is," and they will be proud to make the move. People are used in ways that continually maximize their talents and in combinations with others that offer variety in their work. When the work and the challenges are fresh, flow has a chance to occur in the course of the daily work that needs to be done. Everyone benefits.

3. Today's workers need to continually upgrade their skills. Teams provide intense workshops for learning new skills or disseminating known skills among a wider base of employees. Since workers don't want to disappoint their team-mates (as opposed to wanting to "show up" the boss), they are more likely to seek out training and skills upgrading at their own initiative.

If the work in one area has ended—if some work has been automated, a product has been discontinued or new products need a different combination of skills—people can either offer to stay under reasonable circumstances or choose to move on rather than have their experiences be degraded or diminished. Teams select who will stay on the job and who needs to move on. Better than any after-the-fact managerial evaluation, people know whether or not they fit in or if it is best to move on.

4. Businesses can't afford to staff up and then downsize, time after time. Teams provide a way to maximize performance from a more stable working core of employees. I am just amazed at what people will endure in terms of workload and hours when they are part of something in which they believe. When the performance is there, the employer pays them well; and when things slow down, everyone gets a breather. The team remains intact. Over time, the capabilities and the trust build on one another. The investment pays dividends that far exceed any short-term bottom line.

So, with all these red flags and pitfalls laid out, the real risk, it seems to me, is run when decision makers do not create teams throughout their organization. The flow created in these experiences creates the kind of flexible, responsive, cohesive organization that can truly compete in a fast-paced, changing world. This lesson is lost to decision makers at their own peril.

NOTES

1. Studs Terkel, *Working* (New York: Avon Books, 1972), p. xxix.
2. Jon R. Katzenbach and Douglas K Smith, *The Wisdom of Teams: Creating the High Performance Organization* (New York: Harper Business, 1993), p. 35.
3. Mihaly Csikszentmihalyi, *Flow* (New York: HarperCollins, 1990), p. 210.
4. Katzenbach and Smith, *The Wisdom of Teams*, p. 129.

Chapter 10

Aspire

When the Master governs, the people
are hardly aware that he exists.
Next best is a leader who is loved.
Next, one who is feared.
The worst is one who is despised.
If you don't trust the people,
You make them untrustworthy.
The Master doesn't talk, he acts.
When his work is done,
the People say, "Amazing!
We did it, all by ourselves!"

—Lao-tzu, *Tao te Ching* (17)[1]

MORE THAN A PAY CHECK

Strategic businesses create change because they are aspiring to accomplish something of significance in the marketplace. The people in these businesses constantly envision change—change for the company, its products and markets and for themselves. People working toward the company's goals feel they too are aspiring to higher levels of personal achievement and contribution. Flow is a fitting focus for managerial attention in strategic companies such as these because flow is about change and transformation. If people aspire to new visions and new capability in their work, they will need to work with the sense of completeness and engagement we have described. And once these fundamentals are established, the appetite for the expansive horizons of flow continues to assert itself. Workers will want to "make a difference" and "leave their mark."

They will push ahead to create new, expansive, more nuanced and complex capabilities that are worth more to the company and to themselves.

Successful managers in growing businesses clear the way for people who are willing to change for the sake of something larger. Whether or not the raises, titles and bonuses will be forthcoming is up to the market and lies beyond the control of any one person or company. Still, these people transform their jobs into personal missions, for themselves and the company. And even if you do pay a bonus or promote people for outstanding work that contributes to a successful new product, do those actions really compensate them for the effort it takes to learn new roles or to strive to bring new ideas to fruition? Yet, this is exactly the kind of effort it takes to work in the environments we are describing. The manager's mandate, therefore, is to offer something else—something that creates meaning from that effort, something that comes from the same kind of heart workers are offering by their efforts.

Pushing Back the Limits

I can hear the skeptics now: While this talk about vision and aspiration is all well and good in a fancy book, what about real-life factory jobs or jobs that entail endless paper-pushing? Aren't there just some jobs that are just not interesting? How can you create flow in these situations? Look at the custodian who sweeps the floor at night. Can his work lead to flow? Isn't it mind-numbing work, boring beyond redemption?

Yes, there is no doubt that some work is just plain boring. And it is also true that, at times, the most interesting of work is stressful, disruptive and far from being likely to engender flow. Still, every manager knows that boredom is the enemy of high performance. Mistakes crop in, carelessness overtakes everything. Managers have to deal with the issue of giving people a chance to be engaged in their work, no matter what it is, if there is any prospect for high performance and quality. I have three suggestions to offer:

For one, *automate and reconceive the work*. If a task is so boring and repetitive, there is probably a way to reorganize the work so that mindless tasks can be taken over by computers and the parts that demand more judgment and higher skill will be more prevalent. For another, *elevate people's responsibilities*. Managers who think in mechanistic terms tend to create jobs that are more and more narrow in scope and responsibility, ultimately reducing them down to their most meaningless, assembly line components. Instead, absorb the more boring and pedestrian parts of the work into more interesting kinds of engagements. We saw both of these ideas work their magic in the case of Barry's Sales Purchasing and Receiving Department. Once people elevated their work to taking on responsibility for something important, they themselves pushed for more and more automating of their (once protected and coveted) paper pushing.

For another, *outsource*. It is true that there is always some work that people have to do that doesn't fit with what others in the company are doing. The company has to focus on getting important things done, and there is no way some tasks can fit into the direct line marked out by the Arrow of Value and be accorded high levels of respect or recognition. In a bustling insurance office, for instance, there is very little a manager can do to tie sweeping floors into the mission of providing good service to its customers. By way of contrast, a high-tech facility that makes semi-conductor chips demands that the ambient air in the fabrication areas must have fewer than one particle of dust per millions of parts of air. Here, cleanliness throughout a facility is critical. Sweeping floors is much more highly valued.

The same work has different meanings in the two contexts. There is nothing intrinsically demeaning about this work. The key is to have the work done by people for whom the work is valued. Hire a company for whom the work and the positions required to do the work are meaningful. In this case, a cleaning company will take responsibility for creating some value in the work of its employees. Maybe that value is that this is a job that gets people out of trouble, or maybe it is the first job they held after emigrating to this country. The value in these jobs is that it is work that commands a pay check and puts them into the mainstream of working people. There is pride and dignity in what these people are accomplishing, and the good managers of these companies find ways to harness that pride in order to create value for their customers.

There is just no doubt that there are also limits to the expansiveness and enrichment a company can offer in its work at any point in time. Coaching can help for a while by giving aspiring workers larger responsibilities or greater decision-making discretion, or by rotating people through several positions to expand professional horizons. But there is no denying that eventually even these devices will wear out. Sadly, a manager also has to be willing and able to recognize that sometimes a company can't change at the same pace individuals grow. There does come a time when people have to move on.

When it comes down to the bottom line, our answer to the skeptics is this: If you really want to keep aspiring people, you must be willing to *push back any and all self-imposed limitations on your own aspirations,* then conceive of ideas and act on them in a way that can achieve greatness.

Here we introduce Frank Maris (not his real name), a vice president of Atlantic Wireless Corporation, who has staked his career on the proposition that work is about more than a pay check, that it is about the heart it takes to elevate your life and the lives of those with whom you come into contact in the course of your work. In our story, we see how Frank taps these inner resources in the people that work for him.

Frank's vision is a fitting way to end our presentation, because it summarizes, in so many ways, the kind of managerial effort we have been piecing together throughout this volume. With the images Frank so colorfully spins in our minds, we propose a different kind of career development path for managers. This path is not the vertical route, straight up the hierarchy ladder, but rather a path that circles outward in ever-widening arcs, bringing more and more people into the regime of flow and high performance. This is the path of the "Strategic Heart," in which people's energies are nourished and enriched, creating new horizons for action and fulfillment in everything they and their companies do. It is the path on which strategic organizations drive the value-creating changes that touch all of our lives.

THE STRATEGIC HEART: CREATING THE NEXT CHALLENGE

Frank manages the technicians and engineers who build the network of switches, transmitters and receivers that comprise a wireless communications system. This department spends the lion's share of the company's capital budget and is the branch of the company that has the highest local visibility in the community. Frank resembles the youthful, trim Teddy Roosevelt (without the moustache). The resemblance doesn't stop with looks. Like Roosevelt, Frank drives himself and others to succeed, but succeed with a difference. He is not interested in the narrow sense of success defined as status and position; he irrepressibly and unrelentingly pursues those actions and decisions that make whatever he and his people do count for something—for the company, each other and the community.

When you walk into the capacious switch assembly facility where Frank Maris works, you see more than 30 flags hanging from the rafters high overhead. There are several state flags—Massachusetts, Virginia, Texas, and many more—national flags including Vietnam, and even a flag of the Marine Corps. The sight is inspiring, and the message is liberating, spiritual in many ways. Our eyes are drawn upward. And, instead of seeing steel superstructure and concrete, we see a collage of colorful flags symbolizing that we all have come from somewhere and, by our collaborative actions, we are aspiring to continue on this journey and make a difference in the lives of our customers.

Frank summed up his philosophy of management to me this way: "I can't pay my managers enough for what I have to ask them to do. I can't ask them to work for this," he says, reaching into his pocket and pulling out a wad of dollar bills, "so I've got to ask them to work for something else. I ask them to work for this. . . ." He reaches into a box on the table in front of him and pulls out a black horseshoe.

"Now," he continues in his Southwestern twang, "if I filled up the back of my pick-up truck with thousands of these things and went to the scrap metal yard, I've been told they'll give me about $6.00 for the whole load. So that isn't worth a whole lot of money. So why do I think they'll work for this? Hell, it's not even peanuts, it's just plain old horseshoes. Why? Because of who it is these are given to. These black-painted horseshoes are given out at our monthly managers meeting to those people who have gone above and beyond their job descriptions. And they've done so in one of several ways.

"For example, I gave a horseshoe to the three people I promoted from supervisor to manager. Why them? Wasn't the promotion enough? Well, no it isn't. The promotion says we want you to do this job. The horseshoe says we're counting on you for your heart, not just your time. It's a pledge—if you take the horseshoe you take the pledge. Then there's Trich Binh, he's one of the boat people from Vietnam. He came in here barely able to speak English. Now he's a supervisor. He's got a wall of these horseshoes—for learning English, for going to engineering school at night, for doing whatever the team needed him for, for helping others.

"Can I pay someone for that? Hell, no. Do I need that kind of effort on my team? Hell, yes. How am I going to get that effort? There's only one way: I've got to pay attention and let others know that I'm paying attention.

"I don't believe in rewards like the 'Employee of the Week.' That kind of thing gets too political. I want 100 employees of the week, and I want everyone else knowing that they can be one too. So the horseshoe is only part of the program. I don't choose most of these people. Their peers and reports do. I ask for recommendations, and everyone that is nominated gets something. They also get the letter read about them in front of everyone. Sometimes I have to take matters in my own hands, if I know that someone is really pulling but others haven't quite realized it yet. Binh was in that situation several times.

"That means everyone is paying attention—not to just the work that is getting done, but to the personal spirit, heart that others are putting into it. It means that this person is recognized for the human being he or she is. We try to make 'psychic deposits,' as one of my employees says. Now I've seen people give up their titles or their positions for one reason or another; but try to take their horseshoe away for any reason, and you'll see what these things mean to them.

"I never put a person in a position that he or she has already done for years and years. It's funny, but I'm suspicious about the people with the perfect resumes. In my experience they are never the ones that seem to excel. Maybe it's that the work is just routine for them, another day at the office. Who needs that? It's the ones that have all the basic equipment—the brains, the energy, the knowledge, the heart—but have never done this particular thing before, that succeed according to my definition. These people never fail to accomplish something significant. At a minimum, they're stretching and growing in their jobs. It's not boring for them. Mostly, this philosophy has worked, and these people succeed.

"You know why I think it works out that way? Because they're learning too much to be arrogant, they're too excited about the opportunity to be satisfied and they're too grateful to be insensitive. They're paying attention, too: They have to learn from the people who report to them; they have to keep in touch with me about what is happening; they have to learn what the numbers mean and where the trends might be leading. Now these are the people that are really fun to be with."

MANAGING AND FLOW

No work can ever be an occasion for flow if it does not have an element of aspiration in it. But fostering individual aspirations is as elusive a goal as the mythical grail. A will to aspire to something is beyond most individuals' conscious control, no less managerial control. There are no proven "techniques" or managerial structures that can turn this quality on.

Managers can easily quash the aspirations of those in their charge. In situations where managers fail, this is usually the first thing people point to: The big managerial ego that has to take all the credit, that doesn't allow for experimentation, that just wants people's eight or ten hours a day. Aspirations demand that a person be willing to let go of whomever they were yesterday in service to a greater goal. That goal often goes beyond the control of the manager in charge, puts him in a position where to make the idea work he has to make changes, negotiate with others to change and risk failure or the opprobrium of colleagues and superiors.

The attitude of the person in flow presents the growing business with good news and bad news. The good news is that peak performance is not something that always translates into dollar costs. Frank's horseshoes graphically symbolize this fact. They provide a means to acknowledge and reward what no organization could ever pay for: heart. The bad news is that meeting this more intangible demand can be more difficult for managers. In Mage's work with growing companies, a great deal of our efforts focus on helping managers expand these dimensions of their work. Our approach stems from three basic principles:

- For companies to grow—in revenue, size, market position and complexity—its managers' vision of their roles and interpersonal capabilities have to grow.
- Managers can grow.
- Managers that evolve to higher levels of interpersonal vision and skill can engender flow and thus can manage more complex, more capable organizations.

Our idea of growth focuses on managers fostering the experience of flow in the workplace in order to increase the complexity of both the individual worker and the company as a whole. The growing organization expands its capability, taking on more and more difficult and significant tasks in people's lives and in the marketplace—widening the dimensions of the work each person is able to do and widening the significance and value of that work. To accomplish this managers need to grow by expanding their own ability to use the workplace as a locus of vision, creativity and aspiration. This is not a matter of broadening their technical horizons. Managers need to grow by letting go of their own professional or technical "competence" and letting others' abilities and interests take over. Managers do this by focusing on the people, enriching their experience of what is happening and then blending individual initiative with the company's forward-looking mission and values.

The New Managerial Roles

Doing this kind of work presents a big challenge for managers, a leap into the unknown. Typically, their energies and thoughts have been fixated on other things: succeeding at the task in front of them, pleasing the boss, bucking for that next promotion. Little thought is given to the track of personal development—their own development, no less that of others. Like Phil Jefferies in Chapter 7, young managers find that just multiplying the technical skills they used as workers doesn't lead to success, but instead produces resentment, anger and cynicism. When they arrive at their goal of greater power and influence, they find themselves at a loss for understanding what is expected of them.

In our work with clients, we look at the different roles managers have to adopt if they are going to become more capable of leading people in organized, concerted actions that accomplish larger visions. After helping young managers master basic techniques for measuring and monitoring large-scale production, we focus on developing the skills used in marshalling the spirits and energies of more and more people into more and more interdependent actions.

To make our point, we have distinguished three qualitatively different kinds of roles for managers: "Producing Roles," "Organizational Roles" and, finally, "Strategic Roles." We give a name to each of the roles and cite their organizational function, which highlights the quality of focus each of them demands of those who work for a manager. The "producer," for instance, wants the work to get out on time, within the budget, and drives people to get that done. No exceptions are accepted, just use the approved methods and techniques *consistently* in order to get the job done. The kinds of actions involved in fulfilling these roles are then described in greater detail.

Producing Roles. Producing roles were once thought to comprise the sum total of what managers were supposed to do. In the past, it was the outstanding "producers" who were promoted into management positions and pushed up through the hierarchy. Their vision of managing is to become a "director." These task masters and analysts support and depend on the mechanistic styles of management we see stifling people's strategic initiative and degrading their work into meaningless, disconnected tasks. But for us, these actions constitute only a small part of what is demanded of managers today.

In fact, it is precisely these roles that we advocate be handed over to the workers themselves through the tools we have introduced, including areas of responsibility, CSFs and self-managing teams. The collectors at Eastern Wireless, for instance, were more than capable of monitoring themselves and establishing the kinds of standards and measurements by which to measure their effectiveness. By creating their own meetings and informal networks, they showed how capable they were at coordinating the communications they needed to grow and improve. When these roles are internalized by the workers themselves, however, they take on a different cast. They become a platform for discipline and innovation and open the way for workers to experience flow in their work.

Let's look at the roles we have designated as fitting this level of management. As producers, for instance, the collectors in Eastern Wireless, stuck to the phones and drove themselves to make the calls; but they focused on solving problems and arriving at productive outcomes with each call, rather than on meeting numerical call quotas. Solving problems, and knowing that they have the authority to do so, opens the way to full engagement with the customer, to challenge and creative responsiveness. Thus, each collector adopted the producer manager role and raised that role to a new level of productivity and effectiveness because it opened up the possibility of flow. They were also able directors of the process by being able to analyze their work and make changes that again increased the immediate feedback that lends itself to flow. Their recommendations maintained continuity with the essential mission of the department and with the good tools and practices they had evolved over time, but none of these were sacred when growth and new situations clearly called for improvements to be made. Each step they made along these lines, furthermore, contributed to the department's ability to become more capable, flexible and responsive as the company's exponential growth continued.

While producer roles (see Figure 10.1) are necessary to keep production moving smoothly and economically, they do not need specially designated "managers" to fulfill them. In fact, separating these production management roles from the work that is being done is harmful, detracting from the possibility of creating flow and thus degrading the quality of the work being done (not to mention degrading the work life of the employee). From the organization's perspective, if managerial time and resources are expended in these roles, decision makers are not taking into account the widening influence a manager's actions must have on the experience people have of their work. To restore that balance, we focus on those managerial decisions that effect the conditions, mindset, attitude and energy of workers in ways that either detract or enrich the working experiences they have. These decisions are encompassed in organizational and strategic roles.

Organizational Roles. Organizational roles highlight the ways managers seek out and use the organization's resources to help those who work for them perform at high levels, maximize productivity and optimize conditions for flow (see Figure 10.2). The objective here is to put these resources at the disposal of people who are on the line trying to accomplish something important for the company. Organizational managers are not just inwardly focused on the performance of the department. They are also outwardly focused, sensing what the department needs to be effective and thinking about and planning approaches to peers and superiors for getting these resources. They also "run interference" for the group, making sure that distractions are minimized and that people have a chance to concentrate, focus and do their work with the kind of continuity that can lead to flow. These managers operate on the level of interactive values that emphasize bringing people together.

One example of how organizational management roles are fulfilled involves Mac, the manager from Eastern Wireless who we introduced in the last chapter. As you recall, a task force from among the collectors was created with the charge to negotiate with the MIS Department about changing the screens that

Figure 10.1
Producing Roles

Role	Values Achievement	Action
Monitor	Control	Counts and measures the work that other people do. Uses quantitative standards. A person meets a goal or doesn't. Little more in the way of interaction.
Coordinator	Communications	Meets and greets. Makes sure the right people are present and informed about issues. Uses one-on-one or "broadcast" methods such as memos. Limited interaction.
Marketeer	Customer Consciousness	Surveys and tracks. Uses "academic" or other authoritative means to compile impressive data about the market. Interpersonal action has little influence on actions.
Producer	Consistency	A task master that drives others to perform up to a standard. Interaction is limited to making judgments about others' performance.
Director	Continuity	Analyzes and justifies the actions being done. Interaction is limited to gathering information that can be used in the battles to come.

would be accessed during a call. Early in the process, a manager from MIS approached Mac with a problem. It seemed he was a bit put out by the fact that he wasn't dealing on this problem with Mac, but with nonmanagerial personnel. Mac had to spend quite a bit of time mollifying him. ''The fact is,'' Mac

Figure 10.2
Organizational Roles

Role	Values Achievement	Action
Coach	Choice	Works intensively with others to help them make choices that advance their pursuits. High levels of interaction are needed in order to understand motivations, fears and opportunities and translate into plans for each individual.
Facilitator Broker	Readiness	Exerts focus and drive to assure that proper resources are available to people when needed. A lot of interaction with both those being managed and others in the company to assess and meet needs.
Champion	Innovation	Pulls all needed resources and people together (especially into genuine teams) and creates a "can do" atmosphere in which peak performance is expected and achieved.

explained, "these are the people that have the authority to request these changes and design their screens. I have nothing to add." Here, Mac was fulfilling the roles of facilitator and champion to a tee. He made initial connections for his task force and then went to bat for them so that they could truly fulfill their roles as self-managing producers.

Every organizational success needs these three organizational management roles to be fulfilled well. Facilitators and brokers clear a path for people to make changes. They interpret what a group or team wants to accomplish to those affected by the change and then they channel resources to ventures and programs that have never existed before. They create justifications, not for what has happened but for the kinds of things that need to be done and have not yet been realized as being important. When the going gets tough, they become champions.

Champions are profoundly optimistic people. Managers fulfilling this role conceive the organization in a constructive light—being an "opportunity structure," as one writer put it,[2] rather than a labyrinth of barriers and obstructions. These managers love organizations and exude values that bring people together. They constantly have ideas about how people's talents can be combined and recombined for innovation. Champions become successful organizational managers when getting a "No" for an answer, they keep going back to the drawing board and devise new approaches until they get what they need for their people. When we work with Arrows of Value, the person who gets the "5" is the one who is fully engaged in the action—living and breathing it each and every hour of the day. This is the action's champion, the person whose responsibility it is to make the action happen or die trying. Thus, no action can be successfully completed without this champion being present.

As to the coaching role, when managers act as coaches, they also have to be facilitators and champions. The coach guides the way to the intense and valuable experiences in which people experience flow, and thus change and grow. There is no part of the manager's behavior that is more important on the job. But that means these managers, to keep the faith with those being coached, have to help bring to fruition the resultant initiatives people have devised. The manager's day is thus driven from first acting as the results-producing coach and then extending into the organization, wheeling, dealing and cajoling others to crystalize the department's, team's or individuals' efforts into accomplishment.

When we work with companies, we build on the talents of those managers that are adept at these organizational roles and elevate managers mired in producing roles into organizational roles. These roles can be taken on by any manager. Managers don't need promotions or further authority to adopt them. People that excel are able to envision what the organization is there to do and what more they as managers can do with these resources than with personality or temperament. For instance, our work with Phil Jefferies in Chapter 7 was oriented toward changing his vision of his work from being a producer to a champion. He is, and will always be, an introverted type of personality. But by reorienting his vision of what it takes to create large-scale organizational change, he essentially adopted a different role with everybody involved in the project.

The same process was used with Terry at Barry's Sales. When we started our work with him, he was completely ensconced in the monitor role. He had his people working like bureaucrats and assumed the role of measuring and counting their output. He thought that was what managers did. Our work with him was to elevate him into the role of coach—where he expressed and enforced the kinds of values that demanded that the people in the department grow and become more effective in their work.

Strategic Roles. This next set of roles is qualitatively different from the other two (see Figure 10.3). Not only are they completely interactive and interpersonal but completely "invisible" or "informal." By that I mean that a "superior" can't promote people into positions that have the titles or responsibilities. Quite the opposite, in fact. The titles, exemplar, mentor or master are, in a sense, honorific: they can only be bestowed on someone by the people who are affected by them. There are no official titles that identify these positions, and even the most entry-level person can exhibit the characteristics we describe.

These roles are offered to managers by those whom they manage, and no one else, out of recognition and appreciation. They encompass responsibilities and expectations that go far beyond what any hierarchical title or functional job description can enumerate because they reflect how certain people enrich the working lives of those they touch. They are roles that only exist because they embody values that bring others into an endeavor that is bigger than any one person, an adventure that is mutually envisioned and jointly accomplished, for the benefit of all.

The "exemplar" is a person who has a presence that seems to be able to help get people off the dime, moving, motivated and focused. Many of the exemplars I have met are shy people, never "charismatic" in the classical sense of being "inspirational" in their words or flamboyant in their expression. They bring coherence to the actions people perform out of the force of their own efforts. While they may not inspire creativity or risk-taking from afar, or through the effectiveness of a speech or pep talk, they do inspire imitation of their grit, determination by setting an example in the way they work.

The values of the exemplar are oriented toward keeping things moving. Seemingly out of nowhere, they generate ideas and solutions with ease, carrying the vision and mission on their backs. Their continual activity and drive have a clear and apparent logic to them that is appealing. They embody coherence and determination, while never forgetting that everyone is needed to accomplish the mission.

The "mentor" is a person dedicated to elevating others, through their work, to new levels of excellence, growth and self-esteem. Mentors combine a love of their work with true concern for and belief in other people. As such, they exhibit an unyielding and uncompromising demand for excellence while striking chords of empathy and understanding in people. Mentors foster conditions in which concentration is possible because they a forge a compelling relationship between the work and the people involved in getting the work done. The work and the people matter. "This work isn't much fun, but it matters to my mentor, and I know others are counting on me," the protege thinks. "I'd better do it

Figure 10.3
Strategic Roles

Role	Values Achievement	Action
Exemplar	Cohesion	Gives people a concrete vision of how well things can be done and how great an impact their actions can have. Energizes people by making great efforts seem within reach, and great results genuinely attainable.
Mentor	Concentration	Helps people to envision and grasp a higher purpose and greater sense of opportunity in the work they do.
Master	Constancy	Instills in people a sense of organizational purpose and mission for the long haul. Makes great changes seem not only possible, but necessary and fun. Offers a clear vision of how individual efforts are multiplied by committed and selfless actions and by working in teams.

well.'' Mentoring is completely reciprocal: mentors and proteges choose each other. People who are attracted to mentors are usually also chosen by that mentor who sees the potential for excellence in them.

Finally, the ''master'' is the manager who naturally embodies an organization's highest capabilities, potentials and energy. Nothing seems impossible in the presence of the master. In fact, the outstanding characteristic of the master is that he or she makes dramatic and strategic level change seem like fun, despite the risks. They inspire the question, "What else would I want to be doing but this?" Masters are outgoing, but are often understated and not particularly eloquent; they have a deep conviction and belief about the direction of the company, but they are not ego-driven. They are inclusive, looking only for accomplishment, never credit. People feel in the spell, under the sway and influence of this person, and willingly work within it. Masters exude constancy: that steady, focused, energized work each and every day will accomplish the mission. Those who work for the master manager know this is true.

In my opinion, no organization can succeed for long without having people in prominent leadership positions who are willing, able and accomplished in strategic roles. I would say, an organization that doesn't have these roles filled amidst its ranks is leaderless. Among those we have cited in this chapter, these are the roles that make it possible for organizations to change and grow. Producing roles use the organization to deliver the goods and services that customers demand, organizational roles leverage the organization's resources to raise the level of its people's performance and strategic roles elevate everyone to the task of changing that organization—elevating responsibilities, envisioning new possibilities that can come from change and keeping focused and excited about the tasks and actions performed in order to drive that change.

Of the managers we have talked about so far, I think Norma, the Collections Department Supervisor we profiled in the last chapter, is a highly successful exemplar. As you recall, her senior managers mistakenly identified her as a reason for the department's inability to adapt to Harry's call for a more dynamic and expansive organization. The people in the group were fiercely loyal to her, feeling they had a part in her growth and success. In other words, she exemplified what they could achieve in terms of growth and professional advancement. When she took on the task of creating terms, she once again pointed the way to what was possible if people were willing to adopt new ways of working and interacting. She created a course of action and energized everyone to rise to the occasion. She not only improved people's work performance, she provided a concrete presentation of what it was possible for them all to achieve by growing personally and applying their energies in the workplace.

Frank is an example of the mentor. In fact, for him I would almost be willing to create a new category called "grand mentor." He has a strikingly unique ability to mentor many people, as well as nurture individuals one at a time. Through his meetings and classy, skillful use of symbols, he creates an environment where change is expected, surprises accepted and extra effort unfailingly recognized.

What is so thrilling about Frank's approach is that he takes what might be thought of as mechanical, procedure-bound tasks (his engineering group builds and maintains the towers and switches for Atlantic Wireless), and turns them into expansive opportunities for personal growth. As his personal mission, Frank has taken the task of enriching each step of his people's working lives by dramatizing the appreciation they feel when they envision and act on possibilities for learning and challenge. His ceremonies and speeches show how each step of personal commitment and initiative toward expanding the capabilities of others and the organization contributes to something larger and strengthens everyone involved with the department and the company.

The master role emerges out of being eminently successful at the mentor and exemplar roles. When people have elevated and energized others throughout their careers, they build up the kinds of expectations, trust and stature that thrusts them into the master manager role. Master managers are almost always senior managers—presidents, vice presidents and general managers. They are masters because they are able to reach out and be effective with their whole organization. So they inspire, as does the mentor, but from more of a distance. They provide role models, as do exemplars, but not a path that most people want to imitate. Rather, people see in the master's presence and personality bits and fragments that they can internalize and adopt as their own validation of values and aspirations.

Personal and down to earth on a one-on-one basis, master managers are at once approachable yet, somehow, they stand apart as well. While never losing a "common touch," the master manager is actually guiding a whole organization to new horizons by the powers of conviction, open-hearted understanding and open-minded focus. They are so anchored in their values that people feel safe, even as everything changes around them. Again, master managers are regarded as completely human and fallible, and yet they help people transcend their present circumstances. They lead people into realms never explored before. The people in the company ascribe creating and grasping the vision of what lies ahead to the master managers in their organizations—and they accept that responsibility.

Harry Kaufman is one of the master managers I have met. He was certainly a good production and organizational manager. His prowess as a director and even a champion was immediately evident to us in how well and smoothly his company ran. But, it was by virtue of his complete dissatisfaction with this achievement and his need to have his company be a spirited, vital, alive and heartfelt one, that demonstrated his master status. He was there to enrich lives, not merely to get a product out the door.

Harry coined the term "results-producing coach" because he believed it was the interpersonal contact and attention that managers provided that would lead to superior performance. He instituted the Idea Teams because he wanted everyone to be involved in the process of moving the company forward. He never allowed self-serving politics to diminish the organization's growing capability. How effective is the master manager in terms of delivering to the bottom line? The properties Harry managed had never performed as well as they did under his leadership, and they never performed as well again when he was promoted and had to move on to new corporate challenges.

When he was promoted to a new position and had to leave Eastern Wireless, one of the secretaries explained her tears to me: "Almost every morning he'd walk around carrying his coffee cup and say, 'Hello,' to people. That showed me that he knew who we were, and that it was okay to need a little help getting going in the morning. He just had that touch about him." He provided a way for everyone to find a fragment or piece of something to identify with that could lift them to the level of performance needed.

CONCLUSION: FROM EMPLOYEES TO "PROTEGES"

Aspiring people do not need the carrot of a promotion, but their aspirations do have to be nourished by the sense of possibility. While an ambitious person always wants that tangible reward, that trophy signifying the win, the person who aspires wants an open road. The image of flow captures this sense. Flow is about transformation—transforming a challenge into an opportunity, a fear into a success, one's life from a series of tasks to a field of growth and expansiveness. The aspiring person wants to know that there are more people whose eyes can be lit up, other ways that a message or capability can be disseminated to others, new skills that can open up a heretofore unattainable accomplishment.

The roles we have mapped out are more important for managers to understand and to achieve than ever before. Technical competence has a shorter and shorter time value, while the value of people who can grow in their work and the vision they have of their work is priceless. In today's businesses, managers have to begin with the assumption that however they used to do things, whatever they knew about the work their people are doing, is probably obsolete. The manager is not the expert on the line of fire. Managers provide a global view of the situation, assess priorities, create an atmosphere of urgency and focus, provide encouragement and insight that is specifically appropriate to each person on that line. They are not responsible for generating all the solutions to problems, but they have to provide their people with an understanding of the organization and how things work within it.

There's nothing "hands-off" about this approach at all. Managers are intimately and intensely involved in the work that is being done. It's just that the manager's work is different: it is to focus on the person and that person's ability to achieve optimal experience, flow and performance. The people they work with and manage are not regarded as employees or "subordinates," they are *proteges*—people whose skills, talents and insights are being expanded and integrated into a large field of action and decision making. The protege is the one that still has to perform the tasks. What managers can know, however, is the personality and temperament of their proteges and use that information to spur them on to new levels of performance. They can shape the adversities and difficulties employees face so they are a challenge and not set-ups for defeat. By means of their example, inspiration and attention, they invite the workers' initiative and make it pay for the company and everyone involved.

Ultimately, to imbue others' work with aspiration means bringing to everyone's full attention the service they perform in the course of their work. Of course, people don't work for free (although, I have heard people who experience flow and aspiration in their work exclaim, "I can't believe I am so lucky that I am getting paid for this work!"). It is rather that they aspire to serve a higher purpose in the work they do. That is the point of Frank's horseshoes. He can't pay his people money for their aspiration to perform in the spirit of achievement and service to the company, the community and their co-workers. He can only pay for the work that is in accord with what the company is able to afford before it has realized its profits and growth and for what the market at the present time will bear. Even bonus and profit sharing can't cover all the energy and heart it takes to drive toward greater complexity and capability in our lives.

But Frank realizes he can fully recognize and pay homage to their service with ceremony and ardent appreciation that doesn't get lost in the daily grind. He can work with his colleagues and his bosses to see that something worthwhile, if not worth cash, can really come from this kind of effort that will benefit everyone. He can also work hard to help his people see how their aspirations do matter in the work they have been asked to do. Finally, he can show that these aspirations do matter to him and to everyone involved with the service offered. That demonstration of connection with a person's will to aspire is the essence of the business manager's highest and most challenging (and rewarding) role—tapping into the energy and power of the strategic heart.

NOTES

1. Lao-tzu, *Tao te Ching* (17), trans. Stephen Mitchell (New York: HarperPerennial, 1988).

2. Robert A. Burgelman, "Corporate Entrepreneurship and Strategic Management: Insights from a Process Study," *Management Science* 29, no. 12 (December 1983): 1353.

Chapter 11

Conclusion

And when we start to identify with the evolution of complexity, when we begin to recognize our kinship with the rest of creation, then it will be easier for us to free ourselves from the constricting needs of the self, from the terror of meaningless mortality.
—Mihaly Csikszentmihalyi, *The Evolving Self*[1]

TOWARD GREATNESS: THE ORGANIZATIONAL IMPERATIVE

The mythical lonely entrepreneur can still produce interesting novelties that perform specific and limited functions, but to make an idea into a socially and commercially successful product requires large-scale, distributed authority and integration. The sophistication required to design, manufacture and market today's products and services demands large-scale, open organizations that amplify (not stymie and stifle) human creative energy. Designing technologies and linking together people from around the world in a single communications network, treating disease and increasing agricultural yields through biogenetic engineering, developing new sources of energy, knitting together worldwide financial markets and managing the accelerated pace of trading they offer, all require large scale organization.

I see the trends accelerating in this direction every day. A great deal of Mage's work in recent years has been concentrated on companies that have had to vastly expand the range of their offerings if they were to stay competitive. Companies that once only made products, if they were to remain independent, had to offer service and had to have the means available to provide for continuous improvement (that meant capital to buy another company or an ability to generate improvements internally). These companies immediately became more complex in terms of what their outputs had to be, and the demands made on their employees became more stringent and pressing. The decision makers in these companies had to learn to tap into their "Strategic Hearts" and create dynamic, human-centered organizations. They came to appreciate that organizational thinking had to become a prime focus of managerial attention and be put high up on a list of requirements for reward, recognition and promotion. Demonstrating the ability to nurture organizations that engender flow and enable people to perform at their best became requirements for advancement in these companies that was equal to the ability to generate sales or make production processes efficient (the only recognized paths to promotion in most companies today).

If businesses are to be about greatness, organizational development cannot be relegated to the sidelines as a by-product of production and sales. These demands to create and recreate dynamic organizations won't go away. This is not a fad. It is now our job to conceive and create new ways to collaborate with more and more people on endeavors that only many minds, hearts and talents can accomplish.

Facing decision makers now is the demand to relate to their worlds in new ways. Below we summarize a few of the demands that business leaders now have to meet in order to succeed in the business world that is quickly evolving. We cite the need to reexamine decision-making assumptions and processes around four areas: markets, ethics, the community and the natural environment. These are aspects of the larger world to which the near chaos organization needs to hone its senses and respond in a dynamic, flexible way.

Value Strategy, Not Market Share

No longer are profits solely derived from process efficiencies and economies of scale. Monitoring these aspects of production is necessary in order to optimize an organization's responsiveness and to maximize its realization of potential profits. Now, however, profits are primarily created by offering products or services that drive toward high priority status in customers' lives. In the language of complexity, they act as, or are closely allied to, an "attractor" technology around which an increasingly influential industry is built. In Mage's work with clients, we distinguish this orientation to markets and decision-making, which we call "Value Strategy,"[2] with conventional market share strategies.

The market share strategy is based on the model of driving to accumulate a vast share of the products and services that define the status quo. Economies of scale can be built up because demand is relatively predictable and stable over long periods of time. Fewer and fewer industries have that luxury. With technological innovation pressuring every aspect of business, decision makers have to be able to adjust, make changes quickly and reenvision what products are capable of producing value and how these products and services will be pro-

Figure 11.1
Driving Toward the Center of Influence

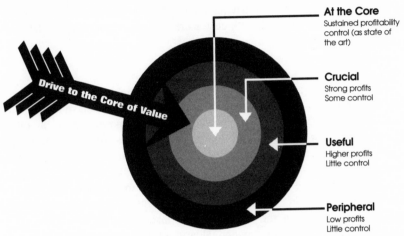

At the Core
Sustained profitability
control (as state of
the art)

Crucial
Strong profits
Some control

Useful
Higher profits
Little control

Peripheral
Low profits
Little control

duced and delivered. Now profits are derived from commanding the resources, talent and expertise to be ahead of the curve, and instead of simply responding to what happens, to actually drive the changes and let others adapt. The new strategy compels decision makers to drive their businesses to occupy a piece of the center of influence, to be capable of affecting the course of development of a whole technology or sector of technology (see Figure 11.1).

This factor weighs heaviest on three aspects of a decision maker's life: investment, research and development (R&D) and risk. As for investment, value strategy entails making the necessary investments that drive the company toward the center of influence or, if already in that center, to keep it moving in a more encompassing and expansive way in order to stay there.

As one moves toward the center of influence in an industry, the barriers to entry get higher (equipment and expertise is more expensive, for instance). Profits are stressed for years and years as decision makers drive the business toward the center of value creation. The risks are always higher because new skills and better organizational capabilities are required in order to succeed in regimes that are closer to the center. And, finally, R&D costs remain high. There is always the risk of failure, and transforming an idea into a viable product is never an easy task. The learning curve remains steep for the foreseeable future.

Stockholders and owners have to be primed to invest for the long term, not quarterly returns. Selling the company is always an option that will provide for a one-time killing, but usually companies that are either swallowed up or are successful in an Initial Public Offering have had to succeed in growing and progressing in just the manner we have talked about. The *status quo* companies, cash cows as they are called, are usually digested and absorbed after having been drained of their vitality. They never command either the high profits, nor the promise of them, that garner large multiples in the mergers and acquisitions world. So a value strategy of driving toward the center of influence is the only strategy that creates both value for customers and reward (in time) for the shareholders.

Ethics

It has never been more important for decision makers to behave in a way that personifies the highest sense of human value and purpose. Simple, moralistic bromides have lost their efficacy in our society. Business life has become more complex, and the ethical and moral demands on decision makers have become more ambiguous.

Deals have become so nuanced and complicated, they require teams of lawyers to figure them out. Many kinds of business transactions can no longer be policed at all. Much of the commerce that takes place around software, for instance, depends on the honesty and integrity of the software users not to pirate the program they install on their personal computers. On another level, as we noted in Chapter 10, much of what we ask of our employees goes beyond what we could ever hope to pay them. What are the ethics of compensation when these kinds of ambiguities assert themselves?

Ethics have recently become a recognized course in many MBA programs. Many believe these courses were introduced in response to a prevalent judgment that graduates of business schools were more concerned about impressing their superiors with results that showed on the bottom line than they were about ethics. However valid that observation is, another reason for elevating ethics in business to the academic level of study is certainly that educators have finally realized that in many business situations, it is often very difficult to figure out the right thing to do.

Today's business questions demand a new kind of thinking and acting. When Mage conducts its values programs with companies, we find that all participants gain new insights into what the business is about and what their roles and responsibilities are. Organizational changes ensue, and people behave with a heightened sense of responsibility. In essence, people work hard to go beyond merely understanding what product or service customers will buy. They also work to sense just what it is that customers, employees and other stakeholders need them to do to be a part of something that is important in their lives. They work to understand what it is the other side in the transaction values in their actions—and they adjust their behavior in order to provide it better. They work to do the most valuable things for everyone involved. None of this happens by way of assumptions or merely by past experience. Business leaders that are able to have conversations about the company's values and the personal values it requires in order to succeed become the masters that elevate the performance of everyone they contact.

Environmentalism

Businesses require a diverse and thriving "natural" (that is, not human-adapted) environment around them. "Nature," even in its human delimited form, has both a symbolic and life-giving force in our lives that cannot be replaced: it provides a symbiotic base for the vital energies we need as humans to be energized and inspired; it offers an intellectual vision of complexity that creates new analogies by which we can continue to create and innovate; it provides an immediate experience of the complex system of life that is larger than any individual and so feeds our imagination as to the scope and depth life encompasses.

If business is about creating life-enhancing products and services, we cannot lose that larger-than-life perspective "nature" offers to our senses and sensibilities. If all we have around us are humanized habitats, we diminish the capacity to transcend our own boundaries.

Exploiting and degrading the remainder of the world's reserves for species other than humans will always be an issue as population explodes. But technology also offers some remedies—recycling, synthetics and bio-engineered materials. In the short term, these products and services add cost to individual products, but in the long run they not only create an industry that itself creates value (necessitated by the overwhelming power of human enterprise), but also preserves the vital source of our own existence. Environmentalism is a core constituent of our endeavoring toward complexity.

New Roles in the Community

With the world moving toward greater complexity, business decision makers, more than any other professionals, are engaged in organizational design and collaborative production. Each and every day they are devising new forms of organization to accomplish ever more challenging ends. This points to a new role for today's business leaders. Now they have the opportunity to become the scions of organizational development and reform. They can revitalize these older, traditional institutions by teaching them how to organize on larger scales in ways that build the kinds of collaboration and open-minded eliciting of performance that makes businesses successful.

Take education, for instance. Governments can no longer act as the sole leaders in this field. Bureaucrats in Washington, state capitals or sitting on politicized school boards do not create the demands for skills and talents that shape the future. They depend on business decision makers to tell them how to match the needs of the community with the demands of new imperatives. Traditional, child-centered education is still within the means of governmentally driven education, since its requirements are basic, elemental and universally required. (Although in recent years the ability of governments to respond to the competing cultural demands on schools, as well as to keep up with the crush of changing learning technologies and methodologies, puts this comfortable assumption in question.)

But the firewall between "liberal education" and business at the level of higher education is losing its purpose. That purpose will entirely disappear when business decision makers themselves appreciate that in order to meet the demands of increasing complexity in their worlds, education needs to be broadly inclusive. Businesses can benefit as much from people with artistic sensibilities (from their ability to envision new possibilities and new understandings of the experience we have of our living worlds), or writing skills (from their ability to organize and articulate concepts and ideas that congeal diffuse impressions into actionable goals and organizational principles) as they can from narrowly focused technologists (whose education has to be continually refreshed in order to keep up with ever accelerating technological changes).

A community responds enthusiastically and supports a business that exemplifies worthwhile values and will guide its children to appreciate its efforts, look forward to working there and learn from it a proper way to plan and organize large-scale initiatives that benefit everyone.

RETHINKING EVOLUTION

As we approach the final pages of this book, we might pause to ask, "What do all these arduous efforts we make to advance and improve our organizations amount to anyway? Are we merely participating in a Sysiphisian effort of pushing a rock up a hill, only to have it roll back down so we have to start all over again?" The complexity model enables us to believe that all these efforts do amount to something, that businesses and the disciplines of guiding organizational growth have an important contribution to make in the grand scheme of things, that these efforts can be about true greatness.

What I am about to propose does have an element of fantasy in it—as all speculations do. But these ideas are sufficiently compatible with the possibilities opened up by the complexity model to warrant some attention. In the Introduction, we observed that business decision makers create institutions in which people work together in an organized way to accomplish shared goals. I would like to elevate this idea to a new level, and invite the reader to join in some speculation about how businesses can achieve not just commercial success, but social, cultural and historical greatness. Consider the possibility that business organizations can build on their already established roles as preeminent places where people collaborate on shared goals to become institutions of evolutionary import.

The "Memetic Code"

To make our case, we introduce a new term that has been coined in complexity circles. That term is "memes." As Csikszentmihalyi points out, the term was coined about twenty years ago by the biologist Richard Dawkins. It comes from the Greek word, *mimesis,* and points to the fact that

> [Our] cultural instructions are passed on from one generation to the next by example and imitation, rather than by the shuffling of genes that occurs between sperm and ova. Perhaps the best definition of a meme is "any permanent pattern of matter or information produced by an act of human intentionality. . . .
>
> At the moment of its creation the meme is part of a conscious process directed by human intentionality. But immediately after a meme has come into existence, it begins to react with and transform the consciousness of its creator, and that of other human beings who come into contact with it.[3]

Memes include all cultural artifacts—objects, tools, ideas, traditions and rituals—that define how we do things, and so give human culture definition and distinctiveness. In the context of the evolution of self-organized systems, *memes* act as a guide for human cultural and intellectual development in the same way that *genes* guide the process of biological evolution. Our intellectual heritage, including literature, science and social institutions are memes, as are the products we make and use in our daily lives. And, just as genetic evolution led to creatures of increasing complexity and then to intelligence, so too can memes develop into new forms of technical, social and organizational complexity.

As an example of how memes work, think about voice and data communications technology. These products and systems didn't even exist 100 years ago, and now we take all forms of communications technology for granted. Not only do we take the technology we use today for granted, we also look forward to the technologies that will evolve from these and more or less eagerly anticipate the changes they will make in our lives. The rapidity with which these innovations are incorporated into our lives seems to point to a human propensity to welcome certain kinds of changes to our life patterns and habits. It seems that our species was "programmed" to drive the incessant production of new memes rather than live in a certain preset way.

No Limits to Self-Organizing Evolution

While quite imposing sounding, the idea that there can be a new regime of evolution that goes beyond the biological is not so farfetched. When we look at the various materials and forms that constitute the universe, we already see how growing complexity creates emergent structures that transcend any capability possessed by its constituent parts. Physical self-organization gives rise to atoms from subatomic particles, molecules from atoms, then from molecules issue forth stars, solar systems and galaxies. When stars explode and release their highly complex molecules, these substances, under the right conditions of just the right amount of excitation, can form living beings.

We all acknowledge that the evolution of living beings constitutes a new, higher level of (complexity) organization over the physical, since these entities exhibit "behaviors," such as instantaneous responses to an environment, that are not observed in the more static physical realm. Another level of evolution starts to emerge when intelligent beings embark on paths to determine (self-organize) what mode of social conditions they live under. So the fact that evolution moves in a direction toward greater complexity means not only that matter combines in a way to create more complex organization, but that this organization of materials can evolve to completely new kinds of beings and entities that have heretofore unimagined capabilities. This is the phenomenon of "emergence" that characterizes complex systems: many entities combine functionality so that a completely new and transcendent capability emerges that none of the constituent elements can do (creating a whole that is truly greater than the sum of its parts).

Scientists can discern neither logical nor natural limits to the processes that yield greater complexity. These scientists cannot tell us why things organize into these ever more complex entities, and they can discern neither a guiding hand to evolution nor a necessity for the formation of more complex entities. That is still a transcendent mystery beyond the reach of our empirical knowledge. But these scientists do observe that a new form of greater complexity and capability emerges (1) when a material or system combines with other materials or systems; (2) when these combined materials are able to withstand being subjected to a high level of energy for an extended amount of time (perserving in a condition that is far beyond equilibrium or near chaos); and (3) when there exists an attractor that is of sufficient complexity and subtlety itself to coalesce these dynamic substances (break their equilibrium and symmetry). According to Prigogine, the Nobel Laureate, the probability that an entity of greater complexity emerges under these conditions is equal to one: that is, it *will* happen.

Each level of complexity relies on the stability of the preceding level. The constituents of a complex system have to be able to withstand the injection of high levels of energy and to combine with (not blend into) other elements in the environment. Still, each level has its own emergent characteristics that are not reducible to those constituents. "No man is an island," means that no individual human being, self-sustaining in some sense, can be complete without immersion and participation in a higher level of organization—a society.

Visible Emergence

For the sake of argument, let's adopt a "complexity cosmologist's" perspective and look at this phenomenon of human intelligence leveraged and amplified by burgeoning technology. Who is to say that the new forms of connection and interaction we observe don't constitute another new kind of self-organizing system? After all, many species form colonies (bees and ants, for instance), and some even have societies (wolves and other primates), so social organization is fully within the range of established forms of complexity. Advancing complexity enabled simple organisms that spawned in warm tidal pools to evolve into creatures that eventually were able to abandon the aquatic environment altogether and become completely terrestrial. Does this kind of trajectory of evolutionary development portend the possibility of a completely new level of evolution beyond the biological adaptation of bodily forms? I don't see what precludes that possibility.

There is nothing to prevent "intelligence" (that is, intelligent beings combined with the memes they have created) from organizing in a new way that constitutes a new evolutionary level. The fact that human beings choose and design the kinds of societies they will live in already points to the possibilities that intelligence opens up for organizational innovation. The first step along this path was taken when Johann Gutenberg invented the printing press and gave rise to the publication of books and newspapers. It allowed our intelligence to become concrete and usable. Our culture is dedicated to creating educational institutions, libraries and whole industries—computers, communications technology and advanced modes of transport—that support these capabilities. These artifacts of daily life, memes, are now being accelerated and more deeply interconnected by new forms of wireless communication, the Internet and a wide variety of ever more personalized broadcasting and publishing services. Taken together, this "exo-neural network" may constitute the basis around which can form a new self-organizing, self-sustaining system that transcends the biological regime.

One scientist, Frank Tipler of Tulane University, has speculated on just this theme. As interpreted by the respected science writers Paul Davies and John Gribbin, Tipler's position is explained this way:

[Intelligence] will eventually spread throughout the cosmos, participating more and more in the workings of nature, until it eventually reaches such an extent that it will have *become* nature. . . . [Intelligent] life—or more likely a network of computing devices—will spread out from its planet of origin (possibly Earth) and slowly but surely gain control over larger and larger domains. . . . Although the process may take trillions of years, in Tipler's scenario the upshot of this creeping "technologization" of nature will be the amalgamation of the whole cosmos into a single intelligent computing system.[4]

The New World and the "University/Business Complex"

Exactly what this new level of organization will look like is hard to predict. The best renderings we have so far are in the annals of science fiction. All we know is that it will be a process given shape by the way we modify and enhance the capabilities of our memes. If we look at the development of our economy from the perspective of our complexity cosmologist, we can see the seeds of something that indeed smacks of a growing complexity in our social/intellectual arrangements. Could this be the significance of the accelerating movement away from agriculturally based subsistence economies, first to industrial societies and then to post-industrial economies based on the development of advanced technologies and services? The reforming of our economic base may well be evidence of the self-developmental process that creates new memes upon which we can use our intelligence as a material around which to create a new level of self-adaptive, self-sustaining complex systems.

Then there is the development within our post-industrial society of what I have already described as the "exo-neural network," the interconnectivity on a massive scale that is taking place through our computer and communications industries. I include in that network everything from wired and wireless voice, image and data transmittal as well as the now multimedia communications available through computers via the Internet. Our complexity cosmologist might see this development as putting what were once internal data signal processing capabilities and/or ephemeral speech emanating from our brains into physical, modifiable, and globally accessible form. It is, in one sense, turning the output human mind into a physical, socially-based system that constitutes the *potential* to coalesce at a new level of self-organization.

Now consider how this scenario envisions an entirely new role and status for business. Businesses are the workhouses that transform these new capabilities into actual memes. They produce the artifacts and commercialize (make accessible, available and useful) the ideas that educated workers produce. They turn the output of raw intelligence into artifacts people find attractive enough to invest in. In so doing, they leverage their hard-earned resources in order to make these changes in their own lives.

Remember that one of the principles of complexity is that it is not the size or mass of the entity that makes it complex, but rather the high level of energy expended by its constituent parts as they coalesce around an attractor into an organized system. And the dramatic progress of world-changing technologies is not just thriving, it exudes an air of inevitability.

This process of life-changing production is the basis of our production system. Businesses either make new products that create value—that is, change people's lives, presumably for the better—or they perish. Just as plants grow upward and outward to be able to capture the sunlight that produces their living tissues, so too do businesses grow in order to create more value. Ideally, everyone involved in the system derives benefits. From the customer side, many people seem to have a natural attraction to technologies that promise to enhance and improve their lives. They are more than willing to expend their hard-earned resources in order to integrate these new products and services into their lives and willingly change certain aspects of their daily activities and reorganize their work and leisure patterns in order to do so.

When people buy these products, well-run businesses are able to realize profits. The complexity cosmologist sees profits as one of the necessary conditions for the emergence of that next level of evolution about which we speculate. The days when profits are seen as wealth expropriated from the social economy for the sake of private enrichment are gone, or certainly need to be. In one direction, when profits are being made, individuals are buying products so that their lives can be enhanced; and, in the other direction, profits feed the innovation businesses promise and so make possible the evolution of memes that can extend human creativity into utterly unlimited realms of possibility.

But Whence the New Attractor?

When value is created in an economy, the energies of our worldwide meme production system are unleashed. We have seen business's power to completely transform so many aspects of our lives. In fact, I see a great deal of today's despair being the result of the way businesses constantly overturn and destabilize the standards and expectations we have about what our lives can actually amount to. These churning, explosive, but value-creating actions push our whole society into a "far from equilibrium" condition that may be exciting, but is also disconcerting. Familiar old places are paved over and turned into sensibility-numbing shopping strips; people lose jobs. The process is out of control. So, what is still lacking on the historical scene, at this point in time, is a suitable attractor around which these volatile forces can coalesce.

It has become clear in recent decades that we are floundering in terms of integrating the changes generated by the business-knowledge complex of our social, cultural and political institutions. They have been slow to grasp the progressive and humanizing implications of what is happening and seem to lurch from one vapid, nostalgic platitude to another. If the myriad businesses and intellectual production houses (universities, think tanks, institutes, etc.) are to congeal into a functional system then, it appears, the farsighted actions of business, community and spiritual leaders will have to lead the way in forging an attractor that is capable of integrating visions and principles around which people can create an expanded collective sense of community, continuity and progress.

It is hard to know what this attractor will look like. Maybe there are some characteristics we can identify, though, that can give us an indication of how such a new level of organization might be possible. To create a force that is capable of congealing the efforts of the already large-minded visionaries that are driving the modern economy will be a challenge of monumental proportions. A sufficient attractor will be one (or combination of several) that will benefit each component of the system. A sufficient attractor will therefore be an *open* one, fluid and capable of sustaining and capturing a wide range of inputs, including ideas, images, technologies, energies and materials. Yet, it will be extremely *robust*. It will hang together with all these inputs blasting away and translate them into a coherent action or set of actions. I tend to think that such an attractor will be an *idea*, one that is even larger and more abstract than the idea of "value" that focuses our economy or "justice" that frames our society. And yet, it will be so *concrete* an image that everyone will be able to partake of it and be enlivened by its inspiration.

And surely no one person, authority or institution will create it or be able to sustain this attractor. In our history, we have benefitted from the visions of singular great individuals—messiahs like Gautama Sidhartha and Jesus, philosophers like Socrates, political leaders like Abraham Lincoln and Mahatma Ghandi. And by saying that business organizers will have to step to the fore, I certainly don't imply that we are counting on the likes of a Ross Perot to point a way to a new future. Rather, our new visionaries will have to find new ways to collaborate in new groups, institutions, councils and other governing bodies around the technologies and actions that are proven to be of such social benefit that competition and egos will be able to take a back seat. Authority in this new system will, therefore, be distributed among many people, groups and institutions.

These kinds of collaborations will point a way to a new sense of the standards of conduct and values required to create successful large-scale social endeavors. We can see this kind of progress already taking shape. Take the world revulsion to the horrors inflicted on the Balkan peoples during the past few years. This kind of ethnic-nationalist conflict was once standard political operating procedure—World Wars I and II being fought largely on the basis of what territory each ethnically demarcated nation sought to claim. Now this standard of national, ethnic or racial identity is thought to be primitive; and war or any kind of violence based on this standard is rightly adjudged as barbaric. Just the fact that this judgment now represents the standard of "civilized" conduct and not just an ideal constitutes progress toward developing higher level principles that support large-scale, open, distributed authority, organization.

While it is too easy to run wild with thoughts such as these—thoughts are free, after all—this speculation shows how "thinking complexity" can open up new vistas to appreciate and grasp the full human potential that businesses are on the threshold of creating. The point is that the "Strategic Heart" points to a vision in which doing business isn't just a matter of busy-work and making money, although there are days, months and years when it seems like it can be nothing else. Businesses can also be the workhouses of our evolution toward a new world of possibilities.

NOTES

1. Mihaly Csikszentmihalyi, *The Evolving Self* (New York: HarperCollins, 1993), p. 292.

2. See Michael Shenkman, *Value and Strategy: Competing Successfully in the Nineties* (New York: Quorum Books, 1992).

3. Csikszentmihalyi, *The Evolving Self*, p. 120.

4. Paul Davies and John Gribbin, *The Matter Myth: Dramatic Discoveries that Challenge Our Understanding of Physical Reality* (New York: Simon and Schuster, 1992), p. 308.

Appendix

Conifer Group, Sample Organizational Documents

CONIFER GROUP PRODUCTION DEPARTMENT MISSION STATEMENT

We promote total customer satisfaction by building and supporting high quality products which have been tested and proven to meet Conifer Group standards while conforming to exact customer specifications.

Through effective internal and external communication, we coordinate all activities of production, including inventory, receiving, testing, integration.

Our commitment to quality continues on to shipping, to deliver exactly what the customer requires, on time—every time—exceeding customers' time and service expectations.

CONIFER GROUP PRODUCTION DEPARTMENT

Area of Responsibility Scheduler

The scheduler assures that expectations of Conifer Group quality and service are met or exceeded by guiding all production stages from order entry, integration and text, through shipping and installation at the customer's site. By carefully reviewing customer order specifications, including components, cabling, system and application software, each order is treated individually and knowledgeably.

We make sure we can keep all our promises to the customer in terms of time, cost and quality assurance. Whenever possible, problems are anticipated or identified early so that delivery dates can be met or exceeded. Trends in terms of production glitches or vendor blockages or quality are noted and remedied;

good ideas that improve productivity, quality and flexibility in the production area are also noted and implemented.

The scheduler works with everyone in the production department, as well as people from Purchasing, Engineering and Technical Operations, so that the most complete knowledge and foresight is applied to each order.

Figure A.1
Conifer Group Complete Arrow of Value Chart: Detail of "Integrate and Assemble Systems"

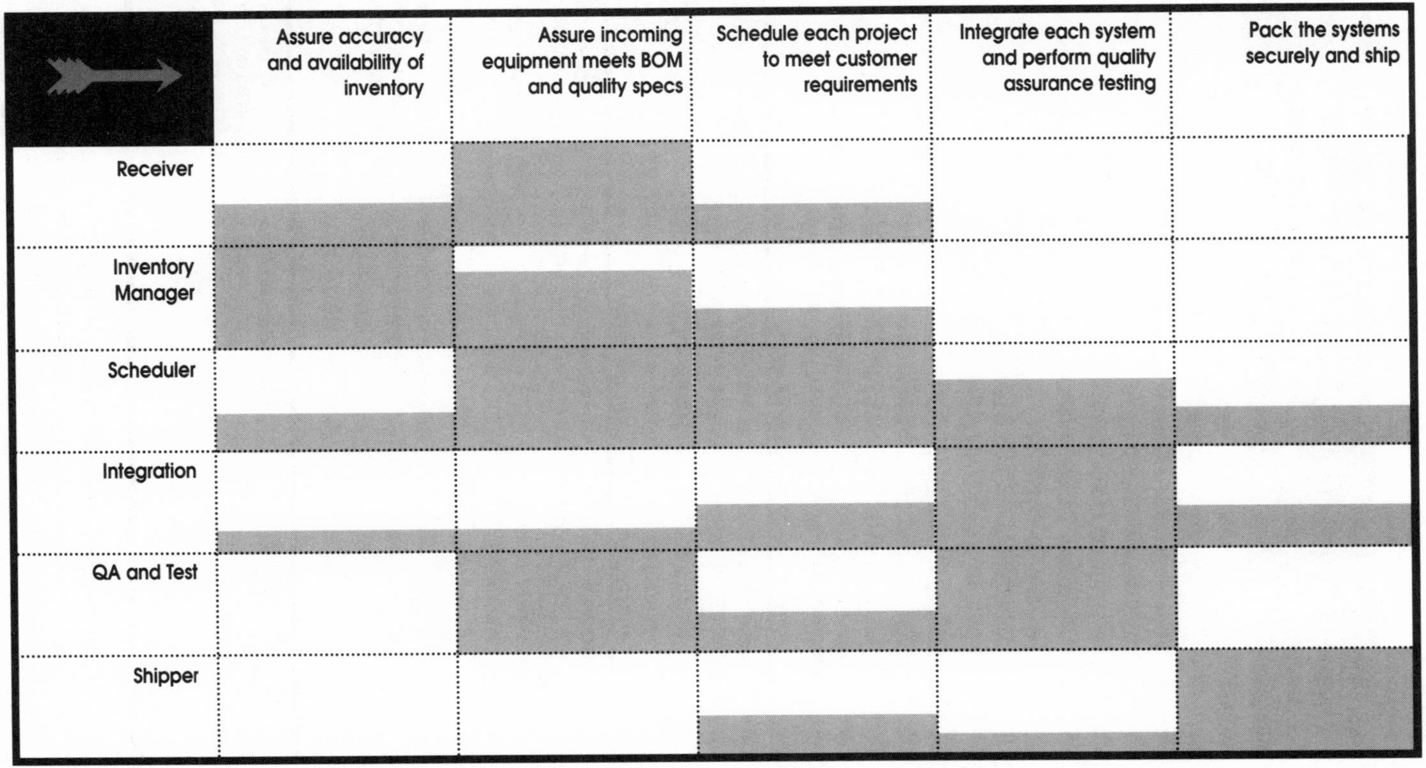

	Assure accuracy and availability of inventory	Assure incoming equipment meets BOM and quality specs	Schedule each project to meet customer requirements	Integrate each system and perform quality assurance testing	Pack the systems securely and ship
Receiver	■	■	■		
Inventory Manager		■	■		
Scheduler	■	■		■	■
Integration		■		■	■
QA and Test	■	■	■	■	■
Shipper			■		■

Figure A.2
Scheduler's Critical Success Factors

Core Action	Load	Critical Success Factors	Deliverable Measurement
Assure accuracy and availability of inventory	2	Verify that bill of materials for each customer's order is itemized and specified correctly	No mistakes due to unnoticed errors on the order
		No delays due to inventory. Inventory matches customers' orders or Purchasing is notified to take immediate action	No delays due to inventory. Purchasing is informed in writing of needs
Assure incoming equipment meets bill of material and quality specifications	5	Schedule for testing incoming new materials is set and coordinated with Incoming Test and Integration Technicians	No scheduling conflicts due to untested stock equipment
Schedule each project to meet customer requirements	5	Customer commitments are made in conjunction with Sales rep; confirmed with Sales, then with customer	No unmet deadlines. High customer satisfaction rating on delivery of systems
Integrate the systems and perform quality assurance testing	3	Aware of changes in the schedule and the reasons for the change	No surprises. Sales rep, customers promptly notified to assure understanding and agreement on the new schedule
		Sales rep and customer called as soon as a change is specified	Problem patterns noted, reported and discussed with appropriate parties
Pack the systems securely and ship	2	Customer satisfaction maintained on delivery time	Problems can be identified and corrected by appropriate parties as soon as possible

Note: This is an example of how CSFs can be used to track and evaluate deliverables, that is, documents, materials and products that are used by others to complete their work.

CSFs can also be used in other ways: (1) personnel evaluations that are updated with each review; (2) tracking operating expenses per action; and (3) mapping out CSFs on a timeline for each project or item.

Bibliography

Bennis, Warren. *On Becoming a Leader.* Reading, MA: Addison-Wesley, 1989.

Bolman, Lee G., and Terrence E. Deal. *Reframing Organizations: Artistry, Choice and Leadership.* San Francisco: Jossey-Bass, 1991.

Burgelman, Robert A. "Corporate Entrepreneurship and Strategic Management: Insights from a Process Study." *Management Science* 29, no. 12 (December 1983).

Csikszentmihalyi, Mihaly. *The Evolving Self.* New York: HarperCollins, 1993.

————. *Flow.* New York: HarperCollins, 1990.

Csikszentmihalyi, Mihaly, and Isabella Selega, eds. *Optimal Experience: Psychological Studies of Flow in Consciousness.* New York: Cambridge University Press, 1992.

Davies, Paul, and John Gribbon. *The Matter Myth: Dramatic Discoveries that Challenge Our Understanding of Physical Reality.* New York: Simon and Schuster, 1992.

Fox, Matthew. *The Reinvention of Work: A New Vision of Livelihood for Our Time.* New York: HarperSanFrancisco, 1994.

Gardner, Howard. *Creating Minds.* New York: Basic Books, 1993.

Gell-Mann, Murray. *The Quark and the Jaguar: Adventures in the Simple and the Complex.* New York: W. H. Freeman and Company, 1994.

Goodwin, Brian. *How the Leopard Changed Its Spots: The Evolution of Complexity.* New York: Charles Scribner & Sons, 1994.

Handy, Charles. *The Age of Unreason.* Cambridge, MA: Harvard Business School Press, 1989.

Katzenbach, Jon R., and Douglas K. Smith. *The Wisdom of Teams: Creating the High Performance Organization.* New York: HarperBusiness, 1993.

Lewin, Roger. *Complexity: Life at the Edge of Chaos.* New York: Macmillan Publishing Company, 1992.

Mainzer, Klaus. *Thinking in Complexity: The Complex Dynamics of Matter, Mind and Mankind.* New York: Springer-Verlag, 1994.

Morgan, Gareth. *Images of Organization.* Newbury Park, CA: Sage Publications, 1986.

Prigogine, Ilya, and Isabelle Stengers. *Order Out of Chaos: Man's New Dialogue With Nature.* New York: Bantam Books, 1984.

Senge, Peter M. *The Fifth Discipline: The Art and Practice of the Learning Organization.* New York: Currency Doubleday, 1990.

Shenkman, Michael H. *Value and Strategy: Competing Successfully in the Nineties.* New York: Quorum Books, 1992.

Suzuki, Shunru. *Zen Mind, Beginner's Mind.* New York: Weatherhill, 1987.

Turkel, Studs. *Working.* New York: Avon Books, 1972.

Waldrop, M. Mitchell. *Complexity: The Emerging Science at the Edge of Order and Chaos.* New York: Simon and Schuster, 1992.

Index

Actions, 49–62; creating value, 49–51; and customers, 116; detailing, 58–59; vision into, 131–132. *See also* Core actions
Adaptive/learning, 11–13
Alienation, x
Architecture of charts, 51–52
Areas of responsibility, 54
Arrow of Value, 50–62, 119; creation of, 55–60
Arthur, W. Brian, 12
Aspirations, 139–155
Assembly lines, 112
Atlantic Transmission, 96
Atlantic Wireless Corporation, 141
Attention, 102–103, 143
Attractors, 7–10; and control, 68; leaders as, 75; new, 167–168; and profits, 158; values and, 20
Authoritarian skills, xxiii
Automation, 140

Balance, 28–29
Barry's Sales, 23–27, 113–120
Bell, Alexander Graham, 34
Bennis, Warren, xii
Beyond equilibrium, 13
"Big Bang," xv

Boredom, 140
Branch managers, 105
Bridges, William, 109
Broad actions, 58
Brokers, 149
Burgleman, Robert, xiii, 69
Businesses: and change, 33–35; cultures of, 21; as emergent social systems, xv–xvi; growing, 66–70; values of, 20–21

Capability, 110
Challenges, 110
Champions, 148–149, 153
Change, 33–35, 118; planning, 128–129
Chaos, 4–5; and complexity, 67; managing in, 68–70
Charisma, 100
Charts: architecture of, 51–52; organizational, 51; "Top Chart," 52
Choice, 65–76, 130–131
"A Christmas Carol" (Dickens), 32
Churning, 34
Clusters, 124
Coaches, 10, 99–106, 149
Commitment, 121–122
Committees, 124
Communication, effective, 46
Community, 161–162

Competition, 14–15

Complex adaptive systems, 11

Complexity, xiv–xvii, xix–xx, 3–16; chaos and, 67; and the growing business, 66–70; and leadership, 74–75

Concentration, 87–88

Conifer Group, Ltd., 38–46; building the new company, 51–55; the process, 44–47; the retreat, 42–44

Constancy, xiv, 105–106

Consumption of resources, 6–7

Control: and choice, 68; moving beyond, 70–73

Control types, 65

Cooperation, 14–15

Core actions, 50–62, 111, 115–116; defined, 50, 56–58; and mission, 119–120

Corporate anorexia, xvi

Creating value, 36–38

Creativity, 84

Critical success factors (CSFs), xviii, 52–55, 57–62, 112, 118–121

Csikszentmihalyi, Mihaly, xix, 76, 81–85, 89, 93, 157, 162–163

Culture, 21

Customers, 7, 111; actions that create value for, 49–51, 116; of merged or acquired companies, 22

Cynicism, 24

Darwin, Charles, 19

Davies, Paul, 165

Dawkins, Richard, 163

Decision makers, xx–xxi; and downsizing, 29–30; and short-term losses, 31–32; traits of, 15–16

Departments, working groups and, 60–61

Detail, 58–59, 61–62

Dickens, Charles, 32

"Downsizing," xvi, 29–30

Dylan, Bob, 11

Dynamism, 15

Eastern Wireless Corporation, 70, 126, 145, 154

Ecological movement, 7

Education, 161–162

Emergent systems, xv, 8–9

Emotions, 13–14; management of, 88–90

Employees: loyalty of, 29; and risks, 14; and vision, 38

Employers, commitment from, xiii–xiv

Empowerment, 69

Energy bombardment, 67

Engage, 93–107

Enjoyment, xix; flow and, 85–86

Entitlement, 96

Entrepreneur, 157; "in the garage," xvi

Entropy, 6; psychic, 84

Environmental business, 7, 161

Environments, and flow, xix

Ethics, xii–xiii, 16, 160

Evolution, xv; business-driven, 34–35; rethinking of, 162–168; self-organizing, 163–164; visible emergence, 164–165

The Evolving Self (Csikszentmihalyi), 81, 157

"Exemplar," xxiii, 151–152

Exo-neural network, 166

Facilitators, xxiii, 148

Fallacies, ix–xiv; mechanistic model, xi–xii; rational enterprises, x–xi; ruthlessness, xii–xiv

Feedback, 88, 103–105; continuous, 132–133; immediate, 116, 120

Financial discipline, 31

"Firing line" level, xi

Flow, xvii–xix, 81–90; basics of, 86–88; commitment and, 121; crafting work for, 99–106; creation of, 130–134; death knell of, 111; and enjoyment, 85–86; and leisure, 83; line managers and, 94–95; managing and, 143–154; terrain of, 123–126; and work, 83–85

Flow (Csikszentmihalyi), 93

Gandhi, Mahatma, 90

Gell-Mann, Murray, 3, 14

Goals, 59, 87; teams choosing, 130–131

Gribbin, John, 165

Gross domestic product, 6

Growth, 6

Hands-on managing, 106–107
Holland, John, 11
Human spirit, xiv
Humanistic managers, 116

Idea teams, 72–74
Ideals, 35
Increasing returns, 12
Innovation, 16
Instincts, 28
Interactive values, 106, 117
Inventory, Phil Jefferies and, 96–99
Investment, 159

Jefferies, Phil, 95–105
Jobs: creating flow from, 130–134; the
    end of, 109–110
Jobs, Steve, xvi

Kaufman, Harry, 69–73, 95, 154

Lao-tzu, 19, 33, 139
Leadership, 10; clearing the way for, 73–
    75; complexity and, 74–75; effective,
    46; magic bullet, 74; rigid, 5; and
    values, 23–25
Learning, and mistakes, 13
LeFevre, Judith, 83
Limits, 140–142
Line managers, xvii–xviii; and charisma,
    100; and constancy, 105; and flow, 94–
    95; hands-on, 106–107; in-depth
    understanding of, 107; as interpreters
    and negotiators, 100; new, 76; and
    subsystems, xxii–xxiii
Loading, 57–58
Loss of self-consciousness, 84
Loyalty, 29

Mage Centers for Management Develop-
    ment, xix, 25–27, 41, 70, 96, 113, 127,
    144, 161
Mainzer, Klaus, 8
Management: in chaos, 68–70; elevation
    to, 24; of emotions, 88–90; hands-on,
    106–107; and flow, 143–154; re-
    sources, 118; self, 9
Managers, xx; branch, 105; as coaches,

10, 99–106, 149; control types, 65; as
    energizers, 13; ethical universe of, xii–
    xiii; and flow, 86–88; humanistic, 16,
    94; line (see Line managers), mandate
    of, 140; new managerial work, xxiii–
    xxiv, 144–154; senior, xxi–xxii, 10;
    strategic minds of, x; successful, 66
Market share strategy, 158
Markets, as complex systems, 11–13
Maslow, Abraham, 28–29
"Master," 151–153
Mechanistic model, xi–xii, xxiii, 12, 25,
    94
Memetic code, 162–163
"Mentor," xxiii, 150–151
Mergers and acquisitions, 22
Mission, 9–10; action and the Arrow of
    Value, 49–62; creating value, 37–38;
    creation of, 41–48; definition of, 35;
    purpose and commitment, 33–48
Mistakes, and learning, 13

"Near chaos" organization, 65–70
New attractor, 167–168
Nonphysical needs, 36

On the Origin of Species by Means of
    Natural Selection (Darwin), 19
Openness, 15
Opportunism, xii
Opportunities, 87
Opportunity structures, xiii, 15, 69
Order Out of Chaos (Prigogine), 3–4
Organization charts, 51
Organizational aphasia, xvi
Organizational imperative, 157–162
Organizational roles, 146–150
Organizations: adaptivity of, 11; contin-
    uum of, 5; meaning of, 3–4; "near
    chaos," 65–70
Outsourcing, 140–141

Panic, 39
Partnerships, xi
Passion, 49–50
Peak performance, 84
People: experience of, 94, 97–99; freely

deciding, 30–31; as primary resources, 13; willing to change, 140

Peter, Tom, 76

Planning, 128–129

Pleasure, 85

Politics, 69; and boundaries, 71; corrosive, 66; good, 73

Positive reinforcement, 85

Potential complexity, 14

Prigogine, Ilya, 3–4, 67

Process, 44–47; taking into the company, 54–55

"Process" consultants, xvii

Producing roles, 145–146

Production skills, xxiii

Productivity, 81

Profits, 7, 158

"Proteges," 150, 154–155

Psychic energy, 102

Psychic entropy, 84

Purchasing and Receiving Department, 113–117

Rational enterprises, x–xi

Recognition, 103–105

"Reengineering" consultants, xvii

Referrals, 60

Relationships, 38

Research and development, 159

Resources, 43; consumption of, 6–7; management, 117–118

Responsibilities, 71, 109–122; division of, 58; elevation of, 140

Results-producing coach, 99–106

Retreat, and creation of company mission, 42–44

Rewards, 133–137

Risks, 14, 134–137, 159

Roles, 144–145; in the community, 162; organizational, 146–150; producing, 145–146; strategic, 150–154

Sales, xi; referrals, 60

Santa Fe Institute, 11

"Scientific management," x

Second law of thermodynamics, 6

Self, 82; as emergent entity, 36–37

Self-esteem, 85

Self-management, 9

Senior managers, xxi–xxii, 10

Short-term losses, 31–32

Skills: authoritarian, xxiii; production, xxiii

Social systems, emergent, xv–xvi

Spin-offs, xvi

"Strategic Heart," xxii, 6; creating the next challenge, 142–143; vision of, 168

"Strategic Minds," x, xxii

Strategic organizations, xix–xxiv, 11

Strategic roles, 150–154

Stress, 82

Success of the most fitting, 19–23

Suzuki, Shunru, 65

Systems, emergent, xv

Tao te Ching (Lao-tzu), 19, 33, 139

Task forces, 124

Teams, 41–42; creation of, 126–130; and flow, 123–126, 130–134; goals of, 130–131; idea, 72–74; and rewards, 133–134; taking charge, 129–130

Terkel, Studs, ix, 123

Termination, xiv

Time, altered sense of, 84

Tipler, Frank, 165

"Top Chart," 52

University/business complex, 165–167

Value strategy, 158–160

Values, 9–10, 19–32; and attractors, 20, 28; and balance, 28–29; a business's, 20–21; conflicting, 22; creating, 36–38; and instincts, 28; interactive, 22; leadership by, 23–25; at work, 21–23

Visible emergence, 164–165

Vision, 13–16, 35, 118, 123–137; into action, 131–132; of Strategic Heart, 168

Waldrop, Michael, 5
Wasniak, Steve, xvi
Wealth, 6
Williams, Ted, 9
Work: boring, 140; flow and, 83–85, 99–
    106; intrinsic rewards of, 133–134;
    tasks and jobs that make up, 117

Working (Terkel), ix, 123
Working groups, 51; and departments,
    60–61; types of, 124

Zen Mind, Beginner's Mind (Suzuki),
    65
"Zone," 83

About the Author

MICHAEL H. SHENKMAN is Vice President of Mage Centers for Management Development, Inc., a consulting firm that specializes in strategic organizational change and individualized management coaching. Dr. Shenkman has introduced innovative organizational management methods and models through books, articles, and college courses. He is the author of *Value and Strategy: Competing Successfully in the Nineties* (Quorum Books, 1992).